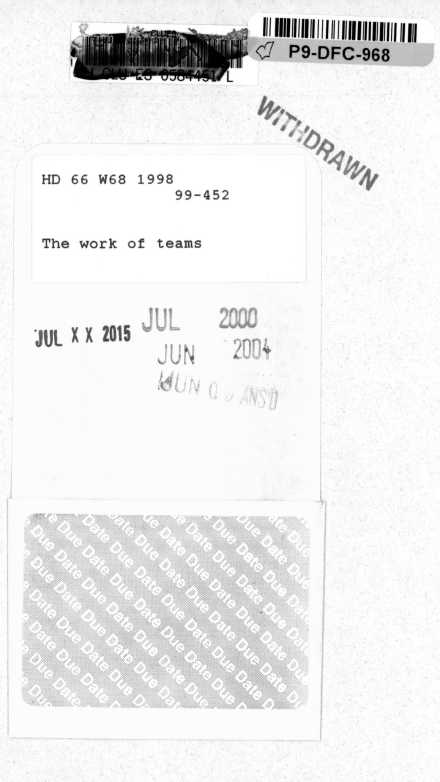

The Work of Teams

The Harvard Business Review Book Series

The
Work of
Teams

Edited with an Introduction by
Jon R. Katzenbach

A Harvard Business Review Book

The *Harvard Business Review* articles in this collection are available as
individual reprints. Discounts apply to quantity purchases. For information
and ordering contact Customer Service, Harvard Business School Publishing,
Boston, MA 02163. Telephone: (617) 496-1449, 8 a.m. to 6 p.m. Eastern
Time, Monday throught Friday. Fax: (617) 496-1029, 24 hours a day.

Library of Congress Cataloging-in-Publication Data

The work of teams / edited with an introduction by Jon R. Katzenbach.
    p.   cm. — (A Harvard business review book)
    Includes index.
    ISBN 0-87584-868-0 (alk. paper)
    1. Teams in the workplace. I. Katzenbach, Jon R., 1932–   .
II. Series: Harvard business review book series.
  HD66.W68   1998
  658.3′128—dc21   98-26760
                                                                    CIP

The paper used in this publication meets the requirements of the American
National Standard for Permanence of Paper for Printed Library Materials
Z39.48-1984.

Contents

Part II   Managing Teams

Part III An Integrated Leadership Approach

Introduction

Jon R. Katzenbach

The work of teams is an increasing concern for top management as well as for leaders all down the line. Real teams offer an attractive potential for boosts in small group performance at all levels. The versatility of a team is well suited to the dynamics of speed, competitive intensity, and rapid change that face more and more high-performing organizations. And yet many companies find working with teams to be fraught with frustration and disappointment. Undisciplined team efforts—still the bulk of teaming activity in most large companies—seldom meet expectations and often create huge problems of confusion and swollen workloads. It's no surprise that many executives continue to view teams with suspicion, despite the scores of books and articles that are written on this topic every year.

This particular collection of articles presents some of the more thoughtful perspectives on when and how teams work. More importantly, it provides broad perspectives on environments that encourage or inhibit the work of teams. Several of the authors comment on the organization, governance, and leadership settings and issues that affect team performance. Within that broader context, they address a fundamental challenge that leaders face with respect to teams: how to integrate legitimate team efforts with the equally legitimate efforts of other important organizational units, governance structures, and management processes.

THE "MISFIT" TEAM

One of my favorite team stories illustrates both the power and the unpredictability of a team, and how difficult it can be to integrate team and enterprise performance. The story appeared in *Business Week* in January of 1990 ("How Sony Pulled Off Its Spectacular Coup"). According to the article, Sony wanted to explore the possibility of adding a small office computer to its product line. Since it wasn't a high priority, the firm decided to assign the task to a group of 11 "misfit" engineers. Left pretty much to their own devices, the engineers decided that developing an office computer wasn't nearly as attractive as crafting an engineering workstation. After all, engineering was their area of expertise and interest; they could even envision using the product themselves. In fact, they became so excited about the prospect that they worked nights and weekends for months to make "their dream" a reality.

Before senior management sponsors picked up on their act, the team had created a market-ready workstation in roughly six months. The normal expected time to develop that kind of product was closer to two years! Moreover, within one year the product took over 20 percent of the Japanese workstation market. It was one of the most successful new product introductions in the history of Japan's computer industry. *It was not, however, the office product line addition that management had asked the team to develop.* Management never got the product it wanted, but it probably got a lot more in performance results than it had expected.

Although it may be an extreme illustration, the Sony "dream team" story highlights the anomaly that teams represent in any organization. They can be powerful as well as versatile units of performance; but they can also be difficult to predict, control, and integrate into a balanced organizational system and leadership approach. Consequently, it's critical that management learn how to use teams in the right places, as well as how to maintain constructive involvement with a team as it develops its own momentum.

WIDELY MISUNDERSTOOD

The work of teams is just plain hard; it need not, however, be complex. In fact, a team is a simple unit—perhaps the most basic performance unit in any organization other than individual performers. Moreover, because a team is a natural unit, formed to address issues requiring multiple skills and leadership roles, it has been relied on literally for centuries. Students of American history can cite numerous team efforts ranging from the Boston Tea Party and the First Continental Congress to NASA astronauts probing the far reaches of space. The simplicity of the team concept is what makes it so powerful—when it is pursued with discipline and resolve.

Unfortunately, today's team efforts are often overcomplicated by well-meaning managers who don't clearly understand the fundamentals required to achieve the extra levels of performance that real teams can deliver. Although people think of many variations of small (and large) group efforts as "teams," few of these efforts would actually qualify if higher performance results were the measure of a real team. Cohesiveness, cooperation, consensus, and collaboration aren't the same thing as—nor do they often produce—higher collective results. Team performance is characterized at least as much by discipline and hard work as it is by empowerment, togetherness, and small group dynamics. Unfortunately, it's easy to lose sight of the fundamentals that lead to the higher levels of performance that a real team is capable of achieving.

For such a simple unit, then, the team remains surprisingly misunderstood and misused. To begin with, a team that delivers higher performance results is not the same thing as teamwork. The latter is an attribute or value that can produce supportive behaviors throughout large and small groups alike; the former is a focused and committed small group (ideally, less than a dozen people). Although teamwork can help individuals and small groups cooperate, it will seldom produce team performance. Though often called a team, a single-leader unit or working group isn't the same thing. The true team draws together the composite skill mix of multiple leaders and members to shape *collective or joint work products,* whereas a working group relies on its leader for task assignment and integration of *individual work products.* Single-leader units are faster (initially, at least) and fit more comfortably with the working approaches of most managers. However, neither the team nor the single-leader unit is "always better" for small group efforts. The best managers and change leaders master the ability to use both. The work of teams isn't always required to realize broader performance aspirations.

To understand where teams fit in any organizational construct (formal or informal), it is very useful to be clear on the terminology. When we are undisciplined in our use of the term *team,* we are likely to be undisciplined in our application of the fundamentals required for team performance. Simply labeling any small group as a "team" or admonishing the members to "become a team" seldom works. Disciplined attention to a few fundamentals is required.

Unfortunately, the higher up they are in the formal organization structure, the more careless managers are about the terminology they use. As a result, senior leadership teams can be the most illusory of all teams, often masquerading as real teams when they are in fact far from it. Yet no self-respecting CEO would deny having his or her own "team at the top." Likewise, most organizational unit managers (at any level) refer to their own "management team." But most of these are mislabeled and fall far short on the performance scale when compared with the results achieved by the more disciplined performance unit that constitutes a real team.

Careless labeling leads executives, consultants, and managers to overlook the differences between teams and single-leader units, and to miss opportunities to use both more effectively. This mislabeling also confuses the rest of the organization, particularly those who have become proficient in the appropriate use of teams. Last, but not least, careless labeling makes it difficult for front-line leaders to communicate with top management about important team opportunities and issues.

It's worthwhile to clean up our language with respect to teams. It doesn't really matter what set of labels or definitions we use, as long as they permit the organization to identify team, single-leader unit, and nonteam situations—and to deal with them appropriately. The use of the term *high-performance team* is a good example. Some companies use that label for what more experienced practitioners would define as a real team. This may be fine, for the true high-performance team is rare and can seldom be created on purpose, but it can be seriously misleading. The high-performance team is more committed, powerful, and rare than any normal team.

Any label works, as long as its meaning is clear to people who must choose among several group options within any institution or discrete work environment. It isn't important what set of labels an organization applies to its small group efforts, as long as its leaders can differentiate between—and effectively integrate—team and nonteam efforts.

MAJOR TOPICS

The articles in this volume are presented within two broad parts: creating teams and managing teams. The articles selected for each part comment on either the requirements or the benefits of creating and managing teams well.

Part I: Creating Teams

Creating a real team requires the determination and persistence of its members and sponsors alike. Those who see "forming a team" as an easy or all-purpose solution will likely be frustrated by the effort and disappointed by the results. The articles in this part support four key guidelines for creating a team:

1. *Apply the fundamentals.* Pay close attention to the fundamentals in identifying the opportunity and in shaping the effort.
2. *Understand the challenge.* Provide for simplicity, conflict, and hard work.
3. *Make the tradeoffs.* Consider the range of small group options.
4. *Integrate the disciplines.* Integrate teams with single-leader units.

APPLY THE FUNDAMENTALS

Bowen H. McCoy's provocative and timeless piece "The Parable of the Sadhu" has become a classic in business ethics courses. It tells the poignant true story of McCoy's participation in a sabbatical tour in 1982 through Nepal and the Himalayas, where his group and three other mountain-climbing groups from different cultures and countries encountered a dying pilgrim, or *sadhu.* Unable to decide whether their first responsibility was to care for the dying man or to continue their difficult climb, they agonized over the situation, its solution, and the problems of the group.

Although McCoy was not directly concerned with team performance, the circumstances he described would have made it literally impossible for these diverse groups to apply certain fundamentals to what was a natural team opportunity. They were victimized by two conflicting purposes, with no clear way to resolve them, had little or no time to work out a common purpose among the groups, had no common leader to whom they could turn for guidance, and were missing capabilities for caring for the dying sadhu. One wonders how their "decision by default" might have differed if some subset of the groups had been able to coalesce as a committed team—or whether the situation might have been best resolved had there been some way to designate a mutually acceptable leader. Nonetheless, the story provides a painful illustration of how difficult it can be for a culturally diverse group to apply team basics, with or without a designated single leader, even when the situation cries out for it.

Suzy Wetlaufer takes us inside the trauma of a dysfunctional team situation in her intriguing piece "The Team That Wasn't." The problem centers on a talented team member who seems determined to undermine the group effort. Seven team experts comment on the situation Wetlaufer poses, each offering different ways to think about the problem and each suggesting different solutions. The primary message, however, is that teaming in a specific working construct is much more difficult than it appears in the abstract, even with a group of talented, hard-working people. By paying attention to the fundamentals, however, we see that a team need not be destroyed by one problem member. We also learn a variety of ways to deal with such disruptions.

The importance of concentrating on a few basic elements or fundamentals is brought out in "The Discipline of Teams," which describes one way of defining these fundamentals. Authors Jon R. Katzenbach and Douglas K. Smith believe that six elements constitute a discipline that must be adhered to by groups that seek real team levels of performance (small size, complementary skills, common levels of member commitment to both a performance purpose and a set of performance goals, a clear working approach, and a strong sense of mutual accountability). A colleague of mine once likened these fundamentals to his Catholic Jesuit high school, where no student could make the honor roll with anything less than straight A's in all of his or her courses. Similarly, a small group must get an A on all six of these team fundamentals to achieve its potential performance as a team. Like many experienced team practitioners, however, the authors also argue that the most important requirement for shaping a team is a clear and compelling performance objective to which all members can commit.

In addition, however, teams need to achieve results that match their purpose. To that end, it is vital to be able to measure those achievements along the way, and some measurements are more important than others. Christopher Meyer, in "How the Right Measures Help Teams Excel," provides several illustrations of how to establish a measurement system that helps teams overcome two major obstacles to effectiveness: getting other functions to provide expertise to teams when they need it and getting team members from different functions to speak a common language. These insights are particularly valuable in helping teams adhere to two critical elements of team basics that are difficult to measure: skills and common commitment.

UNDERSTAND THE CHALLENGE

The simplicity of the unit does not minimize the difficulty of the challenge. From beginning to end, a real team is hard work for everyone involved. Determining when a group should function as a team, recruiting the right members, shaping a compelling performance purpose, setting clear goals, and sustaining common levels of commitment and mutual accountability across the members are all very difficult to achieve.

Executive sponsors work hard to establish the solution space for the team. Team leaders work hard to maintain the group's commitment and focus. Team members work hard at building their skills and delivering collective work products of high value. Many groups are simply not up to the challenge and are unable to sustain the pace and intensity required.

Contrary to popular belief, the work of teams is not about togetherness, compromise, and consensus building. It is about hard work, conflict, integration, and collective results. This makes their challenge even more demanding. Having a good fight is both healthy and unavoidable in real team situations. Kathleen M. Eisenhardt, Jean L. Kahwajy, and L. J. Bourgeois III bring this reality into sharp, useful focus in their article "How Management Teams Can Have a Good Fight." They point out the importance of constructive conflict in resolving tough issues and in bringing the best ideas and approaches to the surface. Their observations remind one of the timeless work of Mary Parker Follett,[1] who perhaps better than any other business writer made a compelling case for struggling to integrate conflicting points of view, rather than driving too soon for compromise—or, perhaps worse, allowing one viewpoint to dominate. The best teams actually thrive on constructive conflict which leads them to creative insights and integrated resolutions. As Eisenhardt, Kahwajy, and Bourgeois point out, this can be of particular value within senior leadership groups.

MAKING THE TRADEOFFS

When confronted with an off-line "small group opportunity," many leaders instinctively turn to a task force or single-leader-unit solution. Most executives continue to believe that, if you pick the right leader, point her at the right target, and hold her accountable, she will drive the "team" to victory. This is an understandable viewpoint because single-leader units are commonly used and fit comfortably within the pervasive mindset of individual accountability. Moreover, the single-leader unit often works very well. A few leaders turn to a real team approach in urgent, unexpected situations, but this, too, is an instinctive reaction. Regrettably, both of these instinctive reactions—even in the very best executives—preclude a conscious consideration of the options or tradeoffs involved.

The instinctive approach sometimes yields the right choice, but without a careful evaluation of the options and tradeoffs, real team performance becomes a random occurrence. Not surprisingly, the random use of teams and single-leader units falls short of the need—particularly at senior leadership levels. Moreover, the options include more than simply choosing between a real team and a single-leader unit. They also include choices among various situational (or one-time) team efforts and an ongoing team effort, or combinations of the two. "The Myth of the Top Management Team" is really based on the simple concept that the "situational" use of the team approach, when integrated within an ongoing single-leader unit, can permit senior leadership groups to capitalize on team performance without sacrificing the speed and efficiency of the more comfortable single-leader approach. Although this article focuses primarily on teams at the top, it is relevant and applicable to teams that run things at any level.

In either the situational or the ongoing team opportunities, three tradeoffs are important to consider: speed versus performance, leadership clarity versus leadership capacity, and skill versus influence. Unless those tradeoffs are made wisely and conscientiously, the result is likely to be a suboptimal, random combination of teams and nonteam efforts. Letting nature take its course at the top of large organizations is most likely to overlook, if not snuff out, important team opportunities.

A real team takes time to form because the members need to learn to appreciate each other's skills, become comfortable in shifting the leadership role, and develop common levels of commitment. A single-leader unit, therefore, has a natural advantage in getting up and running faster, particularly if the leader is experienced at the task at hand. The team is motivated primarily by its performance purpose, whereas the single-leader unit is motivated primarily by its leader. The team depends heavily on collective work products, whereas the

Exhibit I.   *Single Leader Groups vs. Teams*

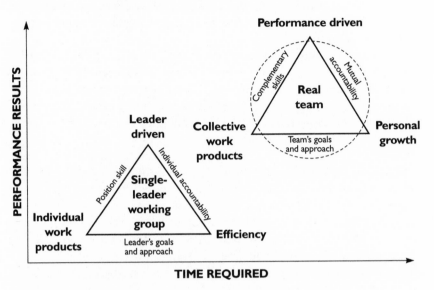

single-leader unit depends heavily on individual work products. The team is better at stimulating personal growth among its members, whereas the single-leader unit is more time-efficient. Exhibit I illustrates these tradeoffs.

The ultimate test of a real team opportunity lies in (1) the potential value of its collective work products; (2) the sharing or shifting of the leadership role among the members (depicted by the circle around the "Real team" triangle); and (3) the common levels of commitment and mutual accountability for results.

These are tough tests to pass, but they invariably determine the degree to which any potential team achieves real team levels of performance.

INTEGRATE THE DISCIPLINES

The discipline of teams has a very important counterpart in any successful organization: the discipline of individual or executive leadership. This discipline is spelled out in "The Myth of the Top Management Team," as it explains why so-called teams at the top of large enterprises seldom achieve real team levels of performance. Simply stated, strong individual leaders adhere to a proven discipline that is often in direct conflict with team basics. Unless executives make determined efforts to integrate the two, the strong single-leader discipline will dominate.

As Follett's seminal writings point out, the integration of two conflicting viewpoints (or disciplines) requires strong conviction, open interactive dialogue, and a degree of patience that many executives don't possess. In "How to Integrate Work *and* Deepen Expertise" (which is cited in more detail and positioned in the second part of this collection), the authors address a different, but relevant integration challenge: how to enforce various leadership disciplines and still maintain functional excellence in global manufacturing settings. The article highlights several team opportunities, including Hewlett-Packard's enigma of getting teams to work across autonomous world-class divisions. This problem is no different from that of getting teams to work within any organizational structure that is based on individual accountability. The issues are the same, but cross-cultural situations are more complex and difficult. Nonetheless, the potential value is well worth the effort required.

Part II: Managing Teams

Clearly, it is a challenge to create even two or three real teams, as the preceding section describes. It's much more challenging, however, for senior leaders to sustain a balanced leadership approach that enables them to design and manage a process for obtaining the performance of dozens of team efforts. Although many companies claim to follow that path, very few have reached their destination. More often than not, they declare victory early, after achieving a random mixture of teams, single-leader units, and pseudo-teams. Because they are unclear as to the causes or significance of the differences between real teams and nonteams, they obtain team performance largely at random—and seldom where they need it most.

To achieve the appropriate balance in an integrated organizational system requires adherence to three fundamental guidelines which the articles in this section suggest:

1. *Sustain a performance focus.* Maintain a relentless focus on performance results, not team building.

2. *Get teams into the right places.* Exploit the versatility of teams, while recognizing their limitations.

3. *Balance the overall leadership approach.* Combine team efforts with structure, process, networks, and other nonteam groups.

SUSTAIN A PERFORMANCE FOCUS

When I first visited Hewlett-Packard several years ago while developing material for *The Wisdom of Teams,* I was surprised when Dean Morton (then president), said that he didn't think the company had very many teams worth researching. Morton had presumed that I was seeking special one-off teams, detached from their normal work to study and recommend something. When I explained that I was actually more interested in teams that run things or make things, he perked up. Many of HP's team efforts reflect the natural team opportunities that arise because of the compelling clarity of the performance challenge they've been asked to address. Such team efforts are a natural product of the company's enviable and well-known performance ethic and of a distributed leadership mindset for which the company is literally world famous.

Nothing is more valuable to a multiple team effort than the existence of a strong performance ethic like Hewlett-Packard's, which is balanced by an equally strong belief in team performance. Even though HP's overall leadership approach is characterized by strong managers who believe in individual accountability and consequence management, their performance ethic doesn't smother or preclude mutual accountability and team results. When a company lacks a strong performance ethic, it must pay particular attention to making sure that each individual team challenge equates to a compelling performance challenge.

Another interesting perspective that bears on the topic is provided in Nitin Nohria and James D. Berkley's "Whatever Happened to the Take-Charge Manager?" Their primary thesis is that managers need to "reclaim managerial responsibility" by emphasizing pragmatic judgment and on-line creative solutions—instead of relying on ready-made answers provided by professional problem solvers, including those who would have management overemphasize teams. Yet their "four faces of pragmatism" actually make a strong argument for the same kind of relentless performance focus in which real teams thrive—and pseudo-teams perish. Their sought-after "effective managers . . . that become adept at making do, and learning to play with possibilities and use available resources to find workable solutions" become the kind of invaluable midlevel change leaders who have learned to use both teams and nonteams in a concerted effort to find "whatever works."

A relentless focus on performance results is what enables companies to get results from teams as well as from take-charge managers. It's also what prevents companies from falling prey to one of the classic problems the authors cite, wherein "teams became a virtue unto themselves, and suddenly all problems had to be solved through teams, whether or not this was the most pragmatic solution." Hence, the notion of a "team-based" organization can be dangerous, because it implies that everything is better done by a team. Team efforts (even by disciplined, performance-focused teams) are only one of the basic performance approaches that leaders should apply. The best rely on a team only where its collective work and versatility advantages fit the situation.

GET TEAMS INTO THE RIGHT PLACES

Although it's important to exploit the versatility, collective skills, and multiple leadership advantages of teams, it's equally important to recognize their limitations. This implies using teams *only* where they really matter, not wherever there are more than two people addressing an issue.

"Information Technology and Tomorrow's Manager," by Linda M. Applegate, James I. Cash, Jr., and D. Quinn Mills, provides a thoughtful look into the future which argues for structures and leadership approaches that can provide both scale and responsiveness. With respect to technology, for example, the authors point out that "while in the past computers primarily supported individual work, the computer systems of the future will also be geared toward groups." Complex organizations will increasingly need to be flexible and responsive while simultaneously seeking processes that ensure stronger integration and central control. This seeming dichotomy is no longer the impossible paradox we once would have thought.

Perhaps the most articulate argument for seeking to combine a broader range of organizational and leadership options comes from the work of James Collins and Jerry Porras in their recent book *Built to*

Last, where they point out the "tyranny of OR" that visionary companies continually reject in favor of "the genius of AND." The reality of dynamic institutions today is not in the replacement of old structures and processes with new ones, but in continually adapting the old and integrating it with the new to optimize the range of choices for leaders at all levels. In this kind of dynamic, fast-paced, and distributed leadership environment, the real team will always have its place. But so will the take-charge manager and the single-leader unit. The management challenge is to design a leadership approach that gets each of them into the right places.

In this respect, it's important to recognize the remarkable flexibility and adaptability of the real team. The potential value of this flexibility often shows up in situations that can't be anticipated in advance or designed into a formal structure and set of management processes. In his book review "Prepare Your Organization to Fight Fires," Karl Weick describes the work, thinking, and writing of Professor Norman Maclean in his provocative book *Young Men and Fire,* which he spent more than a decade researching and writing (it was published posthumously in 1992). Maclean's work brings to our attention the increasing importance of organizations and leaders who develop the ability to improvise and communicate wisely when the unexpected occurs. Formal organizational units will often collapse when they encounter sudden and dangerous "losses of meaning." To make his point, Maclean focuses on the terrible tragedy of the Mann Gulch fire, but less traumatic losses of meaning often occur in fast-paced competitive environments. As Weick observes, "leaders today need to develop resilient groups that are capable of four things: improvisation, wisdom, respectful interaction, and communication." He goes on to point out that, when a small group's formal structure and roles collapse, the primary antidote is communication applied under conditions of trust and time. Thus we need to design structures that are able to "make sense" out of chaos and survive in times of disaster. Because teams are based on discipline and trust, they are likely to be extremely helpful units when the organization has to fight fires.

BALANCE THE OVERALL LEADERSHIP APPROACH

Teams must fit within both formal and informal alignment options—including formal structures, management processes, and informal networks. The latter are of growing importance, as outlined in David Krackhardt and Jeffrey P. Hanson's article "Informal Networks: The Company Behind the Chart." The authors point out the value of understanding three primary informal networks (advice, trust, and communication) before restructuring the formal organization and management processes. The same value and insight should apply in managing and applying team efforts across an enterprise. Teams are invariably an integral part of most effective networks, be they formal or informal. Certainly top management will do a better job of staffing such team efforts, as well as of deciding where to employ a team approach, if it understands the basic informal networks required to make any organization function effectively.

An equally intriguing perspective on the challenge of integration is described in "How to Integrate Work *and* Deepen Expertise," by Dorothy Leonard-Barton, H. Kent Bowen, Kim B. Clark, Charles A. Holloway, and Steven C. Wheelwright. Although the primary challenge posed in this article (referred to earlier) is how to integrate various disciplines and still maintain functional excellence, its perspectives also apply to the integration of team and single-leader disciplines. Moreover, it is clear in the article that many of the tasks required to integrate for functional excellence constitute natural team opportunities and therefore benefit from real team efforts. In an HP example of developing a low-cost computer printer, the authors point out that

> the manufacturing engineers became such valuable team members that the designers even lobbied for more of them. [Moreover,] HP executives also wanted [the project] to signal to the rest of the company that their view of the traditional status of design and manufacturing was changing. [Thus] the project was a model for teamwork, and subsequent projects were organized along similar lines.

This challenge lies at the heart of the transformation in the job of the senior executive. At the same time that companies have discovered the value of process and horizontal organizational thinking, they have been faced with an exploding marketplace need for speed, responsiveness, and flexibility. These forces and their impact on senior executives form the central thesis of "Getting It Done: New Roles for Senior Executives," by Thomas M. Hout and John C. Carter. They make a compelling argument for the growing importance of an executive leadership discipline that is based on more activism and interventionism by top leaders. "They are not just enablers or coaches; they are *doers*." The authors go on to point out how difficult it is for the senior management group to function effectively as a real team, because of the powerful forces that keep them focused on their individual responsibilities.

Yet the article cites a number of examples of senior executives at different companies who also had to work together on collective work products that fueled real team performance. They *were* functioning as real teams, albeit for short periods of time. To handle such situations, senior executives learn to play different roles at different times. The "situational team opportunity" allows leaders more flexibility in recognizing the difference and shifting back and forth between single-leader and real team roles. Playing these different roles is one of the hallmarks of the activist executive of the future.

Hout and Carter go on to illustrate how activist leaders engage in real work. For example, Southland's senior executives not only developed a new strategy themselves, but also set aside exclusive review times wherein the CEO wasn't chairing the review. This is reminiscent of Abraham Zaleznik's classic article, first published in 1989 (reprinted in 1997 with his added commentary), on the value of "Real Work" for executives. Zaleznik defines the real work of executives as "the work of thinking about and acting on ideas relating to products, markets, and customers," which he contrasts with the ritual or "psychopolitics" activities in large organizations. The good news is that Zaleznik's current observations lead him to conclude that "senior executives seem to have reestablished a balance between real work and ritual." The bad news is that maintaining that balance remains a constant challenge because the real work of executives is continually changing and requires a continual readjustment of where and how they will apply their "hard thinking that must precede action."

For the work of teams to be an integral part of the priority real work of executives, teams must fit into the dynamic balance of leadership. Much executive work (such as hard thinking) is *not* best done in a team context. On the other hand, a real team effort, appropriately focused on issues where group thinking and problem solving are essential, is an appropriate and powerful supplement to individual executive efforts. Maintaining the balance, however, is seldom easy.

Last, but by no means least, is the need for leaders to concern themselves with the overall working environment of the enterprise, whatever tools, mechanisms, and leadership approaches they may rely on. The work of Maclean and the commentary by Weick cited earlier illustrate both the complexities and the challenges of maintaining an environment where people can make sense out of and deal with the increasing number of unexpected events, if not crises, that most organizations must face. Helping the workforce find a way to safety in the face of surprise requires leaders to develop incredibly resilient groups.

Clearly this is an opportunity for real teams who can apply the discipline and resourcefulness that characterizes the best team efforts. Maclean's chronicle of Mann Gulch, according to Weick, "teaches us that real action occurs long before decisions ever become visible. By the time a decision needs to be made, sense making processes have already determined its outcome. . . . [Hence] we need to design structures that are resilient sources of collective sense making." I would contend that disciplined, real teams can be an essential part of such structures. More importantly, the need for such structures suggests an environment in which individuals, teams, and single-leader units must all flourish and develop the capacity to rise to the occasion when the unexpected occurs.

Part III: An Integrated Leadership Approach

Our final selection, "Entrepreneurship Reconsidered: The Team as Hero" was written by Robert B. Reich before he became President Bill Clinton's Secretary of Labor. Reich argues that America's long-cherished notion of Horatio Alger's rags-to-riches individual enterpreneurship needs to be redressed in favor of collective entrepreneurship—efforts in which the whole effort is greater than the sum of the individual contributions. *"We need to honor our teams more, our aggressive leaders and maverick geniuses less."*

The basic thesis is appealing, and the arguments are convincing. Surely, unless we become better at integrating real team performance with individual entrepreneurship, our organizations will fail to achieve their full performance potential. It's critical to note, however, that Reich is really arguing for integration and better balance—not for the replacement of individual entrepreneurs with teams. Teams work as powerful performance units, but only in the right places. It is as dangerous to overrely on them as it is to overlook them. I believe the essence of the challenge can be captured in the following four observations:

- A real team is a small, flexible, and versatile unit that can be easily assembled, focused, and disassembled; it is the basic unit of collective performance. It is not, however, as fast or efficient as the more common single-leader unit.

- A team expands leadership capacity by drawing on the leadership and initiative of all its members, and balancing the "flat spots" among them. It cannot, however, replace individual entrepreneurship, creativity, and drive.

- Teams optimize performance within the formal construct of an organization by integrating across formal structures and energizing formal processes. They cannot, however, replace the alignment clarity and consistency of formal structures and management processes.

- Real teams enable the informal (or social) construct of an organization by exploiting natural interactions and energizing informal networks. They cannot, however, replace the action flows of work and information that informal networks provide.

If we are to make teams more heroic, as Reich suggests, we must certainly do it within the context of a balanced leadership approach.

Note

1. Pauline Graham, ed., *Mary Parker Follett—Prophet of Management: A Celebration of Writings from the 1920s* (Boston: Harvard Business School Press, 1995), 69.

PART

I

Creating Teams

1
The Parable of the Sadhu

Bowen H. McCoy

Last year, as the first participant in the new six-month sabbatical program that Morgan Stanley has adopted, I enjoyed a rare opportunity to collect my thoughts as well as do some traveling. I spent the first three months in Nepal, walking 600 miles through 200 villages in the Himalayas and climbing some 120,000 vertical feet. My sole Western companion on the trip was an anthropologist who shed light on the cultural patterns of the villages that we passed through.

During the Nepal hike, something occurred that has had a powerful impact on my thinking about corporate ethics. Although some might argue that the experience has no relevance to business, it was a situation in which a basic ethical dilemma suddenly intruded into the lives of a group of individuals. How the group responded holds a lesson for all organizations, no matter how defined.

The Sadhu

The Nepal experience was more rugged than I had anticipated. Most commercial treks last two or three weeks and cover a quarter of the distance we traveled.

My friend Stephen, the anthropologist, and I were halfway through the sixty-day Himalayan part of the trip when we reached the high

This article was originally published in the September–October 1983 issue of *HBR*. For its republication as an *HBR* Classic, Bowen H. McCoy has written the commentary "When Do We Take a Stand?" (which appears at the end of the article) to update his observations.

point, an 18,000-foot pass over a crest that we'd have to traverse to reach the village of Muklinath, an ancient holy place for pilgrims.

Six years earlier, I had suffered pulmonary edema, an acute form of altitude sickness, at 16,500 feet in the vicinity of Everest base camp—so we were understandably concerned about what would happen at 18,000 feet. Moreover, the Himalayas were having their wettest spring in twenty years; hip-deep powder and ice had already driven us off one ridge. If we failed to cross the pass, I feared that the last half of our once-in-a-lifetime trip would be ruined.

The night before we would try the pass, we camped in a hut at 14,500 feet. In the photos taken at that camp, my face appears wan. The last village we'd passed through was a sturdy two-day walk below us, and I was tired.

During the late afternoon, four backpackers from New Zealand joined us, and we spent most of the night awake, anticipating the climb. Below, we could see the fires of two other parties, which turned out to be two Swiss couples and a Japanese hiking club.

To get over the steep part of the climb before the sun melted the steps cut in the ice, we departed at 3:30 A.M. The New Zealanders left first, followed by Stephen and myself, our porters and Sherpas, and then the Swiss. The Japanese lingered in their camp. The sky was clear, and we were confident that no spring storm would erupt that day to close the pass.

At 15,500 feet, it looked to me as if Stephen were shuffling and staggering a bit, which are symptoms of altitude sickness. (The initial stage of altitude sickness brings a headache and nausea. As the condition worsens, a climber may encounter difficult breathing, disorientation, aphasia, and paralysis.) I felt strong—my adrenaline was flowing—but I was very concerned about my ultimate ability to get across. A couple of our porters were also suffering from the height, and Pasang, our Sherpa sirdar (leader), was worried.

Just after daybreak, while we rested at 15,500 feet, one of the New Zealanders, who had gone ahead, came staggering down toward us with a body slung across his shoulders. He dumped the almost naked, barefoot body of an Indian holy man—a sadhu—at my feet. He had found the pilgrim lying on the ice, shivering and suffering from hypothermia. I cradled the sadhu's head and laid him out on the rocks. The New Zealander was angry. He wanted to get across the pass before the bright sun melted the snow. He said, "Look, I've done what I can. You have porters and Sherpa guides. You care for him. We're going on!" He turned and went back up the mountain to join his friends.

I took a carotid pulse and found that the sadhu was still alive. We figured he had probably visited the holy shrines at Muklinath and was on his way home. It was fruitless to question why he had chosen this desperately high route instead of the safe, heavily traveled caravan route through the Kali Gandaki gorge. Or why he was shoeless and almost naked, or how long he had been lying in the pass. The answers weren't going to solve our problem.

Stephen and the four Swiss began stripping off their outer clothing and opening their packs. The sadhu was soon clothed from head to foot. He was not able to walk, but he was very much alive. I looked down the mountain and spotted the Japanese climbers, marching up with a horse.

Without a great deal of thought, I told Stephen and Pasang that I was concerned about withstanding the heights to come and wanted to get over the pass. I took off after several of our porters who had gone ahead.

On the steep part of the ascent where, if the ice steps had given way, I would have slid down about 3,000 feet, I felt vertigo. I stopped for a breather, allowing the Swiss to catch up with me. I inquired about the sadhu and Stephen. They said that the sadhu was fine and that Stephen was just behind them. I set off again for the summit.

Stephen arrived at the summit an hour after I did. Still exhilarated by victory, I ran down the slope to congratulate him. He was suffering from altitude sickness—walking fifteen steps, then stopping, walking fifteen steps, then stopping. Pasang accompanied him all the way up. When I reached them, Stephen glared at me and said: "How do you feel about contributing to the death of a fellow man?"

I did not completely comprehend what he meant. "Is the sadhu dead?" I inquired.

"No," replied Stephen, "but he surely will be!"

After I had gone, followed not long after by the Swiss, Stephen had remained with the sadhu. When the Japanese had arrived, Stephen had asked to use their horse to transport the sadhu down to the hut. They had refused. He had then asked Pasang to have a group of our porters carry the sadhu. Pasang had resisted the idea, saying that the porters would have to exert all their energy to get themselves over the pass. He believed they could not carry a man down 1,000 feet to the hut, reclimb the slope, and get across safely before the snow melted. Pasang had pressed Stephen not to delay any longer.

The Sherpas had carried the sadhu down to a rock in the sun at about 15,000 feet and pointed out the hut another 500 feet below.

The Japanese had given him food and drink. When they had last seen him, he was listlessly throwing rocks at the Japanese party's dog, which had frightened him.

We do not know if the sadhu lived or died.

For many of the following days and evenings, Stephen and I discussed and debated our behavior toward the sadhu. Stephen is a committed Quaker with deep moral vision. He said, "I feel that what happened with the sadhu is a good example of the breakdown between the individual ethic and the corporate ethic. No one person was willing to assume ultimate responsibility for the sadhu. Each was willing to do his bit just so long as it was not too inconvenient. When it got to be a bother, everyone just passed the buck to someone else and took off. Jesus was relevant to a more individualistic stage of society, but how do we interpret his teaching today in a world filled with large, impersonal organizations and groups?"

I defended the larger group, saying, "Look, we all cared. We all gave aid and comfort. Everyone did his bit. The New Zealander carried him down below the snow line. I took his pulse and suggested we treat him for hypothermia. You and the Swiss gave him clothing and got him warmed up. The Japanese gave him food and water. The Sherpas carried him down to the sun and pointed out the easy trail toward the hut. He was well enough to throw rocks at a dog. What more could we do?"

"You have just described the typical affluent Westerner's response to a problem. Throwing money—in this case, food and sweaters—at it, but not solving the fundamentals!" Stephen retorted.

"What would satisfy you?" I said. "Here we are, a group of New Zealanders, Swiss, Americans, and Japanese who have never met before and who are at the apex of one of the most powerful experiences of our lives. Some years the pass is so bad no one gets over it. What right does an almost naked pilgrim who chooses the wrong trail have to disrupt our lives? Even the Sherpas had no interest in risking the trip to help him beyond a certain point."

Stephen calmly rebutted, "I wonder what the Sherpas would have done if the sadhu had been a well-dressed Nepali, or what the Japanese would have done if the sadhu had been a well-dressed Asian, or what you would have done, Buzz, if the sadhu had been a well-dressed Western woman?"

"Where, in your opinion," I asked, "is the limit of our responsibility in a situation like this? We had our own well-being to worry about. Our Sherpa guides were unwilling to jeopardize us or the porters for the sadhu. No one else on the mountain was willing to commit himself beyond certain self-imposed limits."

Stephen said, "As individual Christians or people with a Western ethical tradition, we can fulfill our obligations in such a situation only if one, the sadhu dies in our care; two, the sadhu demonstrates to us that he can undertake the two-day walk down to the village; or three, we carry the sadhu for two days down to the village and persuade someone there to care for him."

"Leaving the sadhu in the sun with food and clothing—where he demonstrated hand-eye coordination by throwing a rock at a dog—comes close to fulfilling items one and two," I answered. "And it wouldn't have made sense to take him to the village where the people appeared to be far less caring than the Sherpas, so the third condition is impractical. Are you really saying that, no matter what the implications, we should, at the drop of a hat, have changed our entire plan?"

The Individual Versus the Group Ethic

Despite my arguments, I felt and continue to feel guilt about the sadhu. I had literally walked through a classic moral dilemma without fully thinking through the consequences. My excuses for my actions include a high adrenaline flow, a superordinate goal, and a once-in-a-lifetime opportunity—common factors in corporate situations, especially stressful ones.

Real moral dilemmas are ambiguous, and many of us hike right through them, unaware that they exist. When, usually after the fact, someone makes an issue of one, we tend to resent his or her bringing it up. Often, when the full import of what we have done (or not done) hits us, we dig into a defensive position from which it is very difficult to emerge. In rare circumstances, we may contemplate what we have done from inside a prison.

Had we mountaineers been free of stress caused by the effort and the high altitude, we might have treated the sadhu differently. Yet isn't stress the real test of personal and corporate values? The instant decisions that executives make under pressure reveal the most about personal and corporate character.

Among the many questions that occur to me when I ponder my experience with the sadhu are: What are the practical limits of moral imagination and vision? Is there a collective or institutional ethic that

8   *Creating Teams*

differs from the ethics of the individual? At what level of effort or commitment can one discharge one's ethical responsibilities?

Not every ethical dilemma has a right solution. Reasonable people often disagree; otherwise there would be no dilemma. In a business context, however, it is essential that managers agree on a process for dealing with dilemmas.

Our experience with the sadhu offers an interesting parallel to business situations. An immediate response was mandatory. Failure to act was a decision in itself. Up on the mountain we could not resign and submit our résumés to a head-hunter. In contrast to philosophy, business involves action and implementation—getting things done. Managers must come up with answers based on what they see and what they allow to influence their decision-making processes. On the mountain, none of us but Stephen realized the true dimensions of the situation we were facing.

One of our problems was that as a group we had no process for developing a consensus. We had no sense of purpose or plan. The difficulties of dealing with the sadhu were so complex that no one person could handle them. Because the group did not have a set of preconditions that could guide its action to an acceptable resolution, we reacted instinctively as individuals. The cross-cultural nature of the group added a further layer of complexity. We had no leader with whom we could all identify and in whose purpose we believed. Only Stephen was willing to take charge, but he could not gain adequate support from the group to care for the sadhu.

Some organizations do have values that transcend the personal values of their managers. Such values, which go beyond profitability, are usually revealed when the organization is under stress. People throughout the organization generally accept its values, which, because they are not presented as a rigid list of commandments, may be somewhat ambiguous. The stories people tell, rather than printed materials, transmit the organization's conceptions of what is proper behavior.

For twenty years, I have been exposed at senior levels to a variety of corporations and organizations. It is amazing how quickly an outsider can sense the tone and style of an organization and, with that, the degree of tolerated openness and freedom to challenge management.

Organizations that do not have a heritage of mutually accepted, shared values tend to become unhinged during stress, with each individual bailing out for himself or herself. In the great takeover battles we have witnessed during past years, companies that had strong cultures drew the wagons around them and fought it out, while other companies saw executives—supported by golden parachutes—bail out of the struggles.

Because corporations and their members are interdependent, for the corporation to be strong the members need to share a preconceived notion of correct behavior, a "business ethic," and think of it as a positive force, not a constraint.

As an investment banker, I am continually warned by well-meaning lawyers, clients, and associates to be wary of conflicts of interest. Yet if I were to run away from every difficult situation, I wouldn't be an effective investment banker. I have to feel my way through conflicts. An effective manager can't run from risk either; he or she has to confront risk. To feel "safe" in doing that, managers need the guidelines of an agreed-upon process and set of values within the organization.

After my three months in Nepal, I spent three months as an executive-in-residence at both the Stanford Business School and the University of California at Berkeley's Center for Ethics and Social Policy of the Graduate Theological Union. Those six months away from my job gave me time to assimilate twenty years of business experience. My thoughts turned often to the meaning of the leadership role in any large organization. Students at the seminary thought of themselves as antibusiness. But when I questioned them, they agreed that they distrusted all large organizations, including the church. They perceived all large organizations as impersonal and opposed to individual values and needs. Yet we all know of organizations in which people's values and beliefs are respected and their expressions encouraged. What makes the difference? Can we identify the difference and, as a result, manage more effectively?

The word *ethics* turns off many and confuses more. Yet the notions of shared values and an agreed-upon process for dealing with adversity and change—what many people mean when they talk about corporate culture—seem to be at the heart of the ethical issue. People who are in touch with their own core beliefs and the beliefs of others and who are sustained by them can be more comfortable living on the cutting edge. At times, taking a tough line or a decisive stand in a muddle of ambiguity is the only ethical thing to do. If a manager is indecisive about a problem and spends time trying to figure out the "good" thing to do, the enterprise may be lost.

Business ethics, then, has to do with the authenticity and integrity of the enterprise. To be ethical is to follow the business as well as the cultural goals of the corporation, its owners, its employees, and its customers. Those who cannot serve the corporate vision are not authentic businesspeople and, therefore, are not ethical in the business sense.

At this stage of my own business experience, I have a strong interest in organizational behavior. Sociologists are keenly studying what they call corporate stories, legends, and heroes as a way organizations have of transmitting value systems. Corporations such as Arco have even hired consultants to perform an audit of their corporate culture. In a company, a leader is a person who understands, interprets, and manages the corporate value system. Effective managers, therefore, are action-oriented people who resolve conflict, are tolerant of ambiguity, stress, and change, and have a strong sense of purpose for themselves and their organizations.

If all this is true, I wonder about the role of the professional manager who moves from company to company. How can he or she quickly absorb the values and culture of different organizations? Or is there, indeed, an art of management that is totally transportable? Assuming that such fungible managers do exist, is it proper for them to manipulate the values of others?

What would have happened had Stephen and I carried the sadhu for two days back to the village and become involved with the villagers in his care? In four trips to Nepal, my most interesting experience occurred in 1975 when I lived in a Sherpa home in the Khumbu for five days while recovering from altitude sickness. The high point of Stephen's trip was an invitation to participate in a family funeral ceremony in Manang. Neither experience had to do with climbing the high passes of the Himalayas. Why were we so reluctant to try the lower path, the ambiguous trail? Perhaps because we did not have a leader who could reveal the greater purpose of the trip to us.

Why didn't Stephen, with his moral vision, opt to take the sadhu under his personal care? The answer is partly because Stephen was hard-stressed physically himself and partly because, without some support system that encompassed our involuntary and episodic community on the mountain, it was beyond his individual capacity to do so.

I see the current interest in corporate culture and corporate value systems as a positive response to pessimism such as Stephen's about the decline of the role of the individual in large organizations. Individuals who operate from a thoughtful set of personal values provide the foundation for a corporate culture. A corporate tradition that encourages freedom of inquiry, supports personal values, and reinforces a focused sense of direction can fulfill the need to combine individual-ity with the prosperity and success of the group. Without such corpo-rate support, the individual is lost.

That is the lesson of the sadhu. In a complex corporate situation, the individual requires and deserves the support of the group. When people cannot find such support in their organizations, they don't know how to act. If such support is forthcoming, a person has a stake in the success of the group and can add much to the process of estab-lishing and maintaining a corporate culture. Management's challenge is to be sensitive to individual needs, to shape them, and to direct and focus them for the benefit of the group as a whole.

For each of us the sadhu lives. Should we stop what we are doing and comfort him; or should we keep trudging up toward the high pass? Should I pause to help the derelict I pass on the street each night as I walk by the Yale Club en route to Grand Central Station? Am I his brother? What is the nature of our responsibility if we consider our-selves to be ethical persons? Perhaps it is to change the values of the group so that it can, with all its resources, take the other road.

When Do We Take a Stand?

I wrote about my experiences purposely to present an ambiguous situa-tion. I never found out if the sadhu lived or died. I can attest, though, that the sadhu lives on in his story. He lives in the ethics classes I teach each year at business schools and churches. He lives in the classrooms of nu-merous business schools, where professors have taught the case to tens of thousands of students. He lives in several casebooks on ethics and on an educational video. And he lives in organizations such as the American Red Cross and AT&T, which use his story in their ethics training.

As I reflect on the sadhu now, 15 years after the fact, I first have to wonder, What actually happened on that Himalayan slope? When I first wrote about the event, I reported the experience in as much detail as I could remember, but I shaped it to the needs of a good classroom discus-sion. After years of reading my story, viewing it on video, and hearing oth-ers discuss it, I'm not sure I myself know what actually occurred on the mountainside that day!

I've also heard a wide variety of responses to the story. The sadhu, for example, may not have wanted our help at all—he may have been inten-tionally bringing on his own death as a way to holiness. Why had he taken the dangerous way over the pass instead of the caravan route through the gorge? Hindu businesspeople have told me that in trying to assist the sadhu, we were being typically arrogant Westerners imposing our cultural values on the world.

I've learned that each year along the pass, a few Nepali porters are left to freeze to death outside the tents of the unthinking tourists who hired them. A few years ago, a French group even left one of their own, a young French woman, to die there. The difficult pass seems to demonstrate a perverse version of Gresham's law of currency: The bad practices of previous travelers have driven out the values that new travelers might have followed if they were at home. Perhaps that helps to explain why our porters behaved as they did and why it was so difficult for Stephen or anyone else to establish a different approach on the spot.

Our Sherpa sirdar, Pasang, was focused on his responsibility for bringing us up the mountain safe and sound. (His livelihood and status in the Sherpa ethnic group depended on our safe return.) We were weak, our party was split, the porters were well on their way to the top with all our gear and food, and a storm would have separated us irrevocably from our logistical base.

The fact was, we had no plan for dealing with the contingency of the sadhu. There was nothing we could do to unite our multicultural group in the little time we had. An ethical dilemma had come upon us unexpectedly, an element of drama that may explain why the sadhu's story has continued to attract students.

I am often asked for help in teaching the story. I usually advise keeping the details as ambiguous as possible. A true ethical dilemma requires a decision between two hard choices. In the case of the sadhu, we had to decide how much to sacrifice ourselves to take care of a stranger. And given the constraints of our trek, we had to make a group decision, not an individual one. If a large majority of students in a class ends up thinking I'm a bad person because of my decision on the mountain, the instructor may not have given the case its due. The same is true if the majority sees no problem with the choices we made.

Any class's response depends on its setting, whether it's a business school, a church, or a corporation. I've found that younger students are more likely to see the issue as black-and-white, whereas older ones tend to see shades of gray. Some have seen a conflict between the different ethical approaches that we followed at the time. Stephen felt he had to do everything he could to save the sadhu's life, in accordance with his Christian ethic of compassion. I had a utilitarian response: do the greatest good for the greatest number. Give a burst of aid to minimize the sadhu's exposure, then continue on our way.

The basic question of the case remains, When do we take a stand? When do we allow a "sadhu" to intrude into our daily lives? Few of us can afford the time or effort to take care of every needy person we encounter. How much must we give of ourselves? And how do we prepare our organizations and institutions so they will respond appropriately in a crisis? How do we influence them if we do not agree with their points of view?

We cannot quit our jobs over every ethical dilemma, but if we continually ignore our sense of values, who do we become? As a journalist asked at a recent conference on ethics, "Which ditch are we willing to die in?" For each of us, the answer is a bit different. How we act in response to that question defines better than anything else who we are, just as, in a collective sense, our acts define our institutions. In effect, the sadhu is always there, ready to remind us of the tensions between our own goals and the claims of strangers.

2
The Team That Wasn't

Suzy Wetlaufer

The last thing Eric Holt had expected to miss about New York City
was its sunrises. Seeing one usually meant he had pulled another all-
nighter at the consulting firm where, as a vice president, he had managed three teams of manufacturing specialists. But as he stood on the
balcony of his new apartment in the small Indiana city that was now
his home, Eric suddenly felt a pang of nostalgia for the way the dawn
plays off the skyscrapers of Manhattan. In the next moment, though,
he let out a sardonic laugh. The dawn light was *not* what he missed
about New York, he realized. What he missed was the feeling of accomplishment that usually accompanied those sunrises.

An all-nighter in New York had meant hours of intense work with a
cadre of committed, enthusiastic colleagues. Give and take. Humor.
Progress. Here, so far anyway, that was unthinkable. As the director of
strategy at FireArt, Inc., a regional glass manufacturer, Eric spent all
his time trying to get his new team to make it through a meeting
without the tension level becoming unbearable. Six of the top-level
managers involved seemed determined to turn the company around,
but the seventh seemed equally determined to sabotage the process.
Forget camaraderie. There had been three meetings so far, and Eric
hadn't even been able to get everyone on the same side of an issue.

Eric stepped inside his apartment and checked the clock: only three
more hours before he had to watch as Randy Louderback, FireArt's
charismatic director of sales and marketing, either dominated the

---

HBR's cases are derived from the experiences of real companies and real people. As
written, they are hypothetical, and the names used are fictitious.

group's discussion or withdrew entirely, tapping his pen on the table to indicate his boredom. Sometimes he withheld information vital to the group's debate; other times he coolly denigrated people's comments. Still, Eric realized, Randy held the group in such thrall because of his dynamic personality, his almost legendary past, and his close relationship with FireArt's CEO that he could not be ignored. And at least once during each meeting, he offered an insight about the industry or the company that was so perceptive that Eric knew he *shouldn't* be ignored.

As he prepared to leave for the office, Eric felt the familiar frustration that had started building during the team's first meeting a month earlier. It was then that Randy had first insinuated, with what sounded like a joke, that he wasn't cut out to be a team player. "Leaders lead, followers . . . please pipe down!" had been his exact words, although he had smiled winningly as he spoke, and the rest of the group had laughed heartily in response. No one in the group was laughing now, though, least of all Eric.

FireArt, Inc., was in trouble—not deep trouble, but enough for its CEO, Jack Derry, to make strategic repositioning Eric's top and only task. The company, a family-owned maker of wine goblets, beer steins, ashtrays, and other glass novelties had succeeded for nearly eighty years as a high-quality, high-price producer, catering to hundreds of Midwestern clients. It traditionally did big business every football season, selling commemorative knickknacks to the fans of teams such as the Fighting Irish, the Wolverines, and the Golden Gophers. In the spring, there was always a rush of demand for senior prom items—champagne goblets emblazoned with a school's name or beer mugs with a school's crest, for example. Fraternities and sororities were steady customers. Year after year, FireArt showed respectable increases at the top and bottom lines, posting $86 million in revenues and $3 million in earnings three years before Eric arrived.

In the last eighteen months, though, sales and earnings had flattened. Jack, a grandnephew of the company's founder, thought he knew what was happening. Until recently, large national glass companies had been able to make money only through mass production. Now, however, thanks to new technologies in the glassmaking industry, those companies could execute short runs profitably. They had begun to enter FireArt's niche, Jack had told Eric, and, with their superior resources, it was just a matter of time before they would own it.

"You have one responsibility as FireArt's new director of strategy," Jack had said to Eric on his first day. "That's to put together a team of our top people, one person from each division, and have a comprehensive plan for the company's strategic realignment up, running, and winning within six months."

Eric had immediately compiled a list of the senior managers from human resources, manufacturing, finance, distribution, design, and marketing, and had set a date for the first meeting. Then, drawing on his years as a consultant who had worked almost solely in team environments, Eric had carefully prepared a structure and guidelines for the group's discussions, disagreements, and decisions, which he planned to propose to the members for their input before they began working together.

Successful groups are part art, part science, Eric knew, but he also believed that with every member's full commitment, a team proved the adage that the whole is greater than the sum of its parts. Knowing that managers at FireArt were unaccustomed to the team process, however, Eric imagined he might get some resistance from one or two members.

For one, he had been worried about Ray LaPierre of manufacturing. Ray was a giant of a man who had run the furnaces for some thirty-five years, following in his father's footsteps. Although he was a former high school football star who was known among workers in the factory for his hearty laugh and his love of practical jokes, Ray usually didn't say much around FireArt's executives, citing his lack of higher education as the reason. Eric had thought the team atmosphere might intimidate him.

Eric had also anticipated a bit of a fight from Maureen Turner of the design division, who was known to complain that FireArt didn't appreciate its six artists. Eric had expected that Maureen might have a chip on her shoulder about collaborating with people who didn't understand the design process.

Ironically, both those fears had proved groundless, but another, more difficult problem had arisen. The wild card had turned out to be Randy. Eric had met Randy once before the team started its work and had found him to be enormously intelligent, energetic, and good-humored. What's more, Jack Derry had confirmed his impressions, telling him that Randy "had the best mind" at FireArt. It was also from Jack that Eric had first learned of Randy's hardscrabble yet inspirational personal history.

Poor as a child, he had worked as a security guard and short-order cook to put himself through the state college, from which he graduated with top honors. Soon after, he started his own advertising and market research firm in Indianapolis, and within the decade, he had built it into a company employing fifty people to service some of the region's most prestigious accounts. His success brought with it a measure of fame: articles in the local media, invitations to the statehouse, even an honorary degree from an Indiana business college. But in the late 1980s, Randy's firm suffered the same fate as many other advertising shops, and he was forced to declare bankruptcy. FireArt considered it a coup when it landed him as director of marketing, since he had let it be known that he was offered at least two dozen other jobs. "Randy is the future of this company," Jack Derry had told Eric. "If he can't help you, no one can. I look forward to hearing what a team with his kind of horsepower can come up with to steer us away from the mess we're in."

Those words echoed in Eric's mind as he sat, with increasing anxiety, through the team's first and second meetings. Though Eric had planned an agenda for each meeting and tried to keep the discussions on track, Randy always seemed to find a way to disrupt the process. Time and time again, he shot down other people's ideas, or he simply didn't pay attention. He also answered most questions put to him with maddening vagueness. "I'll have my assistant look into it when he gets a moment," he replied when one team member asked him to list FireArt's five largest customers. "Some days you eat the bear, and other days the bear eats you," he joked another time, when asked why sales to fraternities had recently nose-dived.

Randy's negativism, however, was countered by occasional comments so insightful that they stopped the conversation cold or turned it around entirely—comments that demonstrated extraordinary knowledge about competitors or glass technology or customers' buying patterns. The help wouldn't last, though; Randy would quickly revert to his role as team renegade.

The third meeting, last week, had ended in chaos. Ray LaPierre, Maureen Turner, and the distribution director, Carl Simmons, had each planned to present cost-cutting proposals, and at first it looked as though the group were making good progress.

Ray opened the meeting, proposing a plan for FireArt to cut through-put time by 3 percent and raw-materials costs by 2 percent, thereby positioning the company to compete better on price. It was obvious from his detailed presentation that he had put a lot of thought into his comments, and it was evident that he was fighting a certain amount of nervousness as he made them.

"I know I don't have the book smarts of most of you in this room," he had begun, "but here goes anyway." During his presentation, Ray stopped several times to answer questions from the team, and as he went on, his nervousness transformed into his usual ebullience. "That wasn't so bad!" he laughed to himself as he sat down at the end, flashing a grin at Eric. "Maybe we *can* turn this old ship around."

Maureen Turner had followed Ray. While not disagreeing with him—she praised his comments, in fact—she argued that FireArt also needed to invest in new artists, pitching its competitive advantage in better design and wider variety. Unlike Ray, Maureen had made this case to FireArt's top executives many times, only to be rebuffed, and some of her frustration seeped through as she explained her reasoning yet again. At one point, her voice almost broke as she described how hard she had worked in her first ten years at FireArt, hoping that someone in management would recognize the creativity of her designs. "But no one did," she recalled with a sad shake of her head. "That's why when I was made director of the department, I made sure all the artists were respected for what they are—*artists*, not worker ants. There's a difference, you know." However, just as with Ray LaPierre, Maureen's comments lost their defensiveness as the group members, with the exception of Randy, who remained impassive, greeted her words with nods of encouragement.

By the time Carl Simmons of distribution started to speak, the mood in the room was approaching buoyant. Carl, a quiet and meticulous man, jumped from his seat and practically paced the room as he described his ideas. FireArt, he said, should play to its strength as a service-oriented company and restructure its trucking system to increase the speed of delivery. He described how a similar strategy had been adopted with excellent results at his last job at a ceramics plant. Carl had joined FireArt just six months earlier. It was when Carl began to describe those results in detail that Randy brought the meeting to an unpleasant halt by letting out a loud groan. "Let's just do *everything*, why don't we, including redesign the kitchen sink!" he cried with mock enthusiasm. That remark sent Carl back quickly to his seat, where he halfheartedly summed up his comments. A few minutes later, he excused himself, saying he had another meeting. Soon the others made excuses to leave, too, and the room became empty.

No wonder Eric was apprehensive about the fourth meeting. He was therefore surprised when he entered the room and found the whole group, save Randy, already assembled.

Ten minutes passed in awkward small talk, and, looking from face to face, Eric could see his own frustration reflected. He also detected an edge of panic—just what he had hoped to avoid. He decided he had to raise the topic of Randy's attitude openly, but just as he started, Randy ambled into the room, smiling. "Sorry, folks," he said lightly, holding up a cup of coffee as if it were explanation enough for his tardiness.

"Randy, I'm glad you're here," Eric began, "because I think today we should begin by talking about the group itself—"

Randy cut Eric off with a small, sarcastic laugh. "Uh-oh, I knew this was going to happen," he said.

Before Eric could answer, Ray LaPierre stood up and walked over to Randy, bending over to look him in the eye.

"You just don't care, do you?" he began, his voice so angry it startled everyone in the room.

Everyone except Randy. "Quite the contrary—I care very much," he answered breezily. "I just don't believe this is how change should be made. A brilliant idea never came out of a *team*. Brilliant ideas come from brilliant individuals, who then inspire others in the organization to implement them."

"That's a lot of bull," Ray shot back. "You just want all the credit for the success, and you don't want to share it with anyone."

"That's absurd," Randy laughed again. "I'm not trying to impress anyone here at FireArt. I don't need to. I want this company to succeed as much as you do, but I believe, and I believe passionately, that groups are useless. Consensus means mediocrity. I'm sorry, but it does."

"But you haven't even *tried* to reach consensus with us," Maureen interjected. "It's as if you don't care what we all have to say. We can't work alone for a solution—we need to understand each other. Don't you see that?"

The room was silent as Randy shrugged his shoulders noncommittally. He stared at the table, a blank expression on his face.

It was Eric who broke the silence. "Randy, this is a *team*. You are part of it," he said, trying to catch Randy's eye without success. "Perhaps we should start again—"

Randy stopped him by holding up his cup, as if making a toast. "Okay, look, I'll behave from now on," he said. The words held promise, but he was smirking as he spoke them—something no one at the table missed. Eric took a deep breath before he answered; as much as he wanted and needed Randy Louderback's help, he was suddenly struck by the thought that perhaps Randy's personality and his past experiences simply made it impossible for him to participate in the delicate process of ego surrender that any kind of teamwork requires.

"Listen, everyone, I know this is a challenge," Eric began, but he was cut short by Randy's pencil-tapping on the table. A moment later, Ray LaPierre was standing again.

"Forget it. This is never going to work. It's just a waste of time for all of us," he said, more resigned than gruff. "We're all in this together, or there's no point." He headed for the door, and before Eric could stop him, two others were at his heels.

Why Doesn't This Team Work?

Seven experts discuss what teamwork takes.

JON R. KATZENBACH *is a director of McKinsey & Company and co-author, with Douglas K. Smith, of* The Wisdom of Teams: Creating the High-Performance Organization *(Harvard Business School Press, 1993, HarperCollins, 1994). Their video,* The Discipline of Teams, *was published by Harvard Business School Management Productions.*

Eric has his hands full with this team, particularly with Randy. In fact, a skeptic might well advise Eric to throw in the towel now because it is clear that Randy can—and might—destroy the team for good. But there are other factors hindering this team besides Randy, and unless Eric recognizes and addresses them, the team will not make progress, whatever its makeup.

There is no evidence of a common commitment to a team purpose or a working approach. Eric is trying valiantly to hold the members to an agenda based on the CEO's charge: "to have a comprehensive plan for strategic realignment." At best, that's a vague directive. Consequently, the members do not understand the implications of those words, draw any meaningful focus from them, or recognize any need to work together to make "strategic realignment" a performance reality.

The "rules of the road" are extremely unclear. While the team has a good mix of skills and experience, the members do not know how each is expected to contribute, how they will work together, what they will work on together, how the meetings will be conducted, or how each person's "nonteam" responsibilities will be handled.

Eric's consultant "team" experience is misleading. In the past, Eric was really a part of a consultant "working group," which is completely different from a team. For one thing, consultants generally have prior experience dealing with the client assignments they obtain. For another, consultant working groups expect to have leaders; they're usually formed with the understanding that one person knows best how to accomplish the task at hand efficiently with minimal risk. Finally, most of the real work in such a group is done by individuals as individuals, not by individuals relying on one another to accomplish joint tasks. I doubt that Eric's experience in New York was at all similar to the situation that confronts him at FireArt, yet he seems to expect this "team" to gel and operate in a similar fashion.

Eric's group spends more time on feelings and past experiences than on the task at hand. We know little about what they are supposed to be working on and accomplishing. Except for Randy, the members are supportive and helpful—to the point where protecting feelings becomes more important than getting something done. Real teams do not have to get along. They have to get things accomplished.

Eric's group seeks consensus rather than accomplishment. Real teams seldom seek consensus; they decide each issue differently based on who is in the best position to ensure performance. Sometimes the leader decides, sometimes another person, and sometimes more than one. Consensus may happen now and then, but it is not the litmus test for a team's performance.

So what can be done? First, Eric must acknowledge that most would-be teams go through a painful metamorphosis; his group is not uncommon. Having said that, though, he must also recognize that not every group of multiskilled, well-intended people can or should function as a team. In this case, the likelihood of team performance is hard to determine because it has not yet been fully tested. Before giving up on the idea, therefore, Eric can try several things—provided he can also enlist the support of the team's sponsor (CEO Jack Derry) in these attempts.

First, he can decide whether these people should make up a leader-driven "working group" rather than a "team." Is this really a team-performance opportunity? If so, it should be evident that the multiple, diverse skills of the members will make a material difference in the results of their efforts. It must become evident to all members that no one person "knows best"—not even Randy. If the members are to work primarily on individual subassignments and report back to the group, and if the "sum of the individual bests" is good enough, then Eric does not need a team. If it is truly a team opportunity, Eric and/or Jack should:

1. Insist that the team identify specific work "products" that require several members to work together. The value of these products must be significant relative to the group's overall performance, and Randy must recognize both the value and the need for collective work and skills. If this can be accomplished, the team members can be expected to develop trust and respect by working together to those ends, regardless of personal chemistries and past attitudes.

2. Require the team members to determine how to hold themselves mutually accountable for achieving their goals. Teams need mutual or joint accountability in addition to individual accountability. The entire group must believe it can succeed or fail only as a team.

3. Design a more disciplined working approach that enforces "team basics." It should ensure that members do as much real work in team (or subteam) settings as they do separately in preparing for the team sessions. A member giving presentations to the rest of the team seldom constitutes collective work for purposes of increasing team performance. Eric should also set clear and enforceable ground rules to which all members must abide. If Randy still will not follow the rules, either the team or Randy must go. Some people cannot be team members.

The "Randy issue" must be addressed. I suspect Eric has been too quick to assume the worst. Randy may or may not be a team misfit. After all, he has had little chance so far to change his attitude about this team. His bravado tells us only what he thinks of teams in general; many excellent team members begin with this attitude. The only way to find out if this team can include Randy is for him to do real work with other members individually to see if mutual trust and respect develop.

If all else fails, Eric should consider a dual or split working approach that does not include Randy in many of the important working meetings. Otherwise, this "team" may do its best as a leader-driven working group, with Eric playing a stronger leader role. They are not all that bad!

J. RICHARD HACKMAN *is the Cahners-Rabb Professor of Social and Organizational Psychology at Harvard University in Cambridge, Massachusetts. He holds appointments both in the psychology department and at the*

Harvard Business School. His most recent book, Groups That Work (And Those That Don't) *was published in 1990 by Jossey-Bass.*

Some people aren't cut out to be team players. Eric should have paid attention when Randy suggested that he was one of those people.

Eric could have met with Randy privately after that meeting. The first order of business would have been for Eric to assure himself that Randy indeed felt unable to work on a team—and that his self-perception was grounded in reality. That established, the two managers could then have sought a way to capture Randy's insights that did not require him to be a regular team member. Who knows what they might have come up with? Perhaps Eric would meet privately with Randy before and after each team meeting to report progress and seek ideas. Perhaps such briefings would be done by different team members in rotation. Perhaps Randy would be invited to certain meetings, or portions of them, but only when his ideas or reactions were especially needed.

Every organization has some members who make their best contributions as solo performers. These are people who just don't have the skills needed to work constructively in teams—and who are unable or unwilling to acquire those skills. Such people are found in all functions and at all levels, even in senior management. There are only three ways to deal with them when teams are formed. One, keep them at a safe distance from the teams so they can do no damage. (Some companies these days seek to get rid of their solo performers altogether: "Only team players at this company!" is the slogan. As if being a team player were the ultimate measure of anyone's worth, which it is not.) Two, go ahead and put them on teams, install strong leaders to keep things under control, and hope for the best. ("Everybody here works on teams. No exceptions!" is the motto then. As if all people were skilled in teamwork, which they are not.)

Neither of these alternatives has much to recommend it. The first is wasteful. Talent is knowingly withheld from teams. The second is dangerous. Team after team can be sunk by "team destroyers" like Randy—people whose brilliance in individual tasks is matched by their incapacity for collaborative work. (Less talented individuals are less of a problem. If they persist in misbehaving, the team can afford to get rid of them. But it is very hard even to contemplate shunning someone as good as Randy.)

The only realistic alternative, then, is to harvest the contributions of talented people like Randy in a way that does not put the team itself at risk. As I said, Eric should have sought a way to accomplish that immediately after the first meeting. His goal now should be the same. It will be harder now than it would have been then because now he also has considerable repair work to do with Randy and with the team. The task also requires greater care now than it would have then because of the risk of scapegoating.

Teams that encounter frustrating problems as they are working sometimes attach to a single team member all the negative feelings that are rampant in the group. They make that person the scapegoat, the one who is responsible for everything that has gone wrong. If that bad actor could just be removed, the thinking goes, the team's problems would disappear. The impulse to scapegoat someone when the going gets rough can be quite strong; moreover, the scapegoated member often starts to behave in accordance with his or her peers' expectations, which makes things worse all around. Therefore, teams must not too quickly blame any one person for in-process problems. Midcourse corrections in team composition can be accomplished, but they are risky and difficult. It is better to get team composition right when the team is formed than to undertake repair work later.

When reviewing how well a team is doing, I ask three questions. First, does the product or service of the team meet the standards of its clients—those who receive, review, or use the team's work? Second, is the team becoming more capable as a performing unit over time? Third, does membership on the team contribute positively to each person's learning and well-being? Despite an excellent launch, FireArt's strategic repositioning team is now failing on all three criteria.

Eric should once again review the team's direction, its structure, and his own leadership. Such matters should always be considered first, before attributing team problems to the attitudes or skills of individual members. But if Eric finds, as I suspect he will, that the basic performance situation of this team is actually quite favorable, then he will have to confront Randy's apparent incapacity for teamwork directly. Not to do so would be an abdication of his responsibility as team leader.

GENEVIÈVE SEGOL *is a principal scientist in the research and development department at Bechtel Corporation in San Francisco, California.*

People work well as a team, but they don't think well as a team. That is the essence of what Randy is saying in his arrogant way: "A brilliant idea never came out of a team. Brilliant ideas come from brilliant individuals, who then inspire others in the organization to implement them." From this standpoint, Randy is right. The team assembled by Eric would not succeed even if Randy were not bent on sabotaging the process, because its objective is too vague and its leadership is too weak.

The team was given the task of developing a plan for strategic realignment and having it implemented within six months. This guideline is totally insufficient, especially because the members of the team are unaccustomed to working together and probably uncomfortable with conceptual discussions. They are confused by the mandate, and, as a result, they are shooting in all directions. Worse, they do not realize (or want to admit) that they do not understand the issue. No one has asked the basic question: What is the real problem with FireArt's business?

Jack Derry, the CEO, "thought" the company's faltering financial results were caused by the entry of large glassmaking companies into its niche market, but that analysis is superficial. Are customers going to competitors because they offer lower prices, a broader selection, or better service? The solutions proposed by the managers of manufacturing, design, and distribution indicate that each has a different answer to this question. Someone must define the primary cause of FireArt's declining market share and direct the team to focus on that specific issue. That is the first step toward solving the problem presented in this case.

Defining the problem and giving precise directions to the team should have been the responsibility of FireArt's senior management, but clearly the leadership is lacking. The CEO's hands-off attitude is inappropriate, especially considering that the company's future is at stake. Not only did he fail to anticipate and avoid the present downturn, but when the troubles became apparent, he hired an outsider to correct the situation. The CEO is content to "look forward to hearing what [this] team . . . can come up with to steer us away from the mess we're in."

This is not delegation but abdication. Unfortunately, Eric has not so far filled that leadership void. Instead, he has played his prepared script, focusing on the mechanics of the teamwork process and hoping for harmony. He certainly did not control the meetings, and Randy took advantage of his timidity. To his credit, however, Eric has already acknowledged that Randy should not be ignored. He must be kept on the team because he has valuable information and insight, and also because he can do more damage to the team if he is not on it. Keeping Randy involved is the second important step.

Eric can simultaneously address the two key issues—giving the team precise directives and keeping Randy involved—by assigning to the latter the responsibility of researching and documenting the exact nature of FireArt's difficulties. Randy will appreciate this individual task; he's also uniquely qualified for the job because of both his intellect and his position. As director of sales and marketing, he is the closest to customers and competitors, and the data must come from them. What's more, this type of assignment is quite analytical and, for this reason, performed more effectively by one person than by a group.

Purists might argue that permitting one individual to be in the spotlight compromises the team's process, but that is nonsense. Teamwork is a business expedient, not a philosophy, and rules may be bent when necessary. Randy will report his findings to the team, and this event should be used by Eric to relaunch the group's effort on a solid basis, that is, with a precise objective—for example, to cut costs by 10 percent or to be able to fill any order within ten days. Eric must also arrange for the CEO to attend the meeting at which Randy will make his presentation, and a few subsequent team meetings as well, both to control Randy, who is unlikely to be obnoxious in the presence of his boss, and to impress on the group the urgency and importance of its effort.

Eric must act fast, not only because the necessary turnaround of the business cannot wait but also because there is another wild card: Randy might quit. He is an opportunist and an entrepreneur, has little allegiance to FireArt, and enjoys a legendary reputation in the industry, where he has many connections. Eric's job will only be harder if Randy moves to a competitor's team.

PAUL P. BAARD *is an associate professor of communications and management at Fordham University's Graduate School of Business in New York City, with a principal research interest in motivation. He is a former senior corporate executive, and consults with organizations concerning interpersonal issues.*

The truth is, Randy cannot destroy this team unless the other members enable him to do so. Right now, however, an enormous amount of work energy is being lost to reading between the lines, overreacting to perceived slights, pursuing reassurance, and competing instead of cooperating. The group is in danger.

The problem is psychological fusion—a disorder that is running amok in today's stressed corporate environment. In essence, fusion is the failure of one person to separate himself or herself from the words or actions of another. Fusion occurs when we fail to differentiate ourselves emotionally from the opinions and conduct of others. When we allow other people to "make us feel" either good or bad—as a result of compliments or criticism—we have fused with them. Randy was able to drive team members from the room not because he had authority but because they fused with him. These grown adults allowed Randy to make them feel inadequate. They acted as if they *needed* Randy's approval of their ideas. Eric appears to think that he *needs* Randy on the team, which renders Eric unable to interact effectively with him.

Randy, for his part, is caught up in fusion. He clings to the myth that because he is the brightest he is the most effective, and he must have this affirmed continuously by his colleagues. This leaves him unable to acknowledge and support others' good ideas; he is threatened when others have answers too.

Ironically, fusion leads to distance—either overt, as in walking away, or covert, as in withdrawing from a discussion. Because fusion creates pain (from feeling emotionally dependent on others), it leaves people anxious about what others are thinking, saying, and meaning by their words, looks, and even their silences. An individual afflicted with fusion takes on a desperate tone and will usually defend his or her ideas in an emotional way: "That's my baby you're attacking!" Fusion thus inhibits cooperation and understanding, which are essential to a group's productivity.

The condition of the group is not irreversible, however. There are several things Eric can do to turn the situation around. To begin, he must confront Randy with reality in a private conversation.

Eric must make it clear that FireArt needs a new direction and that Eric's group *will recommend* that path. He should tell Randy that his input is indeed desired. But Eric must also tell Randy that if he is to be a member of the team, he must now play a full role. He is to contribute, challenge, and support ideas as appropriate. And he must clarify and take responsibility for his positions. By being sarcastic, Randy may be offering a comment, but he is not taking a stance. We don't know, for example, what specifically about the other team members' proposals Randy doesn't like; we just know he doesn't like them.

Eric must also let Randy know that it's an all-or-nothing proposition. Eric must ask him, "Will you function in the way I have just described?" An affirmative response is usually forthcoming from malcontents who are confronted this way. If the answer is "no," however, Eric must accept Randy's resignation from the group. And he must not worry about Randy's relationship with the CEO. Unless Jack calls him on his actions, Eric has a right and a responsibility to run the group in the way he believes will yield the best results. (If Jack does call Eric on his actions, Eric will have reason on his side. Jack may think Randy is terrific, but he hired Eric to turn the company around.)

After Eric and Randy meet, Eric should turn his attention to damage control with the rest of the group. To get past the recent strain among the members, Eric should start the next meeting, with everyone present, by stating that Randy had not understood his job in the group—namely to help develop a new strategy for the company, but that now he does. Eric should then explain that each member is responsible for taking a position on all matters, sharing and either defending it or modifying it in discussions or debates.

As the team moves forward, Eric ought to expect that Randy will resort at times to his old ways—using sarcasm or tapping his pencil. If he does, Eric should confront Randy immediately with: "Randy, you and I agreed you would make your position clear. I cannot discern your position based on the comment (or gesture) you just made. What are your thoughts on this matter?"

Right now, psychological fusion has created a tense, threatening environment for all members of this team. But over time, they should be able to develop a healthier expectation of appropriate conduct within the group. This, in turn, will support Randy's improved behavior. When fusion has been removed, Randy's only ability to influence the other members will be the strength of his ideas—a scenario that he and the other group members will find much more satisfying and conducive to a creative process.

ED MUSSELWHITE *is the president and chief executive officer of Zenger-Miller, Inc., a San Jose-based international strategic consulting and business training company.* **KATHLEEN HURSON** *is the senior vice president of research and development at Zenger-Miller. They are the co-authors, with John H. Zenger and Craig Perrin, of* Leading Teams: Mastering the New Role *(Irwin Professional Publishing, 1993). Musselwhite is also a coauthor, with Jack Orsburn, Linda Moran, and John H. Zenger, of* Self-Directed Work Teams: The New American Challenge *(Irwin Professional Publishing, 1990).*

Can this team be saved? Maybe. The key will be Eric's ability to focus his unruly team members not on the team itself but on an inspiring goal that only the team can achieve. And the task is enormously important. The success of the organization may hinge on the success of this team.

For many people contemplating teams, this case represents their darkest nightmare: the brilliant loner refusing to cooperate, the other members goaded into personal attack, the leader powerless to control the situation, and the hoped-for progress dashed. In our experience, few team members behave so outrageously. What's more common—and more insidious—is that some people's concerns go underground, where they harden into resistance and outright sabotage. In fact, in a 1994 independent Zenger-Miller survey conducted by the American Institutes for Research, more than one-third of the 1,000-plus respondent organizations reported that strong internal resistance and/or sabotage is a significant barrier to be overcome on the road to successful team implementations.

This case confirms our belief that shortchanging a team launch—especially an executive team launch—is always a mistake. Eric's guidelines for group debate do not begin to cover the orientation, skills training, and goal setting that an effective team launch must contain. We suspect that Eric gave in to deadline pressure and a fear that executive team members would not stand for any touchy-feely stuff. Nevertheless, we have found that executives must receive careful training if they are to function as effective members of a team (as opposed to a traditional executive committee). By and large, these are men and women whose individually focused competitiveness and ability to advance the interests of their own departments have gotten them where they are. The team format represents a radical departure from the environs in which they have previously excelled.

By skipping the critical team-launch process, Eric has gotten himself into a classic team-leadership pickle. To renew trust and foster cohesiveness, he probably should open things up through a series of team meetings in which a progress check is made, mistakes are admitted (including his own), everyone's reactions and feelings are elicited, and agreement is reached on next steps. However, in order to reach the

CEO's six-month goal for the company, we recommend that Eric take a few immediate shortcuts.

First, he should have a serious talk with Jack, the CEO. Eric needs to make it clear that without more involvement from Jack, this team is history, and Eric will be headed back to those Manhattan sunrises he misses so much. Having captured Jack's attention, Eric needs to spell out what Jack, and only Jack, can do: provide a lot more visible and behind-the-scenes support for team activities *and* neutralize Randy. Jack's message to Randy should be: (1) this company can't succeed without you; (2) the team is a fact of life; and (3) you don't have to be on it, but you can't sabotage it, either. (At the same time, Jack must be careful not to give other team members the idea that membership is elective.)

Although it's tempting to try to turn Randy into a team player, we think the team stands a better chance of reaching its goal if Eric doesn't focus too much on that one problem. Thus far, Randy has chosen to bring along antiteam baggage. Instead of forcing that issue prematurely—which could trigger Randy's untimely resignation—Eric first should try to create a useful and compatible role for Randy as a special consultant to the team, called in for review or advice whenever the team needs his expertise. As he begins to see the team's successes and feels more and more cut off from its decisions and camaraderie, Randy may eventually want to get more involved. He should be encouraged to do so, although we don't think he will ever be a consummate team player. Not everyone is.

With Randy neutralized for a bit, Eric's next challenges will be to get himself and his team trained and to help the team members create a compelling and results-oriented realignment strategy. The problems facing this organization cry out for effective cross-functional team solutions and innovations.

Instead of the uninspiring department-focused improvements presented by Maureen, Ray, and Carl, we'd like to see the team trained to take a bigger-picture, cross-departmental approach to its realignment task. Working to create cross-functional improvements will jar the executives out of their departmental allegiances and give them a much-needed companywide perspective.

What are the key strategic processes that cut across all departments? How do they affect customers? How should they? Where are the opportunities for improvement? For example, how can Maureen's artists and Ray's furnace workers get together to cut costs, streamline processes, and create new and better products? How can manufacturing and distribution cooperate to make delivery speed a real competitive advantage? High-level cross-functional teams such as this one can meaningfully explore these kinds of questions. And the answers usually produce the biggest organizational improvements.

MICHAEL GARBER *is the manager of quality and employee involvement and training at USG Corporation in Chicago, Illinois.*

Eric is not leading a team. He is facilitating a meeting of a group of individuals who don't really understand the concepts, methods, or importance of teamwork—individuals who are each lobbying for their own personal goals. In fact, it's somewhat surprising that the CEO, Jack Derry, decided to solve FireArt's problems with a team in the first place. The company clearly operates with a traditional, hierarchical management structure, not a structure that supports teamwork.

Teamwork does not occur simply by mandate from above. Nor does it occur overnight. It requires a supportive corporate culture, certain management and interpersonal skills, and practice. Eric has none of these at his disposal except his own experience, so in a sense he must start from scratch at FireArt. I suggest the following action plan:

First, Jack Derry must visit the team to champion its efforts. He must also request periodic updates from the team. His doing that will link the team to the organization and show the group that the company is genuinely interested in and supports its efforts.

Then, Ray, Maureen, et al., need to learn more about the concepts behind teamwork and the benefits of working on a team. They need to know what's in it for them as well as what's in it for the organization. They should hear about successful team efforts in other companies and be educated about common obstacles teams face and specific tools that can help build consensus. To accomplish this, Eric might consider holding an on-site workshop (run by Eric or by an outsider with expertise) that features discussions about the theory behind team management, a review of current literature on the subject, and simulations of various team situations.

The team members must come to understand that teams, by definition, don't require members to surrender their individuality. Rather, teams work best when members respect one another and believe that each is unique and has something important to add. Therefore, the workshop should also include time to evaluate and improve the members' interpersonal skills—skills such as listening, communicating, and giving and receiving feedback. Of course, most members of the FireArt team would probably argue (as most people do) that they already know how to listen and communicate. But the fact is, when Ray LaPierre says something, Maureen Turner has to do more than nod supportively. She must understand his most important points, grasp their implications, and perhaps even formulate a rebuttal. This is a skill, and it can be taught.

With the workshop complete, the team should focus on developing a mission statement. This is necessary to provide the group with a common purpose, and it should help reduce individual lobbying efforts. Once a mission statement is formed, specific goals can be determined to narrow the team's focus of activity. Each member will then better understand his or her role, and real progress can begin.

Randy is a difficult character, mainly because the CEO has put him on a pedestal—a fact that he is exploiting. But with a new foundation in place, Eric will have increased leverage with Randy because he, along with the other members, will recognize the importance of teamwork and be more supportive of it. Together, then, they will be able to begin the process of developing a strategic plan to attack the deteriorating business situation.

3
The Discipline of Teams

Jon R. Katzenbach and Douglas K. Smith

Early in the 1980s, Bill Greenwood and a small band of rebel rail-roaders took on most of the top management of Burlington Northern and created a multibillion-dollar business in "piggybacking" rail ser-vices despite widespread resistance, even resentment, within the com-pany. The Medical Products Group at Hewlett-Packard owes most of its leading performance to the remarkable efforts of Dean Morton, Lew Platt, Ben Holmes, Dick Alberting, and a handful of their col-leagues who revitalized a health care business that most others had written off. At Knight-Ridder, Jim Batten's "customer obsession" vi-sion took root at the *Tallahassee Democrat* when 14 frontline enthusi-asts turned a charter to eliminate errors into a mission of major change and took the entire paper along with them.

Such are the stories and the work of teams—real teams that per-form, not amorphous groups that we call teams because we think that the label is motivating and energizing. The difference between teams that perform and other groups that don't is a subject to which most of us pay far too little attention. Part of the problem is that *team* is a word and concept so familiar to everyone.

Or at least that's what we thought when we set out to do research for our book *The Wisdom of Teams*. We wanted to discover what differ-entiates various levels of team performance, where and how teams work best, and what top management can do to enhance their effec-tiveness. We talked with hundreds of people on more than 50 differ-ent teams in 30 companies and beyond, from Motorola and Hewlett-Packard to Operation Desert Storm and the Girl Scouts.

We found that there is a basic discipline that makes teams work. We also found that teams and good performance are inseparable; you cannot have one without the other. But people use the word *team* so loosely that it gets in the way of learning and applying the discipline that leads to good performance. For managers to make better decisions about whether, when, or how to encourage and use teams, it is important to be more precise about what a team is and what it isn't.

Most executives advocate teamwork. And they should. Teamwork represents a set of values that encourage listening and responding constructively to views expressed by others, giving others the benefit of the doubt, providing support, and recognizing the interests and achievements of others. Such values help teams perform, and they also promote individual performance as well as the performance of an entire organization. But teamwork values by themselves are not exclusive to teams, nor are they enough to ensure team performance.

Nor is a team just any group working together. Committees, councils, and task forces are not necessarily teams. Groups do not become teams simply because that is what someone calls them. The entire work force of any large and complex organization is *never* a team, but think about how often that platitude is offered up.

To understand how teams deliver extra performance, we must distinguish between teams and other forms of working groups. (See Exhibit I.) That distinction turns on performance results. A working group's performance is a function of what its members do as individuals. A team's performance includes both individual results and what we call "collective work-products." A collective work-product is what two or more members must work on together, such as interviews, surveys, or experiments. Whatever it is, a collective work-product reflects the joint, real contribution of team members.

Working groups are both prevalent and effective in large organizations where individual accountability is most important. The best working groups come together to share information, perspectives, and insights; to make decisions that help each person do his or her job better; and to reinforce individual performance standards. But the focus is always on individual goals and accountabilities. Working-group members don't take responsibility for results other than their own. Nor do they try to develop incremental performance contributions requiring the combined work of two or more members.

Teams differ fundamentally from working groups because they require both individual and mutual accountability. Teams rely on more than group discussion, debate, and decision; on more than sharing in-

Exhibit I. Not All Groups Are Teams: How to Tell the Difference

Working Group	Team
Strong, clearly focused leader	Shared leadership roles
Individual accountability	Individual and mutual accountability
The group's purpose is the same as the broader organizational mission	Specific team purpose that the team itself delivers
Individual work-products	Collective work-products
Runs efficient meetings	Encourages open-ended discussion and active problem-solving meetings
Measures its effectiveness indirectly by its influence on others (e.g., financial performance of the business)	Measures performance directly by assessing collective work-products
Discusses, decides, and delegates	Discusses, decides, and does real work together

formation and best practice performance standards. Teams produce discrete work-products through the joint contributions of their members. This is what makes possible performance levels greater than the sum of all the individual bests of team members. Simply stated, a team is more than the sum of its parts.

The first step in developing a disciplined approach to team management is to think about teams as discrete units of performance and not just as positive sets of values. Having observed and worked with scores of teams in action, both successes and failures, we offer the following. Think of it as a working definition or, better still, an essential discipline that real teams share.

A team is a small number of people with complementary skills who are committed to a common purpose, set of performance goals, and approach for which they hold themselves mutually accountable.

The essence of a team is common commitment. Without it, groups perform as individuals; with it, they become a powerful unit of collective performance. This kind of commitment requires a purpose in which team members can believe. Whether the purpose is to "transform the contributions of suppliers into the satisfaction of customers," to "make our company one we can be proud of again," or to "prove that all children can learn," credible team purposes have an element related to winning, being first, revolutionizing, or being on the cutting edge.

Teams develop direction, momentum, and commitment by working to shape a meaningful purpose. Building ownership and commitment to team purpose, however, is not incompatible with taking initial direction from outside the team. The often-asserted assumption that a team cannot "own" its purpose unless management leaves it alone actually confuses more potential teams than it helps. In fact, it is the exceptional case—for example, entrepreneurial situations—when a team creates a purpose entirely on its own.

Most successful teams shape their purposes in response to a demand or opportunity put in their path, usually by higher management. This helps teams get started by broadly framing the company's performance expectation. Management is responsible for clarifying the charter, rationale, and performance challenge for the team, but management must also leave enough flexibility for the team to develop commitment around its own spin on that purpose, set of specific goals, timing, and approach.

The best teams invest a tremendous amount of time and effort exploring, shaping, and agreeing on a purpose that belongs to them both collectively and individually. This "purposing" activity continues throughout the life of the team. In contrast, failed teams rarely develop a common purpose. For whatever reason—an insufficient focus on performance, lack of effort, poor leadership—they do not coalesce around a challenging aspiration.

The best teams also translate their common purpose into specific performance goals, such as reducing the reject rate from suppliers by 50 percent or increasing the math scores of graduates from 40 percent to 95 percent. Indeed, if a team fails to establish specific performance goals or if those goals do not relate directly to the team's overall purpose, team members become confused, pull apart, and revert to mediocre performance. By contrast, when purposes and goals build on one another and are combined with team commitment, they become a powerful engine of performance.

Transforming broad directives into specific and measurable performance goals is the surest first step for a team trying to shape a purpose meaningful to its members. Specific goals, such as getting a new product to market in less than half the normal time, responding to all customers within twenty-four hours, or achieving a zero-defect rate while simultaneously cutting costs by 40 percent, all provide firm footholds for teams. There are several reasons:

- Specific team performance goals help to define a set of work-products that are different both from an organizationwide mission and from individual job objectives. As a result, such work-products require the collective effort of team members to make something specific happen that, in and of itself, adds real value to results. By contrast, simply gathering from time to time to make decisions will not sustain team performance.

- The specificity of performance objectives facilitates clear communication and constructive conflict within the team. When a plant-level team, for example, sets a goal of reducing average machine changeover time to two hours, the clarity of the goal forces the team to concentrate on what it would take either to achieve or to reconsider the goal. When such goals are clear, discussions can focus on how to pursue them or whether to change them; when goals are ambiguous or nonexistent, such discussions are much less productive.

- The attainability of specific goals helps teams maintain their focus on getting results. A product-development team at Eli Lilly's Peripheral Systems Division set definite yardsticks for the market introduction of an ultrasonic probe to help doctors locate deep veins and arteries. The probe had to have an audible signal through a specified depth of tissue, be capable of being manufactured at a rate of 100 per day, and have a unit cost less than a preestablished amount. Because the team could measure its progress against each of these specific objectives, the team knew throughout the development process where it stood. Either it had achieved its goals or not.

- As Outward Bound and other team-building programs illustrate, specific objectives have a leveling effect conducive to team behavior. When a small group of people challenge themselves to get over a wall or to reduce cycle time by 50 percent, their respective titles, perks, and other stripes fade into the background. The teams that succeed evaluate what and how each individual can best contribute to the team's goal and, more important, do so in terms of the performance objective itself rather than a person's status or personality.

- Specific goals allow a team to achieve small wins as it pursues its broader purpose. These small wins are invaluable to building commitment and overcoming the inevitable obstacles that get in the way of a long-term purpose. For example, the Knight-Ridder team mentioned at the outset turned a narrow goal to eliminate errors into a compelling customer-service purpose.

• Performance goals are compelling. They are symbols of accomplishment that motivate and energize. They challenge the people on a team to commit themselves, as a team, to make a difference. Drama, urgency, and a healthy fear of failure combine to drive teams who have their collective eye on an attainable, but challenging, goal. Nobody but the team can make it happen. It is their challenge.

The combination of purpose and specific goals is essential to performance. Each depends on the other to remain relevant and vital. Clear performance goals help a team keep track of progress and hold itself accountable; the broader, even nobler, aspirations in a team's purpose supply both meaning and emotional energy.

Virtually all effective teams we have met, read or heard about, or been members of have ranged between two and twenty-five people. For example, the Burlington Northern "piggybacking" team had seven members, the Knight-Ridder newspaper team, fourteen. The majority of them have numbered less than ten. Small size is admittedly more of a pragmatic guide than an absolute necessity for success. A large number of people, say fifty or more, can theoretically become a team. But groups of such size are more likely to break into subteams rather than function as a single unit.

Why? Large numbers of people have trouble interacting constructively as a group, much less doing real work together. Ten people are far more likely than fifty are to work through their individual, functional, and hierarchical differences toward a common plan and to hold themselves jointly accountable for the results.

Large groups also face logistical issues, such as finding enough physical space and time to meet. And they confront more complex constraints, like crowd or herd behaviors, which prevent the intense sharing of viewpoints needed to build a team. As a result, when they try to develop a common purpose, they usually produce only superficial "missions" and well-meaning intentions that cannot be translated into concrete objectives. They tend fairly quickly to reach a point when meetings become a chore, a clear sign that most of the people in the group are uncertain why they have gathered, beyond some notion of getting along better. Anyone who has been through one of these exercises knows how frustrating it can be. This kind of failure tends to foster cynicism, which gets in the way of future team efforts.

In addition to finding the right size, teams must develop the right mix of skills, that is, each of the complementary skills necessary to do the team's job. As obvious as it sounds, it is a common failing in potential teams. Skill requirements fall into three fairly self-evident categories:

Technical or functional expertise. It would make little sense for a group of doctors to litigate an employment discrimination case in a court of law. Yet teams of doctors and lawyers often try medical malpractice or personal injury cases. Similarly, product-development groups that include only marketers or engineers are less likely to succeed than those with the complementary skills of both.

Problem-solving and decision-making skills. Teams must be able to identify the problems and opportunities they face, evaluate the options they have for moving forward, and then make necessary trade-offs and decisions about how to proceed. Most teams need some members with these skills to begin with, although many will develop them best on the job.

Interpersonal skills. Common understanding and purpose cannot arise without effective communication and constructive conflict, which in turn depend on interpersonal skills. These include risk taking, helpful criticism, objectivity, active listening, giving the benefit of the doubt, and recognizing the interests and achievements of others.

Obviously, a team cannot get started without some minimum complement of skills, especially technical and functional ones. Still, think about how often you've been part of a team whose members were chosen primarily on the basis of personal compatibility or formal position in the organization, and in which the skill mix of its members wasn't given much thought.

It is equally common to overemphasize skills in team selection. Yet in all the successful teams we've encountered, not one had all the needed skills at the outset. The Burlington Northern team, for example, initially had no members who were skilled marketers despite the fact that their performance challenge was a marketing one. In fact, we discovered that teams are powerful vehicles for developing the skills needed to meet the team's performance challenge. Accordingly, team member selection ought to ride as much on skill potential as on skills already proven.

Effective teams develop strong commitment to a common approach, that is, to how they will work together to accomplish their purpose. Team members must agree on who will do particular jobs, how schedules will be set and adhered to, what skills need to be developed, how continuing membership in the team is to be earned, and how the group will make and modify decisions. This element of commitment is as important to team performance as is the team's commitment to its purpose and goals.

Agreeing on the specifics of work and how they fit together to integrate individual skills and advance team performance lies at the heart of shaping a common approach. It is perhaps self-evident that an approach that delegates all the real work to a few members (or staff outsiders), and thus relies on reviews and meetings for its only "work together" aspects, cannot sustain a real team. Every member of a successful team does equivalent amounts of real work; all members, including the team leader, contribute in concrete ways to the team's work-product. This is a very important element of the emotional logic that drives team performance.

When individuals approach a team situation, especially in a business setting, each has preexisting job assignments as well as strengths and weaknesses reflecting a variety of backgrounds, talents, personalities, and prejudices. Only through the mutual discovery and understanding of how to apply all its human resources to a common purpose can a team develop and agree on the best approach to achieve its goals. At the heart of such long and, at times, difficult interactions lies a commitment-building process in which the team candidly explores who is best suited to each task as well as how individual roles will come together. In effect, the team establishes a social contract among members that relates to their purpose and guides and obligates how they must work together.

No group ever becomes a team until it can hold itself accountable as a team. Like common purpose and approach, mutual accountability is a stiff test. Think, for example, about the subtle but critical difference between "the boss holds me accountable" and "we hold ourselves accountable." The first case can lead to the second; but without the second, there can be no team.

Companies like Hewlett-Packard and Motorola have an ingrained performance ethic that enables teams to form "organically" whenever there is a clear performance challenge requiring collective rather than individual effort. In these companies, the factor of mutual accountability is commonplace. "Being in the boat together" is how their performance game is played.

At its core, team accountability is about the sincere promises we make to ourselves and others, promises that underpin two critical aspects of effective teams: commitment and trust. Most of us enter a potential team situation cautiously because ingrained individualism and experience discourage us from putting our fates in the hands of others or accepting responsibility for others. Teams do not succeed by ignoring or wishing away such behavior.

Mutual accountability cannot be coerced any more than people can be made to trust one another. But when a team shares a common purpose, goals, and approach, mutual accountability grows as a natural counterpart. Accountability arises from and reinforces the time, energy, and action invested in figuring out what the team is trying to accomplish and how best to get it done.

When people work together toward a common objective, trust and commitment follow. Consequently, teams enjoying a strong common purpose and approach inevitably hold themselves responsible, both as individuals and as a team, for the team's performance. This sense of mutual accountability also produces the rich rewards of mutual achievement in which all members share. What we heard over and over from members of effective teams is that they found the experience energizing and motivating in ways that their "normal" jobs never could match.

On the other hand, groups established primarily for the sake of becoming a team or for job enhancement, communication, organizational effectiveness, or excellence rarely become effective teams, as demonstrated by the bad feelings left in many companies after experimenting with quality circles that never translated "quality" into specific goals. Only when appropriate performance goals are set does the process of discussing the goals and the approaches to them give team members a clearer and clearer choice: they can disagree with a goal and the path that the team selects and, in effect, opt out, or they can pitch in and become accountable with and to their teammates.

The discipline of teams we've outlined is critical to the success of all teams. Yet it is also useful to go one step further. Most teams can be classified in one of three ways: teams that recommend things, teams that make or do things, and teams that run things. In our experience, each type faces a characteristic set of challenges.

Teams that recommend things. These teams include task forces, project groups, and audit, quality, or safety groups asked to study and solve particular problems. Teams that recommend things almost always have predetermined completion dates. Two critical issues are unique to such teams: getting off to a fast and constructive start and dealing with the ultimate handoff required to get recommendations implemented.

The key to the first issue lies in the clarity of the team's charter and the composition of its membership. In addition to wanting to know why and how their efforts are important, task forces need a clear definition of whom management expects to participate and the time commitment required. Management can help by ensuring that the team includes people with the skills and influence necessary for crafting practical recommendations that will carry weight throughout the organization. Moreover, management can help the team get the necessary cooperation by opening doors and dealing with political obstacles.

Missing the handoff is almost always the problem that stymies teams that recommend things. To avoid this, the transfer of responsibility for recommendations to those who must implement them demands top management's time and attention. The more top managers assume that recommendations will "just happen," the less likely it is that they will. The more involvement task force members have in implementing their recommendations, the more likely they are to get implemented.

To the extent that people outside the task force will have to carry the ball, it is critical to involve them in the process early and often, certainly well before recommendations are finalized. Such involvement may take many forms, including participating in interviews, helping with analyses, contributing and critiquing ideas, and conducting experiments and trials. At a minimum, anyone responsible for implementation should receive a briefing on the task force's purpose, approach, and objectives at the beginning of the effort as well as regular reviews of progress.

Teams that make or do things. These teams include people at or near the front lines who are responsible for doing the basic manufacturing, development, operations, marketing, sales, service, and other value-adding activities of a business. With some exceptions, like new-product development or process design teams, teams that make or do things tend to have no set completion dates because their activities are ongoing.

In deciding where team performance might have the greatest impact, top management should concentrate on what we call the company's "critical delivery points," that is, places in the organization where the cost and value of the company's products and services are most directly determined. Such critical delivery points might include where accounts get managed, customer service performed, products designed, and productivity determined. If performance at critical delivery points depends on combining multiple skills, perspectives, and judgments in real time, then the team option is the smartest one.

When an organization does require a significant number of teams at these points, the sheer challenge of maximizing the performance of so many groups will demand a carefully constructed and performance-focused set of management processes. The issue here for top management is how to build the necessary systems and process supports without falling into the trap of appearing to promote teams for their own sake.

The imperative here, returning to our earlier discussion of the basic discipline of teams, is a relentless focus on performance. If management fails to pay persistent attention to the link between teams and performance, the organization becomes convinced that "this year we are doing 'teams.'" Top management can help by instituting processes like pay schemes and training for teams responsive to their real time needs, but more than anything else, top management must make clear and compelling demands on the teams themselves and then pay constant attention to their progress with respect to both team basics and performance results. This means focusing on specific teams and specific performance challenges. Otherwise "performance," like "team," will become a cliché.

Teams that run things. Despite the fact that many leaders refer to the group reporting to them as a team, few groups really are. And groups that become real teams seldom think of themselves as a team because they are so focused on performance results. Yet the opportunity for such teams includes groups from the top of the enterprise down through the divisional or functional level. Whether it is in charge of thousands of people or a handful, as long as the group oversees some business, ongoing program, or significant functional activity, it is a team that runs things.

The main issue these teams face is determining whether a real team approach is the right one. Many groups that run things can be more effective as working groups than as teams. The key judgment is whether the sum of individual bests will suffice for the performance challenge at hand or whether the group must deliver substantial incremental performance requiring real, joint work-products. Although the team option promises greater performance, it also brings more risk, and managers must be brutally honest in assessing the trade-offs.

Members may have to overcome a natural reluctance to trust their fate to others. The price of faking the team approach is high: at best, members get diverted from their individual goals, costs outweigh benefits, and people resent the imposition on their time and priorities; at worst, serious animosities develop that undercut even the potential personal bests of the working-group approach.

Working groups present fewer risks. Effective working groups need little time to shape their purpose since the leader usually establishes it. Meetings are run against well-prioritized agendas. And decisions are implemented through specific individual assignments and account-abilities. Most of the time, therefore, if performance aspirations can be met through individuals doing their respective jobs well, the working-group approach is more comfortable, less risky, and less dis-ruptive than trying for more elusive team performance levels. Indeed, if there is no performance need for the team approach, efforts spent to improve the effectiveness of the working group make much more sense than floundering around trying to become a team.

Having said that, we believe the extra level of performance teams can achieve is becoming critical for a growing number of companies, especially as they move through major changes during which com-pany performance depends on broad-based behavioral change. When top management uses teams to run things, it should make sure the team succeeds in identifying specific purposes and goals.

This is a second major issue for teams that run things. Too often, such teams confuse the broad mission of the total organization with the specific purpose of their small group at the top. The discipline of teams tells us that for a real team to form there must be a *team* pur-pose that is distinctive and specific to the small group and that re-quires its members to roll up their sleeves and accomplish something beyond individual end-products. If a group of managers looks only at the economic performance of the part of the organization it runs to assess overall effectiveness, the group will not have any team per-formance goals of its own.

While the basic discipline of teams does not differ for them, teams at the top are certainly the most difficult. The complexities of long-term challenges, heavy demands on executive time, and the deep-seated individualism of senior people conspire against teams at the top. At the same time, teams at the top are the most powerful. At first we thought such teams were nearly impossible. That is because we were looking at the teams as defined by the formal organizational structure, that is, the leader and all his or her direct reports equals the team. Then we discovered that real teams at the top were often smaller and less formalized—Whitehead and Weinberg at Goldman, Sachs; Hewlett and Packard at HP; Krasnoff, Pall, and Hardy at Pall Corp; Kendall, Pearson, and Calloway at Pepsi; Haas and Haas at Levi Strauss; Batten and Ridder at Knight-Ridder. They were mostly twos and threes, with an occasional fourth.

Nonetheless, real teams at the top of large, complex organizations are still few and far between. Far too many groups at the top of large corporations needlessly constrain themselves from achieving real team levels of performance because they assume that all direct reports must be on the team; that team goals must be identical to corporate goals; that the team members' positions rather than skills determine their respective roles; that a team must be a team all the time; and that the team leader is above doing real work.

As understandable as these assumptions may be, most of them are unwarranted. They do not apply to the teams at the top we have observed, and when replaced with more realistic and flexible assumptions that permit the team discipline to be applied, real team performance at the top can and does occur. Moreover, as more and more companies are confronted with the need to manage major change across their organizations, we will see more real teams at the top.

We believe that teams will become the primary unit of performance in high-performance organizations. But that does not mean that teams will crowd out individual opportunity or formal hierarchy and process. Rather, teams will enhance existing structures without replacing them. A team opportunity exists anywhere hierarchy or organizational boundaries inhibit the skills and perspectives needed for optimal results. Thus, new-product innovation requires preserving functional excellence through structure while eradicating functional bias through teams. And frontline productivity requires preserving direction and guidance through hierarchy while drawing on energy and flexibility through self-managing teams.

We are convinced that every company faces specific performance challenges for which teams are the most practical and powerful vehicle at top management's disposal. The critical role for senior managers, therefore, is to worry about company performance and the kinds of teams that can deliver it. This means that top management must recognize a team's unique potential to deliver results, deploy teams strategically when they are the best tool for the job, and foster the basic discipline of teams that will make them effective. By doing so, top management creates the kind of environment that enables team as well as individual and organizational performance.

Building Team Performance

Although there is no guaranteed how-to recipe for building team performance, we observed a number of approaches shared by many successful teams.

Establish urgency, demanding performance standards, and direction. All team members need to believe the team has urgent and worthwhile purposes, and they want to know what the expectations are. Indeed, the more urgent and meaningful the rationale, the more likely it is that the team will live up to its performance potential, as was the case for a customer-service team that was told that further growth for the entire company would be impossible without major improvements in that area. Teams work best in a compelling context. That is why companies with strong performance ethics usually form teams readily.

Select members for skill and skill potential, not personality. No team succeeds without all the skills needed to meet its purpose and performance goals. Yet most teams figure out the skills they will need after they are formed. The wise manager will choose people both for their existing skills and their potential to improve existing skills and learn new ones.

Pay particular attention to first meetings and actions. Initial impressions always mean a great deal. When potential teams first gather, everyone monitors the signals given by others to confirm, suspend, or dispel assumptions and concerns. They pay particular attention to those in authority: the team leader and any executives who set up, oversee, or otherwise influence the team. And, as always, what such leaders do is more important than what they say. If a senior executive leaves the team kickoff to take a phone call ten minutes after the session has begun and he never returns, people get the message.

Set some clear rules of behavior. All effective teams develop rules of conduct at the outset to help them achieve their purpose and performance goals. The most critical initial rules pertain to attendance (for example, "no interruptions to take phone calls"), discussion ("no sacred cows"), confidentiality ("the only things to leave this room are what we agree on"), analytic approach ("facts are friendly"), end-product orientation ("everyone gets assignments and does them"), constructive confrontation ("no finger pointing"), and, often the most important, contributions ("everyone does real work").

Set and seize upon a few immediate performance-oriented tasks and goals. Most effective teams trace their advancement to key performance-oriented events. Such events can be set in motion by immediately establishing a few challenging goals that can be reached early on. There is no such thing as a real team without performance results, so the sooner such results occur, the sooner the team congeals.

Challenge the group regularly with fresh facts and information. New information causes a team to redefine and enrich its understanding of the performance challenge, thereby helping the team shape a common purpose, set clearer goals, and improve its common approach. A plant quality improvement team knew the cost of poor quality was high, but it wasn't until they researched the different types of defects and put a price tag on each one that they knew where to go next. Conversely, teams err when they assume that all the information needed exists in the collective experience and knowledge of their members.

Spend lots of time together. Common sense tells us that team members must spend a lot of time together, scheduled and unscheduled, especially in the beginning. Indeed, creative insights as well as personal bonding require impromptu and casual interactions just as much as analyzing spreadsheets and interviewing customers. Busy executives and managers too often intentionally minimize the time they spend together. The successful teams we've observed all gave themselves the time to learn to be a team. This time need not always be spent together physically; electronic, fax, and phone time can also count as time spent together.

Exploit the power of positive feedback, recognition, and reward. Positive reinforcement works as well in a team context as elsewhere. "Giving out gold stars" helps to shape new behaviors critical to team performance. If people in the group, for example, are alert to a shy person's initial efforts to speak up and contribute, they can give the honest positive reinforcement that encourages continued contributions. There are many ways to recognize and reward team performance beyond direct compensation, from having a senior executive speak directly to the team about the urgency of its mission to using awards to recognize contributions. Ultimately, however, the satisfaction shared by a team in its own performance becomes the most cherished reward.

4
How the Right Measures Help Teams Excel

Christopher Meyer

Many executives have realized that process-focused, multifunctional teams can dramatically improve the way their companies deliver products and services to customers. Most executives have not yet realized, however, that such teams need new performance-measurement systems to fulfill their promise.

The design of any performance-measurement system should reflect the basic operating assumptions of the organization it supports. If the organization changes and the measurement system doesn't, the latter will be at best ineffective or, more likely, counterproductive. At many companies that have moved from control-oriented, functional hierarchies to a faster and flatter team-based approach, traditional performance-measurement systems not only fail to support the new teams but also undermine them. Indeed, traditional systems often heighten the conflicts between multifunctional teams and functions that are vexing many organizations today.

Ideally, a measurement system designed to support a team-based organization should help teams overcome two major obstacles to their effectiveness: getting functions to provide expertise to teams when they need it and getting people from different functions on a team to speak a common language. Traditional measurement systems don't solve those problems.

The primary role of traditional measurement systems, which are still used in most companies, is to pull "good information" up so that

The author would like to thank Steven C. Wheelwright, who provided valuable guidance for this article.

senior managers can make "good decisions" that flow down. To that end, each relatively independent function has its own set of measures, whose main purpose is to inform top managers about its activities. Marketing tracks market share, operations watches inventory, finance monitors costs, and so on.

Such *results measures* tell an organization where it stands in its effort to achieve goals but not how it got there or, even more important, what it should do differently. Most results measures track what goes on within a function, not what happens across functions. The few cross-functional results measures in organizations are typically financial, like revenues, gross margins, costs of goods sold, capital assets, and debt, and they exist only to help top managers. In contrast, *process measures* monitor the tasks and activities throughout an organization that produce a given result. Such measures are essential for cross-functional teams that are responsible for processes that deliver an entire service or product to customers, like order fulfillment or new-product development. Unlike a traditional, functional organization, a team-based organization not only makes it possible to use process measures but also requires them.

How should performance-measurement systems be overhauled to maximize the effectiveness of teams? Here are four guiding principles:

1. The overarching purpose of a measurement system should be to help a team, rather than top managers, gauge its progress. A team's measurement system should primarily be a tool for telling the team when it must take corrective action. The measurement system must also provide top managers with a means to intervene if the team runs into problems it cannot solve by itself. But even if a team has good measures, they will be of little use if senior managers use them to control the team. A measurement system is not only the measures but also the way they are used.

2. A truly empowered team must play the lead role in designing its own measurement system. A team will know best what sort of measurement system it needs, but the team should not design this system in isolation. Senior managers must ensure that the resulting measurement system is consistent with the company's strategy.

3. Because a team is responsible for a value-delivery process that cuts across several functions (like product development, order fulfillment, or customer service), it must create measures to track that process. In a traditional functional organization, no single function is responsible for a total value-delivery process; thus there are no good ways to measure those processes. In contrast, the purpose of the multifunctional team approach is to create a structure—the team—that is responsible for a complete value-delivery process. Teams must create measures that support their mission, or they will not fully exploit their ability to perform the process faster and in a way that is more responsive to customer demands.

A process measure that a product-development team might use is one that tracks staffing levels to make sure that the necessary people are on a given team at the right time. Another measure is the number or percentage of new or unique parts to be used in a product. While such parts may offer a performance advantage, the more a product contains, the greater the likelihood that there will be difficult design, integration, inventory, manufacturing, and assembly issues.

Having sung the praises of process measures, let me throw in a qualification: while such measures are extremely important, teams still need to use some traditional measures, like one that tracks receivables, to ensure that functional and team results are achieved. Functional excellence is a prerequisite for team excellence.

4. A team should adopt only a handful of measures. The long-held view that "what gets measured gets done" has spurred managers to react to intensifying competition by piling more and more measures on their operations in a bid to encourage employees to work harder. As a result, team members end up spending too much time collecting data and monitoring their activities and not enough time managing the project. I have seen dozens of teams spend too much time at meetings discussing the mechanics of the measurement system instead of discussing what to *do*. As a general rule, if a team has more than fifteen measures, it should take a fresh look at the importance of each one.

Trying to run a team without a good, simple guidance system is like trying to drive a car without a dashboard. We might do it in a pinch but not as a matter of practice, because we'd lack the necessary information—the speed, the amount of fuel, the engine temperature—to ensure that we reach our destination. Companies may find it helpful to create a computerized "dashboard," which inexpensive graphics software has made easy to do. (See "The Team Dashboard.")

The lack of an effective measurement system, or dashboard, can even prevent teams from making it much past the starting line. After companies first adopt the team approach, teams must typically prove to skeptical senior and middle managers that the power these managers have wielded can be handed to the teams without the business spinning out of control. A team can offer no such proof if it lacks the tools to track its performance.

The Team Dashboard

Spreadsheets are the most common format companies use to display their performance measures. But if a measurement system should function like a car's dashboard by providing a multifunctional team with the information it needs to complete its journey, why not actually construct a dashboard? The dashboard format, complete with colorful graphic indicators and other easy-to-read gauges, makes it much easier for a team to monitor its progress and know when it must change direction. A multifunctional team called Lethal, which designed and built a 2.5-inch disk drive for the Quantum Corporation in Milpitas, California, used the displayed dashboard. (See Exhibit I.)

Quantum had begun using multifunctional development teams only nine months before it established the Lethal team late in 1989. Lethal's core group included representatives from marketing, manufacturing, engineering, quality assurance, finance, and human resources. While Quantum was a strong player in the 3.5-inch drive segment, it had never made 2.5-inch drives. On top of this technical challenge, managers wanted Lethal to deliver the drive in fourteen months—ten months less than similar projects had taken.

Larry, the team's principal leader, who came from engineering, was very skeptical about whether or not Quantum's past development practices would enable Lethal to reach its fourteen-month goal. When he asked leaders from previous teams what they would do differently, all said they would try to find a better way to detect problems early. The teams would gather all the right players, but too many problems still ended up being resolved in the functions. Larry recognized one reason for that situation: the teams had used measurement systems designed for hierarchical, functional organizations. He thought Lethal could do better.

When the team began trying to establish a schedule, its members quickly discovered that development engineering was the only function that had provided a complete schedule for performing its tasks. The others had only sketched out major milestones. In addition, individual team members were often unsure what the others' schedules meant, and none of the schedules had been integrated. Marketing had even gone ahead and set a date for the product launch without consulting development engineering!

After this revelation, the team members decided to spell out the details of all the functional schedules in terms that everyone could understand. They then integrated those schedules into one master product-development schedule, which product-development programs often lack.

Exhibit I. Lethal's Dashboard

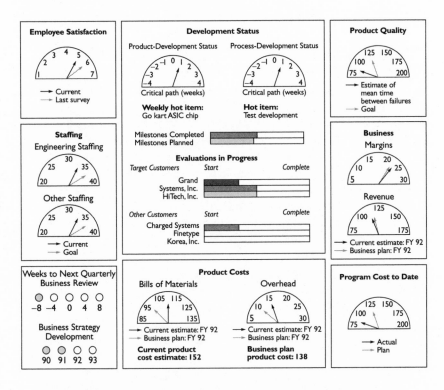

In addition to this schedule monitor and a milestone gauge, the dashboard contains a variety of other results measures, which development teams typically use to track their progress in achieving the key strategic goals that will determine whether or not top managers consider the project a success. Lethal's goals included creating a product that could be manufactured at a targeted cost (tracked by the "Overhead" and "Bills of Materials" gauges) and had a competitive quality level (tracked by the "Product Quality" gauge). The dashboard also has results measures for tracking the product's success in achieving profit margin and revenue targets once it is on the market. But such results measures tell a team only where it stands, not why it stands there. To do the latter, Lethal adopted the first process measures used by multifunctional teams in the company.

Previous teams at Quantum had focused on developing the product and treated as secondary such tasks as developing the methods and equipment for testing. Only after teams discovered that early prototypes couldn't be adequately tested did those issues receive attention. To avoid such a bottleneck, Lethal adopted a separate process-development gauge for all the tasks involved in manufacturing, including testing.

A similar discussion resulted in a decision to include staffing gauges on the dashboard. People for areas like testing, manufacturing, and marketing had to be hired early enough so that they would be on board when the team needed them. If the team waited until the development of testing methods and equipment were supposed to start before hiring test engineers, the schedule could slip by at least six weeks.

Larry's motive for suggesting the employee-satisfaction gauge was simple: unhappy team members won't keep to an ambitious schedule. The position of the "Current" needle reflects the team leaders' opinion of the team's morale. The position of the "Last survey" needle reflects the most recent survey of all team members. By forcing themselves to monitor morale, the leaders discovered that people were concerned about such things as the shortage of lab space and access to the workstations and were able to do something about those issues before they hurt morale.

The indicator lights in the lower left-hand corner of the dashboard were designed to ensure that the team allocated enough time to planning. While weekly team meetings were adequate for dealing with many issues, some, like product-launch planning, required more preparation. Because of the program's intensity, team members worried that issues that couldn't be solved quickly would eventually cause a bottleneck. Scheduling a half- or full-day meeting that everyone could attend would often take at least four weeks. John from marketing suggested that the team use the indicator lights as a reminder to schedule time for planning sessions.

The team quickly realized which gauges were not useful. John from finance argued that determining Lethal's expenses for the "Program Cost to Date" gauge was nearly impossible since the company did not have a project-based accounting system. Moreover, top managers rarely asked about an individual program's costs because they hardly varied from project to project. Since nobody on the team changed his or her behavior if the program-cost gauge dropped or increased, the team decided to eliminate it.

The team succeeded in getting potential customers for the 2.5-inch disk drive to approve the company as a qualified supplier in sixteen months—two months over the original target date but still 33 percent faster than previous teams. However, the drive took longer to move through the actual qualification phase than previous drives. The "Evaluations in Progress" gauges helped Lethal track its progress with potential customers but did not help the team discover a key problem until relatively late: Lethal's test procedures were more rigorous than those used by potential customers, which made it look as if the drives' failure rate was relatively high. On the basis of these data, potential customers would not qualify the company as a supplier.

Could a dashboard with different gauges have detected the problem early enough to solve it? Probably not. Like any performance-measurement tool, the dashboard is not a replacement for the decision maker.

What operations executive, for example, would be willing to let a new-product development team manage the transition from an existing product to a new one if the team did not have a measure that tracked old product inventory from the factory throughout the distribution channel? Without such information, the company might end up stuck with lots of an unsellable old product. And what development executive would be willing to hand over responsibility for a project if he or she did not see that the product-development team was able to track cost, quality, and schedule?

Many managers fail to realize that results measures like profits, market share, and cost, which may help them keep score on the performance of their businesses, do not help a multifunctional team, or any organization, monitor the activities or capabilities that enable it to perform a given process. Nor do such measures tell team members what they must do to improve their performance.

An 8 percent drop in quarterly profits accompanied by a 10 percent rise in service costs, for example, does not tell a customer-service team what its service technicians should do differently on their next call. Process measures, however, examine the actions and capabilities that contributed to the situation. Knowing that the average time spent per service call rose 15 percent last month and that, as a result, the number of late calls rose 10 percent would explain to the technicians why service costs had gone up and customer satisfaction and profits had gone down.

The most commonly used results measures in product development are schedule and cost. But the fact that a program is six months late and $2 million over budget doesn't tell anyone what went wrong or what to do differently. In contrast, tracking staffing levels during the course of a project—a process measure that might include not only the number of bodies but also the years of experience in major job categories—can radically affect a team's performance. Many product-development teams, for example, do a poor job planning exactly when they will need people with a certain functional expertise. Not having all the necessary people at a particular stage often leads to expensive and time-consuming efforts to fix problems that the right people would have detected earlier.

This is exactly what I saw happen at a company that had given a multifunctional team seven months to develop a consumer product for testing blood-sugar levels. The team began work on July 1 and had a February 1 target date for launching the product. Although the company had named the people from the critical functions who would serve on the team well before the effort got under way, Mary, the manufacturing representative, did not join the team until mid-August. By then, people from marketing and development engineering had already made some best-guess decisions about significant packaging and manufacturing issues. After one week on the team, Mary raised serious questions about many of those decisions, and the team decided to adopt her suggestions and retrace its steps. Not only was Mary's arrival on the team very awkward, but also the program slipped by three weeks within the first two months.

A team's reliance on traditional measures can also cause its members to forget the team's goal and revert to their old functional way of working—or fighting—with one another. Consider the case of Ford Motor Company during the development of a luxury model in 1991. The project was one of Ford's first attempts to use multifunctional teams for product development. By and large, the team's measurement system was a collection of the individual measures that each function on the team (styling, body engineering, power train, purchasing, finance, etc.) had used for years.

Shortly before team members were to sign off on the car's design and begin engineering the body, a controversy developed over the door handle, which was different from the ones Ford had been using. One reason for the controversy was that each function made different assumptions about the relative importance of the factors contributing to the product's costs and competitiveness.

Members from the purchasing and finance departments feared that the handle would be too expensive. Their gauges were the cost of manufacturing the handle and its warranty costs. The people from design and body engineering responded that the handle's design was no more complex than that of existing handles. And because there was no basis for assuming that its warranty costs would be higher, they argued, the cost of manufacturing the handle should be the main issue in the cost debate. They submitted a bid from a vendor on Ford's approved vendor list as proof that the handle would be no more expensive to make. In addition, they argued, purchasing and finance were not giving enough weight to the importance of the handle's design in the overall design of the car.

The purchasing representative was still not satisfied about the warranty costs. He said that handles made by other approved vendors had had lower warranty costs than handles made by the vendor whose bid had been submitted. After a short shouting match, the design and engineering people gave up.

During the debate, no one asked the critical question: Would the new handle increase the car's ability to compete in the marketplace? Since the model's distinctive styling was a critical competitive element, the new handle might have helped the vehicle capture enough additional customers to more than compensate for higher warranty costs. Adopting the old handle was not necessarily the best decision, and this last-minute design change, which in turn required other changes, added at least one week to the development process. The members of this product-development team were still thinking as they did in their functions, where nobody had an overview of what would make the product succeed in the marketplace.

What kind of measures could have helped the team avoid its win-lose battle over cost versus style? One possibility would have been a measure that incorporated several product attributes, such as product cost, features, service, and packaging, to enable the team to assess trade-offs. This may have helped the team realize that an undetermined factor—the proposed handle's warranty costs—should not have influenced the decision so heavily.

When cross-functional teams are being established, many companies do not institute a measurement system that supports the company's strategy, ensures senior managers that there won't be unpleasant surprises, and, last but not least, truly empowers the teams. Let me offer a generic process that most companies can implement. I'll start with the role of top managers.

In two articles on the *balanced scorecard* ("The Balanced Scorecard—Measures That Drive Performance," *HBR* January–February 1992, and "Putting the Balanced Scorecard to Work," *HBR* September–October 1993), Robert S. Kaplan and David P. Norton provide managers with a valuable framework for integrating a company's strategic objectives and competitive demands into its performance-measurement system. They urge managers to augment their traditional financial measures with measures of customer satisfaction, internal processes, and innovation and improvement activities.

What Kaplan and Norton do not explain is how such an approach can be applied to team-based organizations. I believe that it can, with one caveat: senior managers should create the strategic context for the teams but not the measures. Senior managers should dictate strategic goals, ensure that each team understands how its job fits into the strategy, and provide training so that the team can devise its own measures. But to ensure that ownership of and accountability for performance remains with the teams, managers must require the teams to decide which measures will best help them perform their jobs.

For example, the managers of a multinational computer company established an ambitious strategic goal for all of the company's product-development teams to reduce their cycle times by more than 50 percent within three years. But rather than dictating how the teams measure cycle time, managers asked each team to select its own measures. To help the teams in this effort, managers provided training in cycle-time reduction and a very broad selection of measures from which the teams could choose.

Top managers and a team should jointly establish rules about when or under what circumstances managers will review the team's performance and its measurement system. A team should know at the outset that it will have to review the measures it has selected with top managers to ensure that they are consistent with corporate strategy and that it may have to adjust its measures. The team should also promise to renegotiate with managers any major changes in the measures made during the course of the project. As I will discuss later, measures should not be carved in stone.

The team and senior managers should also set boundaries, which, if crossed, will signal that the team has run into trouble serious enough to trigger an "out-of-bounds" management review. Such an approach keeps managers informed without disenfranchising the team.

During an out-of-bounds review, teams and managers must define the problem and decide what corrective action to take. The team must retain responsibility for calling and running the review and executing any decisions. It must be clear that the purpose of the reviews is for senior managers to help the teams solve problems, not to find fault.

Some product-development teams actually negotiate written contracts with senior managers at the start of a project. The contracts define the product, including features and quality targets; the targeted cost to the customer; the program cost; financial information like revenues, gross margins, and cost of goods sold; and the schedule. During the contract negotiations, management ensures that the overall program, including the measures, supports the company's strategy.

The contract also establishes rules for management reviews. For example, one company requires only two planned reviews. The first comes at the end of the design phase so that management can confirm that the product still meets the market need before the company invests in expensive tooling. The second review is after production is under way so that management can learn about and pass on to other teams any advances that the team has made, like designing a particular component to be manufactured easily, and can solve unforeseen production problems early on. During the entire design phase, the team is free to proceed without any contact with management unless it has broken or knows it will break its commitments on product features, performance, product and development costs, or schedule.

The main problem at most companies that now use multifunctional teams is that top managers use a team's measurement system to monitor and control projects or processes. Even if unintentional, such behavior will inevitably undermine the effectiveness of any team.

This is what happened when a Ford manufacturing plant turned to multifunctional teams to improve product quality but didn't change management's command-and-control mind-set.

The company grouped line workers from various functional areas into teams and trained them to collect and analyze data so that they could resolve quality problems on their own. But then came the mistake: the division managers asked quality engineers, who supposedly had been sent to assist the teams, to send a monthly report on the plant's quality and plans for improving it. In turn, the quality engineers asked the teams for their data.

Over time, the teams began to depend on the quality engineers to analyze the data and waited for the engineers' directions before taking action. The engineers recognized what was happening but felt caught in a bind because the division managers wanted them, rather than the teams, to provide the reports. Problems that the teams had been able to resolve on their own in a day or two began to require the involvement of the quality engineers and twice the time. And the quality engineers asked for more engineers to help them support the teams.

The division managers became very frustrated. Given all their verbal support for empowering teams, they couldn't understand why the teams didn't act empowered.

When a group of people builds a measurement system, it also builds a team. One benefit of having a team create its own measurement system is that members who hail from different functions end up creating a common language, which they need in order to work as an effective team. Until a group creates a common language, it can't reach a common definition of goals or problems. Instead of acting like a team, the group will act like a collection of functions.

As a first step, the team should develop a work plan that can serve as a process map of the critical tasks and capabilities required to complete the project. The second step is to make sure that everyone understands the team's goals in the same way. Team members frequently start out believing that they share an understanding of their goals only to discover when they begin developing performance measures how wrong they were.

After the goals have been confirmed, the appropriate team members should develop individual measures for gauging the team's progress in achieving a given goal and identifying the conditions that would trigger an out-of-bounds review. In addition, each member should come to the next meeting with two or three gauges that he or she considers most effective for monitoring his or her functional area. In an attempt to push team members to focus on overall goals and the total value-delivery process as they develop measures, they should be encouraged to include process measures. (See "Creating Process Measures.")

At the next meeting, each member should explain what his or her proposed measures track and why they are important. Everyone should make an effort to define any terms or concepts that are unfamiliar to others. One important rule is that no question is a "dumb question." So-called dumb questions are often the most valuable because they test the potential value of each measure in the most obvious terms.

Creating Process Measures

There are four basic steps to creating process measures: defining what kinds of factors, such as time, cost, quality, and product performance, are critical to satisfying customers; mapping the cross-functional process used to deliver results; identifying the critical tasks and capabilities required to complete the process successfully; and, finally, designing measures that track those tasks and capabilities. The most effective process measures are often those that express relative terms. For example, a measure that tracks the percentage of new or unique parts is usually more valuable than one that tracks the absolute number.

Here's how the parts and service operation of a Europe-based car company created process measures.

The warehousing function had traditionally measured its performance by tracking how often parts ordered by dealers could be filled immediately from the warehouse shelf. If a stock picker found a gasket on the warehouse shelf—meaning that it did not have to be ordered—that counted as a "first fill."

When the organization began using teams, it put the warehousing and the dealer-service groups on a multifunctional team charged with improving the total service process, from product breakdown through repair. The team reexamined the current performance measures and concluded that, from the dealer's perspective, the first-fill measure was meaningless. Dealers—and the final customers—didn't care where the part came from; they just wanted to know when they'd receive it. And just because a part was on the warehouse shelf did not ensure that it would get to a dealer quickly; the sloppy handling of orders and shipping problems could also cause delays.

Because the new team was responsible for the entire process, it mapped all the steps in the service cycle, from the moment the warehouse received a dealer's order to the moment the dealer received the part, and the time each step took. The team then identified its critical tasks and capabilities, which included the order-entry operation, the management-information system for tracking orders and inventories, warehouse operations, and shipping. The team created cycle-time measures for six to eight sub-processes, which helped the team see how much time was being spent on each step of the process relative to the value of that process. With this information, the team could begin figuring out how to reduce cycle time without sacrificing quality. The resulting changes included reducing the copies made of each order and the number of signatures required to authorize filling it. Within six months, the team was able to reduce the service cycle considerably. Not coincidentally, dealer complaints fell by a comparable amount.

Some measures will be either eliminated or agreed on very quickly. The hard work will be assessing those that fall in between. No final decisions should be made until all the gauges accepted or still in contention are tested as a unit against the following criteria:

- Are critical team objectives (like filling an order within 24 hours) tracked?
- Are all out-of-bounds conditions monitored?

- Are the critical variables required to reach the goal (like having enough skilled personnel to run an order-entry system) tracked?
- Would management approve the system as is or seek changes?
- Is there any gauge that wouldn't cause the team to change its behavior if the needle swung from one side to another? If so, eliminate it.
- Are there too many gauges? As I mentioned earlier, if a team has more than 15 measures, it should take a second look at each one.

After a team's measures have passed this test, the system is ready for the management review.

A team can preserve the value of its performance-measurement system by diligently adding and eliminating gauges, as required, during the project or task.

Measures that were relevant during the early stages in the development of a new product will undoubtedly become irrelevant as the product nears production. In most cases, teams realize that and plan for changes during the development of their measurement systems. But priorities often change during a project, which means that measures should be changed too. And sometimes measures prove not to be so useful after all and should be dropped. A team should also regularly audit the data being fed into its measurement system to make sure they are accurate and timely.

Managers are still in the early stages of learning how to maximize the effectiveness of multifunctional teams that are incorporated into their functional organizations. The same applies to the measurement systems used to guide both. As companies gain experience, they will discover that some specific measures can be used over and over again by different teams undertaking similar tasks or projects. But managers should be on their guard lest they do with performance-measurement systems what they have done with so many management tools: assume that one size fits all. Managers can systematize the process that teams use to create their measurement systems. They can also catalog the measures that appear to have been most effective in particular applications. But managers must never make the mistake of thinking that they know what is best for the team. If they do, they will have crossed the line and returned to the command-and-control ways of yore. And they will have rendered their empowered teams powerless.

5

How Management Teams Can Have
a Good Fight

Kathleen M. Eisenhardt, Jean L. Kahwajy, and
L. J. Bourgeois III

Top managers are often stymied by the difficulties of managing conflict. They know that conflict over issues is natural and even necessary. Reasonable people, making decisions under conditions of uncertainty, are likely to have honest disagreements over the best path for their company's future. Management teams whose members challenge one another's thinking develop a more complete understanding of the choices, create a richer range of options, and ultimately make the kinds of effective decisions necessary in today's competitive environments.

But, unfortunately, healthy conflict can quickly turn unproductive. A comment meant as a substantive remark can be interpreted as a personal attack. Anxiety and frustration over difficult choices can evolve into anger directed at colleagues. Personalities frequently become intertwined with issues. Because most executives pride themselves on being rational decision makers, they find it difficult even to acknowledge—let alone manage—this emotional, irrational dimension of their behavior.

The challenge—familiar to anyone who has ever been part of a management team—is to keep constructive conflict over issues from degenerating into dysfunctional interpersonal conflict, to encourage managers to argue without destroying their ability to work as a team.

We have been researching the interplay of conflict, politics, and speed in strategic decision making by top-management teams for the past ten years. In one study, we had the opportunity to observe closely the work of a dozen top-management teams in technology-based companies. All the companies competed in fast changing, competitive global markets. Thus all the teams had to make high-stakes decisions in the face of considerable uncertainty and under pressure to move quickly. Each team consisted of between five and nine executives; we were allowed to question them individually and also to observe their interactions firsthand as we tracked specific strategic decisions in the making. The study's design gives us a window on conflict as top-management teams actually experience it and highlights the role of emotion in business decision making.

In four of the twelve companies, there was little or no substantive disagreement over major issues and therefore little conflict to observe. But the other eight companies experienced considerable conflict. In four of them, the top-management teams handled conflict in a way that avoided interpersonal hostility or discord. We've called those companies Bravo Microsystems, Premier Technologies, Star Electronics, and Triumph Computers. Executives in those companies referred to their colleagues as "smart," "team player," and "best in the business." They described the way they work as a team as "open," "fun," and "productive." The executives vigorously debated the issues, but they wasted little time on politicking and posturing. As one put it, "I really don't have time." Another said, "We don't gloss over the issues; we hit them straight on. But we're not political." Still another observed of her company's management team, "We scream a lot, then laugh, and then resolve the issue."

The other four companies in which issues were contested were less successful at avoiding interpersonal conflict. We've called those companies Andromeda Processing, Mega Software, Mercury Microdevices, and Solo Systems. Their top teams were plagued by intense animosity. Executives often failed to cooperate, rarely talking with one another, tending to fragment into cliques, and openly displaying their frustration and anger. When executives described their colleagues to us, they used words such as "manipulative," "secretive," "burned out," and "political."

The teams with minimal interpersonal conflict were able to separate substantive issues from those based on personalities. They managed to disagree over questions of strategic significance and still get along with one another. How did they do that? After analyzing our observations of the teams' behavior, we found that their companies used the same six tactics for managing interpersonal conflict. Team members

- worked with more, rather than less, information and debated on the basis of facts;

Exhibit I. How Teams Argue but Still Get Along

Tactic ⟶	Strategy
Base discussion on current, factual information. Develop multiple alternatives to enrich the debate.	} Focus on issues, not personalities.
Rally around goals. Inject humor into decision-making process.	} Frame decisions as collaborations aimed at achieving the best possible solution for the company.
Maintain a balanced power structure. Resolve issues without forcing consensus.	} Establish a sense of fairness and equity in the process.

- developed multiple alternatives to enrich the level of debate;
- shared commonly agreed-upon goals;
- injected humor into the decision process;
- maintained a balanced power structure;
- resolved issues without forcing consensus.

Those tactics were usually more implicit than explicit in the decision-making work of the management teams, and if the tactics were given names, the names varied from one organization to the next. Nonetheless, the consistency with which all four companies employed all six tactics is testimony to their effectiveness. Perhaps most surprising was the fact that the tactics did not delay—and often accelerated—the pace at which the teams were able to make decisions. (See Exhibit I.)

Focus on the Facts

Some managers believe that working with too much data will increase interpersonal conflict by expanding the range of issues for debate. We found that more information is better—if the data are objective and up-to-date—because it encourages people to focus on issues, not personalities. At Star Electronics, for example, the members of the top-management team typically examined a wide variety of operating measures on a monthly, weekly, and even daily basis. They claimed to "measure everything." In particular, every week they fixed their attention on indicators such as bookings, backlogs, margins, engineering milestones, cash, scrap, and work-in-process. Every month, they reviewed an even more comprehensive set of measures that gave them extensive knowledge of what was actually happening in the corporation. As one executive noted, "We have very strong controls."

Star's team also relied on facts about the external environment. One senior executive was charged with tracking such moves by competitors as product introductions, price changes, and ad campaigns. A second followed the latest technical developments through his network of contacts in universities and other companies. "We over-M.B.A. it," said the CEO, characterizing Star's zealous pursuit of data. Armed with the facts, Star's executives had an extraordinary grasp of the details of their business, allowing them to focus debate on critical issues and avoid useless arguments rooted in ignorance.

At Triumph Computer, we found a similar dedication to current facts. The first person the new CEO hired was an individual to track the progress of engineering-development projects, the new-product lifeblood of the company. Such knowledge allowed the top-management team to work from a common base of facts.

In the absence of good data, executives waste time in pointless debate over opinions. Some resort to self-aggrandizement and ill-formed guesses about how the world might be. People—and not issues—become the focus of disagreement. The result is interpersonal conflict. In such companies, top managers are often poorly informed both about internal operations, such as bookings and engineering milestones, and about external issues, such as competing products. They collect data narrowly and infrequently. In these companies, the vice presidents of finance, who oversee internal data collection, are usually weak. They were often described by people in the companies we studied as "inexperienced" or "detached." In contrast, the vice president of finance at Premier Technologies, a company with little interpersonal conflict, was described as being central to taking "the constant pulse of how the firm is doing."

Management teams troubled by interpersonal conflict rely more on hunches and guesses than on current data. When they consider facts, they are more likely to examine a past measure, such as profitability, which is both historical and highly refined. These teams favor planning based on extrapolation and intuitive attempts to predict the future, neither of which yields current or factual results. Their conversations are more subjective. The CEO of one of the four high-conflict teams told us his interest in operating numbers was "minimal," and he described his goals as "subjective." At another such company, senior managers saw the CEO as "visionary" and "a little detached from the day-to-day operations." Compare those executives with the CEO of Bravo Microsystems, who had a reputation for being a "pragmatic numbers guy."

There is a direct link between reliance on facts and low levels of interpersonal conflict. Facts let people move quickly to the central issues surrounding a strategic choice. Decision makers don't become bogged down in arguments over what the facts *might* be. More important, reliance on current data grounds strategic discussions in reality. Facts (such as current sales, market share, R&D expenses, competitors' behavior, and manufacturing yields) depersonalize the discussion because they are not someone's fantasies, guesses, or self-serving desires. In the absence of facts, individuals' motives are likely to become suspect. Building decisions on facts creates a culture that emphasizes issues instead of personalities.

Multiply the Alternatives

Some managers believe that they can reduce conflict by focusing on only one or two alternatives, thus minimizing the dimensions over which people can disagree. But, in fact, teams with low incidences of interpersonal conflict do just the opposite. They deliberately develop multiple alternatives, often considering four or five options at once. To promote debate, managers will even introduce options they do not support.

For example, Triumph's new CEO was determined to improve the company's lackluster performance. When he arrived, new products were stuck in development, and investors were getting anxious. He launched a fact-gathering exercise and asked senior executives to develop alternatives. In less than two months, they developed four. The first was to sell some of the company's technology. The second was to undertake a major strategic redirection, using the base technology to enter a new market. The third was to redeploy engineering resources and adjust the marketing approach. The final option was to sell the company.

Working together to shape those options enhanced the group's sense of teamwork while promoting a more creative view of Triumph's competitive situation and its technical competencies. As a result, the team ended up combining elements of several options in a way that was more robust than any of the options were individually.

The other teams we observed with low levels of interpersonal conflict also tended to develop multiple options to make major decisions. Star, for example, faced a cash flow crisis caused by explosive growth. Its executives considered, among other choices, arranging for lines of credit from banks, selling additional stock, and forming strategic alliances with several partners. At Bravo, managers explicitly relied on three kinds of alternatives: sincere proposals that the proponent actually backed; support for someone else's proposal, even if only for the sake of argument; and insincere alternatives proposed just to expand the number of options.

There are several reasons why considering multiple alternatives may lower interpersonal conflict. For one, it diffuses conflict: choices become less black and white, and individuals gain more room to vary the degree of their support over a range of choices. Managers can more easily shift positions without losing face.

Generating options is also a way to bring managers together in a common and inherently stimulating task. It concentrates their energy on solving problems, and it increases the likelihood of obtaining integrative solutions—alternatives that incorporate the views of a greater number of the decision makers. In generating multiple alternatives, managers do not stop at obvious solutions; rather, they continue generating further—usually more original—options. The process in itself is creative and fun, setting a positive tone for substantive, instead of interpersonal, conflict.

By contrast, in teams that vigorously debate just one or two options, conflict often does turn personal. At Solo Systems, for instance, the top-management team considered entering a new business area as a way to boost the company's performance. They debated this alternative versus the status quo but failed to consider other options. Individual executives became increasingly entrenched on one side of the debate or the other. As positions hardened, the conflict became more pointed and personal. The animosity grew so great that a major proponent of change quit the company in disgust while the rest of the team either disengaged or slipped into intense and dysfunctional politicking.

Create Common Goals

A third tactic for minimizing destructive conflict involves framing strategic choices as collaborative, rather than competitive, exercises. Elements of collaboration and competition coexist within any management team: executives share a stake in the company's performance, yet their personal ambitions may make them rivals for power. The successful groups we studied consistently framed their decisions as collaborations in which it was in everyone's interest to achieve the best possible solution for the collective.

They did so by creating a common goal around which the team could rally. Such goals do not imply homogeneous thinking, but they do require everyone to share a vision. As Steve Jobs, who is associated with three high-profile Silicon Valley companies—Apple, NeXT, and Pixar—has advised, "It's okay to spend a lot of time arguing about which route to take to San Francisco when everyone wants to end up there, but a lot of time gets wasted in such arguments if one person wants to go to San Francisco and another secretly wants to go to San Diego."

Teams hobbled by conflict lack common goals. Team members perceive themselves to be in competition with one another and, surprisingly, tend to frame decisions negatively, as reactions to threats. At Andromeda Processing, for instance, the team focused on responding to a particular instance of poor performance, and team members tried to pin the blame on one another. That negative framing contrasts with the positive approach taken by Star Electronics executives, who, sharing a common goal, viewed a cash crisis not as a threat but as an opportunity to "build the biggest war chest" for an impending competitive battle. At a broad level, Star's executives shared the goal of creating "*the* computer firm of the decade." As one Star executive told us, "We take a corporate, not a functional, viewpoint most of the time."

Likewise, all the management team members we interviewed at Premier Technologies agreed that their common goal—their rallying cry—was to build "the best damn machine on the market." Thus in their debates they could disagree about critical technical alternatives—in-house versus offshore manufacturing options, for example, or alternative distribution channels—without letting the conflict turn personal.

Many studies of group decision making and intergroup conflict demonstrate that common goals build team cohesion by stressing the shared interest of all team members in the outcome of the debate. When team members are working toward a common goal, they are less likely to see themselves as individual winners and losers and are far more likely to perceive the opinions of others correctly and to learn from them. We observed that when executives lacked common goals, they tended to be closed-minded and more likely to misinterpret and blame one another.

Use Humor

Teams that handle conflict well make explicit—and often even contrived—attempts to relieve tension and at the same time promote a collaborative esprit by making their business fun. They emphasize the excitement of fast-paced competition, not the stress of competing in brutally tough and uncertain markets.

All the teams with low interpersonal conflict described ways in which they used humor on the job. Executives at Bravo Microsystems enjoyed playing gags around the office. For example, pink plastic flamingos—souvenirs from a customer—graced Bravo's otherwise impeccably decorated headquarters. Similarly, Triumph Computers' top managers held a monthly "dessert pig-out," followed by group weight watching. Those seemingly trivial activities were part of the CEO's deliberate plan to make work more fun, despite the pressures of the industry. At Star Electronics, making the company "a fun place" was an explicit goal for the top-management team. Laughter was common during management meetings. Practical jokes were popular at Star, where executives—along with other employees—always celebrated Halloween and April Fools' Day.

At each of these companies, executives acknowledged that at least some of the attempts at humor were contrived—even forced. Even so, they helped to release tension and promote collaboration.

Humor was strikingly absent in the teams marked by high interpersonal conflict. Although pairs of individuals were sometimes friends, team members shared no group social activities beyond a standard holiday party or two, and there were no conscious attempts to create humor. Indeed, the climate in which decisions were made was often just the opposite—hostile and stressful.

Humor works as a defense mechanism to protect people from the stressful and threatening situations that commonly arise in the course of making strategic decisions. It helps people distance themselves psychologically by putting those situations into a broader life context, often through the use of irony. Humor—with its ambiguity—can also blunt the threatening edge of negative information. Speakers can say in jest things that might otherwise give offense because the message is simultaneously serious and not serious. The recipient is allowed to save face by receiving the serious message while appearing not to do so. The result is communication of difficult information in a more tactful and less personally threatening way.

Humor can also move decision making into a collaborative rather than competitive frame through its powerful effect on mood. According to a large body of research, people in a positive mood tend to be not only more optimistic but also more forgiving of others and creative in seeking solutions. A positive mood triggers a more accurate perception of others' arguments because people in a good mood tend to relax their defensive barriers and so can listen more effectively.

Balance the Power Structure

We found that managers who believe that their team's decision-making process is fair are more likely to accept decisions without resentment, even when they do not agree with them. But when they believe the process is unfair, ill will easily grows into interpersonal conflict. A fifth tactic for taming interpersonal conflict, then, is to create a sense of fairness by balancing power within the management team.

Our research suggests that autocratic leaders who manage through highly centralized power structures often generate high levels of interpersonal friction. At the other extreme, weak leaders also engender interpersonal conflict because the power vacuum at the top encourages managers to jockey for position. Interpersonal conflict is lowest in what we call *balanced power structures,* those in which the CEO is more powerful than the other members of the top-management team, but the members do wield substantial power, especially in their own well-defined areas of responsibility. In balanced power structures, all executives participate in strategic decisions.

At Premier Technologies, for example, the CEO—described by others as a "team player"—was definitely the most powerful figure. But each executive was the most powerful decision maker in some clearly defined area. In addition, the entire team participated in all significant decisions. The CEO, one executive observed, "depends on picking good people and letting them operate."

The CEO of Bravo Microsystems, another company with a balanced power structure, summarized his philosophy as "making quick decisions involving as many people as possible." We watched the Bravo team over several months as it grappled with a major strategic redirection. After many group discussions, the final decision was made at a multiday retreat involving the whole team.

In contrast, the leaders of the teams marked by extensive interpersonal conflict were either highly autocratic or weak. The CEO at Mercury Microdevices, for example, was the principal decision maker. There was a substantial gap in power between him and the rest of the team. In the decision we tracked, the CEO dominated the process from start to finish, identifying the problem, defining the analysis, and making the choice. Team members described the CEO as "strong" and "dogmatic." As one of them put it, "When Bruce makes a decision, it's like God!"

At Andromeda, the CEO exercised only modest power, and areas of responsibility were blurred within the top-management team, where power was diffuse and ambiguous. Senior executives had to politick amongst themselves to get anything accomplished, and they reported intense frustration with the confusion that existed at the top.

Most executives expected to control some significant aspect of their business but not the entirety. When they lacked power—because of either an autocrat or a power vacuum—they became frustrated by their inability to make significant decisions. Instead of team members, they became politicians. As one executive explained, "We're all jockeying for our spot in the pecking order." Another described "maneuvering for the CEO's ear."

The situations we observed are consistent with classic social-psychology studies of leadership. For example, in a study from the 1960s, Ralph White and Ronald Lippitt examined the effects of different leadership styles on boys in social clubs. They found that boys with democratic leaders—the situation closest to our balanced power structure—showed spontaneous interest in their activities. The boys were highly satisfied, and within their groups there were many friendly remarks, much praise, and significant collaboration. Under weak leaders, the boys were disorganized, inefficient, and dissatisfied. But the worst case was autocratic rule, under which the boys were hostile and aggressive, occasionally directing physical violence against innocent scapegoats. In imbalanced power situations, we observed adult displays of verbal aggression that colleagues described as violent. One executive talked about being "caught in the cross fire." Another described a colleague as "a gun about to go off." A third spoke about "being beat up" by the CEO.

Seek Consensus with Qualification

Balancing power is one tactic for building a sense of fairness. Finding an appropriate way to resolve conflict over issues is another—and, perhaps, the more crucial. In our research, the teams that managed conflict effectively all used the same approach to resolving substantive conflict. It is a two-step process that some executives call *consensus with qualification.* It works like this: executives talk over an issue and try to reach consensus. If they can, the decision is made. If they can't, the most relevant senior manager makes the decision, guided by input from the rest of the group.

When a competitor launched a new product attacking Premier Technologies in its biggest market, for example, there was sharp disagreement about how to respond. Some executives wanted to shift R&D resources to counter this competitive move, even at the risk of diverting engineering talent from a more innovative product then in design. Others argued that Premier should simply repackage an existing product, adding a few novel features. A third group felt that the threat was not serious enough to warrant a major response.

After a series of meetings over several weeks, the group failed to reach consensus. So the CEO and his marketing vice president made the decision. As the CEO explained, "The functional heads do the talking. I pull the trigger." Premier's executives were comfortable with this arrangement—even those who did not agree with the outcome—because everyone had had a voice in the process.

People usually associate consensus with harmony, but we found the opposite: teams that insisted on resolving substantive conflict by forcing consensus tended to display the most interpersonal conflict. Executives sometimes have the unrealistic view that consensus is always possible, but such a naïve insistence on consensus can lead to endless haggling. As the vice president of engineering at Mega Software put it, "Consensus means that everyone has veto power. Our products were too late, and they were too expensive." At Andromeda, the CEO wanted his executives to reach consensus, but persistent differences of opinion remained. The debate dragged on for months, and the frustration mounted until some top managers simply gave up. They just wanted a decision, any decision. One was finally made when several executives who favored one point of view left the company. The price of consensus was a decimated team.

In a team that insists on consensus, deadlines can cause executives to sacrifice fairness and thus weaken the team's support for the final decision. At Andromeda, executives spent months analyzing their industry and developing a shared perspective on important trends for the future, but they could never focus on making the decision. The decision-making process dragged on. Finally, as the deadline of a board meeting drew imminent, the CEO formulated and announced a choice—one that had never even been mentioned in the earlier discussions. Not surprisingly, his team was angry and upset. Had he been less insistent on reaching a consensus, the CEO would not have felt forced by the deadline to act so arbitrarily.

How does consensus with qualification create a sense of fairness? A body of research on procedural justice shows that process fairness, which involves significant participation and influence by all concerned, is enormously important to most people. Individuals are willing to accept outcomes they dislike if they believe that the process by which those results came about was fair. Most people want their opinions to be considered seriously but are willing to accept that those opinions cannot always prevail. That is precisely what occurs in consensus with qualification. As one executive at Star said, "I'm happy just to bring up my opinions."

Apart from fairness, there are several other reasons why consensus with qualification is an important deterrent to interpersonal conflict. It assumes that conflict is natural and not a sign of interpersonal dysfunction. It gives managers added influence when the decision affects their part of the organization in particular, thus balancing managers' desires to be heard with the need to make a choice. It is an equitable and egalitarian process of decision making that encourages everyone to bring ideas to the table but clearly delineates how the decision will be made.

Finally, consensus with qualification is fast. Processes that require consensus tend to drag on endlessly, frustrating managers with what they see as time-consuming and useless debate. It's not surprising that the managers end up blaming their frustration on the shortcomings of their colleagues and not on the poor conflict-resolution process.

Linking Conflict, Speed, and Performance

A considerable body of academic research has demonstrated that conflict over issues is not only likely within top-management teams but also valuable. Such conflict provides executives with a more inclusive range of information, a deeper understanding of the issues, and a richer set of possible solutions. That was certainly the case in the companies we studied. The evidence also overwhelmingly indicates that where there is little conflict over issues, there is also likely to be poor decision making. "Groupthink" has been a primary cause of major corporate- and public-policy debacles. And although it may seem counterintuitive, we found that the teams that engaged in healthy conflict over issues not only made better decisions but moved more quickly as well.

Without conflict, groups lose their effectiveness. Managers often become withdrawn and only superficially harmonious. Indeed, we found that the alternative to conflict is usually not agreement but apathy and disengagement. Teams unable to foster substantive conflict ultimately achieve, on average, lower performance. Among the companies that we observed, low-conflict teams tended to forget to consider key issues or were simply unaware of important aspects of their strategic situation. They missed opportunities to question falsely limiting assumptions or to generate significantly different alternatives. Not surprisingly, their actions were often easy for competitors to anticipate.

In fast-paced markets, successful strategic decisions are most likely to be made by teams that promote active and broad conflict over issues without sacrificing speed. The key to doing so is to mitigate interpersonal conflict.

Building a Fighting Team

How can managers encourage the kind of substantive debate over issues that leads to better decision making? We found five approaches that help generate constructive disagreement within a team:

1. **Assemble a heterogeneous team, including diverse ages, genders, functional backgrounds, and industry experience.** If everyone in the executive meetings looks alike and sounds alike, then the chances are excellent that they probably think alike, too.

2. Meet together as a team regularly and often. Team members that don't know one another well don't know one another's positions on issues, impairing their ability to argue effectively. Frequent interaction builds the mutual confidence and familiarity team members require to express dissent.

3. Encourage team members to assume roles beyond their obvious product, geographic, or functional responsibilities. Devil's advocates, sky-gazing visionaries, and action-oriented executives can work together to ensure that all sides of an issue are considered.

4. Apply multiple mind-sets to any issue. Try role-playing, putting yourself in your competitors' shoes, or conducting war games. Such techniques create fresh perspectives and engage team members, spurring interest in problem solving.

5. Actively manage conflict. Don't let the team acquiesce too soon or too easily. Identify and treat apathy early, and don't confuse a lack of conflict with agreement. Often, what passes for consensus is really disengagement.

6
The Myth of the Top Management Team

Jon R. Katzenbach

Companies all across the economic spectrum are making use of teams. Self-directed work teams, product design teams, sales account teams, cross-functional teams, process redesign teams—you name it, you are likely to find it. And you are just as likely to find the group at the very top of an organization professing to be a team.

But walk into almost any organization and ask anyone about the "team at the top." The immediate response is likely to be a knowing, skeptical smile, followed by a comment along the lines of "Well, they are not *really* a team, but. . . ." Even in the best of companies, a so-called top team seldom functions as a *real* team. The fact is, a team's know-how and experience inevitably lose power and focus at the top of the corporate hierarchy. And simply labeling the leadership group a team does not make it one.

The idea of a team at the top still remains a seductive notion. There are very few CEOs who do not refer often—both privately and publicly—to their "top team." New CEOs shape their own version of a team at the top to fit their idea about the support they will need from their leadership group. And the business press perpetuates the view that CEOs of large organizations put together a top team of executives to spearhead their enterprises.

But *team at the top* is a badly misused term that obscures both what teams can actually accomplish and what is required to make them work. The terminology is important: when we are undisciplined in our language, we become undisciplined in our thinking and actions. Real teams must follow a well-defined discipline in order to achieve their performance potential.

And performance is the key issue. Not long ago, the corporate world was victimized by an army of gurus proclaiming the virtues of such "team values" as involvement, empowerment, and sensitivity. The focus on performance was lost temporarily, and in many companies, it still is. The *team-based organization* became a dangerous idea—if not a dirty word—in the minds of those who saw it lead to the undiscriminating pursuit of new teams everywhere. But in well-managed enterprises today, the notion of performance is central to team efforts. And the closer a team is to its marketplace, the easier it is to maintain that critical focus on performance—because customers and competitors energize a team's natural instincts more than any other source. As one moves up the leadership ladder, however, one can easily lose sight of the collective results that differentiate real teams from pseudoteams.

It is critical to be precise: A real team is a *small number* of people with *complementary skills* who are *committed to a common purpose, performance goals,* and an *approach* for which they hold themselves *mutually accountable.* Each phrase in that definition represents an explicit element of a discipline—what I've referred to in the past as the *discipline of team basics*—that is absolutely essential if a group at any level is to obtain the extra measure of performance results that real teams can deliver.

There is little doubt that many senior executives and CEOs become frustrated in their efforts to form teams at the top. Too often, they see few gains in performance from their attempts to become more teamlike. And they recognize that the rest of the organization knows that the senior group doesn't really work together as a team.

My message, then, might come as a welcome relief to those who have been struggling with their frustration over top teams. Indeed, trying to shoehorn a group of top-level executives into a team *can* be frustrating. More important, it can be pointless. But it's also true that when the conditions are right, a team effort at the top can be essential to capturing the highest performance results possible. Good leadership requires differentiating between team and nonteam opportunities, and then acting accordingly. (See "The Myths That Hamper Team Performance.")

The Myths That Hamper Team Performance

Among top-level executives today, there is a set of strongly held beliefs about the importance and potential value of teams at the top. Ironically, these myths hamper the very team performance they are designed to stimulate.

Teamwork at the top will lead to team performance. This myth argues for more attention to the "four Cs" of effective teamwork: communication, cooperation, collaboration, and compromise.

The reality is that *teamwork* is not the same thing as *team performance*. Teamwork is broad-based cooperation and supportive behavior; a team is a tightly focused performance unit. By concentrating all its attention on teamwork, the senior group is actually less likely to be discriminating about when and where it needs to apply the discipline required to achieve real team performance. Members of the group may improve their ability to communicate and support one another, but they will not obtain team performance without applying the discipline.

Teams at the top need to spend more time together building consensus. This myth assumes that time spent together will lead to team performance and that decisions built on consensus are better than those handed down by individuals. In addition, it assumes that building consensus is synonymous with reducing conflict—and that less conflict somehow leads to more teamlike behavior.

The truth is that most executives have little time to spare, and the idea of spending more time struggling to build consensus simply makes no sense to them. In fact, many decisions are better made individually than collectively. Moreover, spending time together seeking consensus is not the same thing as doing real work. Most important, real teams do not avoid conflict—they thrive on it. And conflict is virtually unavoidable at the top.

The senior group should function as a team whenever it is together. This myth suggests that every task to be tackled by the executive leadership group qualifies as a team opportunity.

In fact, most senior-leadership interactions are not real team opportunities. A lot of time can be wasted attempting to apply team behaviors to situations that require approaches driven by a single leader. Nonteam efforts can often be faster and more effective—particularly when the value of the collective work-products is either difficult to identify or less than compelling.

Why Nonteam Behavior Prevails at the Top

The typical pattern of behavior in the top leadership group of all kinds of enterprises is familiar and well established: The CEO designates his or her direct reports as some kind of executive council. That council's primary purpose is to shape strategic priorities, enforce operating standards, establish corporate policy, and develop management talent; its members set the direction, mission, and policies for the business. The group meets at least weekly to discuss operating matters; individuals also come together periodically to discuss major strategy and policy matters. The CEO chairs the meetings, controls the agenda, and gains support for decisions from members. Agendas are circulated in advance, allowing only modest amounts of time for unscheduled subjects. In short, the executive council functions as an efficient, effective working group with a single leader. It seldom applies the discipline of team basics either to the full group or to its occasional subgroups. Why, despite the increasing value of team performance down the line, do nonteam behaviors continue to prevail at the top? There are a number of reasons for this apparent paradox.

First, a meaningful purpose for a team at the top is difficult to define. A real team must be deeply committed to a purpose that not only provides a sense of direction to its members but also justifies and clarifies the kind of extra collective efforts required for the team to achieve its performance potential. A frontline team on the plant floor can relatively easily articulate a meaningful purpose—for example, one that might involve making full use of a machine's capacity or improving a product's quality. A team effort at the top, however, cannot be tied to a machine or a single product line. And abstract goals—such as "improve the company's performance" or "implement the company's strategy"—are much too broad to provide the appropriate focus or mutual accountability that is necessary for a real team effort.

Second, tangible performance goals are hard to articulate. The goals of frontline teams are clear, specific, recurring, and measurable. They cover, for example, downtime, changeover speeds, yields, costs, and outputs. At the top, however, team goals are much harder to determine. Appropriate goals must be culled from targets for corporate and business-unit objectives, long-term finances, market share, and executive performance. As a result, goal setting for a so-called team at the top is often vague, and the process is rarely compelling to results-oriented senior executives.

Third, the right mix of skills is often absent. The extra performance capability that a real team provides comes largely from a complementary mixing of its members' skills. As a result, team members should be selected primarily on the basis of the set of skills they will bring to the group. But that's not how it usually works at the top, where team assignments are often based more on members' formal position than on actual skills. (See "The 'All My Direct Reports' Fallacy.") And although any group of executives can bring a good mix of skills to a team, it is simply wrong to presume that a senior leadership group will possess the right skills for *any* given project.

Fourth, most teams require a heavy time commitment. Each team needs to shape a working approach that takes into account its members' available time, as well as their different skills and roles. The members must become as committed to that approach as they are to the team's overall purpose and goals. Most frontline teams have the advantage of full-time members, whereas most top teams consist of busy executives who have trouble making the kind of time commitment that real teams deserve and who therefore devote only part of their time to the team's assignment.

The "All My Direct Reports" Fallacy

Many CEOs tend to think of their group of direct reports as a team. But shaping collective work of high value that fits the group's mix of skills is difficult. It is analogous to searching for a market after a product has been designed, rather than first identifying what the market needs and then designing the product to fill that need.

Top-level executives are chosen because their individual capabilities and experiences qualify them for extremely demanding primary responsibilities. Team challenges at the top seldom require the particular mix of skills represented by a CEO's direct reports, and such challenges do not usually take clear priority over the individual executives' formal responsibilities. In other words, it is hard to find collective work-products that justify top-level executives doing real work together. As long as senior leaders instinctively hold to the "all my direct reports" assumption about team composition, their experience with teams at the top will remain disappointing.

Consider the case of a large multinational company that recently confronted a disaster in its management-information-systems function. Years of inept leadership, misallocation of resources, and procrastination had produced an intolerable situation. When senior managers finally acknowledged the magnitude of the problem, the company was in critical condition. Without a major transformation in the MIS function, there was little doubt that the company would lose its competitive edge and would either go out of business or be acquired by another company.

The leadership group convened in several intensive sessions to evaluate the options and decide on a course of action. None of the group's members had any MIS experience, yet the group proceeded without any changes to its composition. The members simply assumed that the CFO would be able to provide the necessary MIS knowledge and judgment. Early on, they concluded that they should retain outside consultants. Soon after, they entered into a five-year contract for nearly $100 million to reengineer the function. Several months later, the CEO had to bring in a hired gun to straighten out the mess. By that time, the company was practically at a standstill.

Who is to say that top management might not have resolved the issue differently had it consulted the company's own MIS experts? Skeptics will argue that the internal experts were precisely the people who had created the mess, so they could hardly be counted on to decide how it should be cleaned up. But the organization's MIS professionals knew what "the mess" consisted of and realized that a consultant-intensive solution would meet with crippling resistance.

The company's actions reflect the prevailing mind-set in many top-leadership groups: somehow the collective judgment and experience of those on the so-called top team will make up for a lack of more specific and relevant skills. All of a CEO's direct reports can seldom, if ever, constitute an ongoing real team. Nor should they be trying to become one in their quest to build and maintain a high-performing enterprise. It simply does not work that way at the top.

Fifth, real teams rely on mutual accountability. By the time executives reach top management positions, they have mastered an *executive leadership discipline* that is grounded in the principle of individual accountability. They believe that individual accountability is essential to maintaining control over performance—and they can point to results over time to back up that belief. Mutual accountability, by contrast, is much harder to develop and is not as battle tested. In fact, most executives distrust the entire notion.

Sixth, nonteams fit the power structure. The single leader approach fits the expectations of the hierarchy that governs most organizations. Top-level executives are natural overachievers who master the art of working within an orderly hierarchy early in their careers; at the same time, they are uncomfortable collaborating in amorphous groups with overlapping accountabilities.

In any hierarchical organization, a "power alley" exists that consists of the individuals who have the most clout, make the critical decisions, and are expected to align the decisions and actions of others with corporate priorities. Working groups and organizational units with a single leader fit within this model much better than real teams do because of their clarity about leadership and accountability. In this situation, such groups tend to be formed at random—not by design. And when they do become visible, they usually are seen as forums for communication or for building morale rather than as true performance units.

Seventh, nonteams are fast and efficient. The unit or working group with a single leader can be energized and aligned relatively quickly. A seasoned leader usually knows what the group's goals and basic working approach should be. As a result, the group hits the ground running. It can rely on the experience and formal position of its leader to make individual assignments clearly and wisely, to protect it from unfriendly outside elements, and to keep its members on track. The group is likely to make few mistakes, because of the leader's knowledge and experience regarding the task at hand. Moreover, the members seek out and rely on the formal leader's know-how. By contrast, real teams, especially during the initial phase of shaping goals and brainstorming about working approaches, need more time to develop. Many executives have little patience for the time-consuming "forming, norming, and storming" activities that team efforts commonly require at the start.

Executive Leadership Discipline Versus Team Discipline

For all the reasons just cited, "teaming at the top" is an unnatural act. Rather than seeing nonteam behavior as a failure, however, wise leaders recognize the inherent value of both behaviors, and the fundamentally different disciplines required for strong executive leadership on the one hand and for true team performance on the other. Top-level executives can and do learn to integrate the two instead of replacing one with the other.

The best CEOs apply an executive leadership discipline that places a premium on individual accountability for profit, market results, speed, and growth. The business press expects it, Wall Street rewards it, and boards of directors demand it. Consequently, CEOs organize senior executives in a group in order to take full advantage of their experience and skills. They establish efficient processes and forums that bring their best leaders together to contribute their experiences, insights, and judgments to shaping the company's strategy and policy. And they set high standards of performance—and expect executives to meet them.

Most executives at the top are conditioned to this set of leadership rules. They have proved over time their ability to produce consistently good results. But the discipline of executive leadership is often in direct conflict with the discipline required for team performance. The two are uncomfortable bedfellows. Consider the following differences:

- Top executives are individually accountable for whatever happens on their watch; they enforce such accountability in the organization by rewarding and punishing managers according to how well they meet clear-cut individual objectives. A team learns to hold its members mutually accountable for collective results.

- Top executives are primarily responsible for broad corporate strategy, policy, and objectives. A team's purpose and goals must be tightly focused on specific performance results.

- Top executives must create and maintain a sense of urgency about resolving those issues that are critical to overall company performance. A team mobilizes around a meaningful purpose and a commitment to specific, common goals; a team's purpose and goals may be important without being either urgent or critical.

- Top executives make decisions on their own; they exercise personal judgment about risks, resources, and strategic options. A team makes collective judgments by means of open dialogue, conflict resolution, and collective *real work*.[1]

- Top executives assign people to tasks based largely on their position in the organization. Members of a team are assigned on the basis of the specific skills required by the task at hand, regardless of their formal role in the company.

- Top executives leverage their time and experience by means of efficient organizational and managerial processes; as executives become more efficient and thus more valuable, they are given responsibility for more people and greater assets. A team is seldom the most efficient way of getting something accomplished.

These contrasting disciplines produce conflicts that are difficult to resolve. The fundamental point, however, is that each has its place in the senior leadership of any performance-oriented organization—although it takes perceptive executive judgment to determine when and how each discipline should be applied. In fact, the best leaders make a conscious effort to apply both disciplines, recognizing that they will not always make the right call.

Litmus Tests for Teams

Three litmus tests determine whether a group can achieve real team performance. These tests are valid regardless of a potential team's position within its company—at the top, in the middle, or on the front line. First, the group must focus its attention on shaping *collective work-products* of clear value to the company. Second, its members must learn how to shift and share leadership roles. Third, those members must be mutually accountable for the group's results. Let's examine each test in turn.

SHAPING COLLECTIVE WORK-PRODUCTS

A collective work-product for a top leadership group is relatively easy to define: it is the tangible result of the group applying different skills to produce a performance improvement not achievable by the members of the group working on their own. Let me be clear: team performance at the top is not the same thing as open discussion, debate, decision making, or delegation of authority.

Collective work-products are not as easy to come by at the top as they are down the line. A company undergoing major change, however, will invariably encounter some obvious opportunities for collective work at the top. For example, in 1993, executives at Citicorp formed a team to help redesign the company's credit-management process after a collapse in the real estate market created a serious financial crisis throughout the industry. And in 1995, four executives at Browning-Ferris Industries, the second-largest global waste-management and recycling company, functioned as a real team in order to raise several hundred million dollars in new financing—a sum critical to the company's future growth. Those success stories, however, were energized by urgency, if not by a crisis. Without a need for urgent action, a top leadership group can seldom carve out collective work-products that match its mix of skills and also justify the diversion of executives' time from their primary responsibilities. And keep in mind that not all collective work-products constitute a real team opportunity: if the leadership role does not need to shift, collective work can be directed by a single leader.

SHIFTING THE LEADERSHIP ROLE

A real team is never leaderless. Instead, it is able to draw on the leadership ability of each of its members at different times and in different ways.

A working group or an organizational-unit "team" operates under the guidance and direction of its formal leader. Although the leader may opt to delegate primary responsibility for a particular assignment, the formal leader is still accountable for the group's results—and all the members know it. Seldom does a member take an initiative that is not strongly endorsed and supported by the formal leader. This approach provides lines of leadership that are crystal clear, and it is a time-honored way for organizations to maintain order and accountability as they become larger.

Real teams, by contrast, boost their leadership capacity by shifting the leader's role back and forth among members depending on the task. The leader's mantle falls naturally on the shoulders of whichever executive has the knowledge or experience most relevant to the particular issue at hand. In the major refinancing effort at Browning-Ferris Industries, for instance, the top team was often led by the CFO during discussions with the board, by the CEO in meetings with key investors, and by the COO when crafting events to build cross-organizational support for initiatives.

BUILDING MUTUAL ACCOUNTABILITY

True mutual accountability is critical to the success of teams. Best characterized by the phrase "We hold one another accountable" rather than "The boss holds us accountable," it demonstrates the high degree of commitment that all members of a real team must share. People at the top of an organization are accustomed to being held individually accountable for whatever happens on their watch; when they are on a true team, they must subordinate that approach in order to pursue a collective result.

When Teams at the Top Make Sense

The contrasting disciplines of team and executive performance help explain why the best senior-leadership groups rarely function as ongoing true teams. But we often see such groups functioning as real teams when major, unexpected events arise—particularly when a sudden change breaks up the natural order at the top of an organization.

Consider, for example, what happens in a merger or acquisition. The opportunity to acquire or merge with another company creates a number of real team opportunities at the top of both companies—not only during the negotiating process but also while the two organizations integrate their operations. Groups of people from both sides come together to exchange information, eliminate duplication, and meld the best practices of the merging companies. The performance challenges of a merger or an acquisition naturally give rise to team acts. Those challenges almost always include

- a compelling sense of urgency throughout both organizations;
- new imperatives to improve performance, including many that are measurable;
- critical issues that cannot be resolved without integrating the skill sets of both organizations;
- overlapping formal structures and processes that require new informal networks; and
- temporary leadership roles that differ from permanent leadership roles.

Given those challenges, it is natural for executives at the top of two merging companies to engage in team behavior as a complement to their usual single-leader approach. Indeed, mobilized by a major change, the right executives often come together to function as a real team. But those who wait for a cataclysmic event to spawn a team at the top are likely to miss important opportunities to exploit team performance. Those opportunities are to be found wherever there is collective real work to be done by the company's top-level executives.

DOING COLLECTIVE WORK AT MOBIL

Despite the long and successful history of single-executive leadership at Mobil Oil Corporation, in 1994 CEO Lucio Noto believed that it was time to try for more team performance at the top. The company was at a critical juncture in its development: the industry was undergoing significant changes, competitors were modifying both strategies and structures, and growth prospects were becoming more difficult to identify and realize. In short, Noto wanted all the senior-level help he could get to strengthen Mobil's strategic position and leadership capacity for the next generation of the company's senior managers.

The first credible team challenge for Noto's senior-leadership group was to create a new process for accelerating the development of the company's leadership capacity. The members of the executive office began by forming a team to evaluate the company's future leaders. All team members, including Noto, were required to conduct extensive interviews about the candidates assigned to them and to review a new base of performance facts about those they had not worked with recently. This was a real-work role for the team members. Moreover, once they had developed the base of information they needed for their assigned candidates, the members of the top team had to come together and work collectively to complete the evaluations.

During those efforts, Noto functioned as both a team member and a team leader—but seldom as *the* leader. Other members of the senior group also learned how to act as leaders and team players. Noto filled the gaps whenever the group's progress seemed to falter, and he was diligent about subtly reminding the group of the main reason for its effort: to accelerate the development of the next generation of Mobil's leaders.

As these efforts evolved, the team coalesced around a few simple messages that enabled it to improve the balance between collective work and individual tasks. Perhaps the most powerful of these messages can be described in the statement "Our primary focus is development, not evaluation." That message shifted the balance of the team's collective work from evaluation to development. It became clear that the evaluation work could be delegated to organizational-unit leaders and to teams in the organization's formal structure and that the executive office should concentrate on addressing the company's high-level development needs.

At the same time, the simple message that helped the team coalesce also enabled it to identify collective work-products that it otherwise might have overlooked. One such work-product was a new leadership-development profile: the executive-office team completely redesigned the criteria and evidence required for evaluating the leadership accomplishments of middle and senior managers.

Another work-product was a more rigorous evaluation process for candidates for the top 100 or so positions in the company. The new process not only included 360-degree evaluations but also required senior executives to conduct intensive interviews and to review fact-based information on candidates that went well beyond the usual human-resources evaluations.

A third work-product was a new opportunity-development and assignment-matching process. A group called the Opportunity Development Council was established to uncover development opportunities for leadership candidates of high potential.

Top leadership groups that do real work together, such as the one at Mobil, are much like musical ensembles that sing or play together: as members gain a firsthand appreciation for the talent each possesses, they develop mutual respect for one another and a strong conviction about the value of what they can accomplish together. Unless a group continues to do substantive work together, however, it will lose its ability to shape collective work-products.

RESPONDING TO THE MARKETPLACE AT TEXAS INSTRUMENTS

The collective work of teams at the top can be particularly powerful when the direction of the marketplace is hard to comprehend and no single member of the leadership group can clearly see the way forward. Consider the case of Texas Instruments in 1986. A small team took over the leadership of the company's rapidly eroding calculator business at a time when both the market and Texas Instruments itself were rapidly moving away from handheld calculators in favor of personal computers. The market was in such turmoil that few thought calculators would survive at all. Resorting to dark humor amid this doom and gloom, the team referred to its regular Friday afternoon meetings as "window-jumping sessions." Over time, however, the team's collective sense of the marketplace allowed it to accomplish more than its members could have accomplished working on their own. Mobilizing its collective skills in engineering and marketing, the team succeeded in redesigning the product and resegmenting the market. Most important, it persuaded the company that it needed to make use of technology from outside Texas Instruments. Most so-called teams at the top do not immerse themselves in the marketplace the way the team at Texas Instruments did.

Guidelines for Initiating a Real Team

A simple set of guidelines can help any group—at the top, in the middle, or on the front line—find its hidden potential for team performance.

PICK YOUR SHOTS WISELY

Operating as a team is not the only way leadership groups can improve performance. Remember: team efforts work only when collective work-products and shifting leadership contributions offer high value.

Avoid the trap of picking hollow opportunities for your top team. Doing so not only distracts the team from the real issues that justify taking up executives' time but also builds skepticism among other employees about the value of the team's efforts. The best leadership groups learn to avoid such situations and focus instead on spotting real team opportunities in advance rather than waiting to be jolted into action by a major event.

CONSIDER YOUR OPTIONS CAREFULLY

Teams go by a variety of different names according to their various purposes and goals. Although many fail to meet the vigorous litmus tests of real team performance, such groups are not without value within a balanced approach to leadership. They may be composed of a unit leader's direct reports, a cross-functional selection of managers, or an entire enterprise. The different types of small-group efforts all have their place within a high-performing organization. The best leadership groups are never wedded to one approach; they make a concerted effort to master and modify several approaches.

MAKE THE CRITICAL TRADE-OFFS CONSCIOUSLY

Executives must grapple with three important trade-offs when thinking about establishing a top team. First, they must consider whether the expenditure of time needed to get real team performance is worth it. Groups with a single leader are fast, efficient, and powerful when the person in charge really does know best. Second, executives must keep in mind that it is more important to a team's performance to choose individuals based on their mix of skills rather than on their formal titles. Projects that do not require a composite mix of skills for collective work-products are best handled by individuals in a working group, each tackling a piece of the puzzle largely on his or her own. Third, executives must consider the leadership trade-off. Real teams—in which the leadership role shifts—can help build an organization's overall leadership capacity by allowing both a number of different individuals to lead and a number of potential leaders to develop their capabilities. In many situations, executives will decide to forgo teams and will instead opt for the clear line of accountability provided by a single leader.

APPLY THE DISCIPLINE THAT FITS

It is usually more natural to apply the executive leadership discipline the higher up in the organization you go, simply because that is how large organizations are expected to work. But high-level executives tend to overuse that discipline to the detriment of potential team performance. The right balance is a moving target that is never easy to hit. Once groups at the top experience the power of team discipline, their members can easily start to overuse that approach.

LEARN DIFFERENT LEADERSHIP ROLES

Top-level executives should be wary of their personal preferences when it comes to leadership approaches. Most people who have attempted to be team leaders in a situation that demanded strong direction will remember the frustration and confusion that resulted. The reverse is equally true. Those who are wedded to what has worked for them in the past will always find it difficult to succeed in a new leadership role.

Note

1. For a discussion of what constitutes real work, see the *HBR* Classic, Part II, Chapter 7, "Real Work," by Abraham Zaleznik.

PART

II

Managing Teams

1
Whatever Happened to the
Take-Charge Manager?

Nitin Nohria and James D. Berkley

Many managers felt that the emergence of new managerial ideas during the 1980s signaled the rejuvenation of U.S. business. By readily adopting innovations such as total quality programs and self-managed teams, managers believed that they were demonstrating the kind of decisive leadership that kept companies competitive. But such thinking doesn't jibe with the facts. American managers did not take charge in the 1980s. Instead, they abdicated their responsibility to a burgeoning industry of management professionals.

The 1980s witnessed the spectacular rise of management schools, consultants, media, and gurus who fed on the insecurities of American managers fearful of foreign competition and economic decline. (See Exhibit I.) Mistrustful of their own judgment, many managers latched on to these self-appointed pundits, readily adopting their latest panaceas. Off-the-shelf programs addressing quality, customer satisfaction, time-to-market, strategic focus, core competencies, alliances, global competitiveness, organizational culture, and empowerment swept through U.S. corporations with alarming speed.

Adopting "new" ideas became a way for companies to signal to the world that they were progressive, that they had come to grips with their misguided pasts, and that they were committed to change. After all, the worst thing one could do was stick with the status quo.

For some businesses, the new ideas worked. They enabled companies to stem decline and challenge their foreign competitors. But in the majority of cases, research shows, the management fads of the last fifteen years rarely produced the promised results.

Between 1980 and 1990, market share in most key U.S. industries

Exhibit I.   The Rise of the Management Industry

	1982	1992	Growth
Management Schools and MBAs			
Number of management schools	545	670	23%
Number of MBAs granted	60,000	80,000	33
Consulting Industry			
Number of consulting firms	780	1,533	97
Number of consultants	30,000	81,000	170
Total consulting revenues	$3.5 billion	$15.2 billion	334
Corporate Training			
Number of people trained	33.5 million	40.9 million	22
Total training hours	1.1 billion	1.3 billion	18
Total corporate expenditures	$10 billion	$45 billion	350
Business Media			
Number of business stories	125,000	680,000	444
Number of new business books	1,327	1,831	38
Sales of business books	$225 million	$490 million	118

Source: Authors' estimates, drawn from multiple sources. The authors gratefully acknowledge the assistance of Michael Stevenson and George Jenkins, both business information analysts at the Harvard Business School, in compiling these data.

declined as much as or more than it had between 1970 and 1980. (See Exhibit II.) Recent surveys at the Harvard Business School, McKinsey & Company, and Ernst & Young and the American Quality Foundation suggest that managers themselves are dissatisfied with the new management programs. In a study we conducted in 1993 at the Harvard Business School, we polled managers at nearly 100 companies on more than twenty-one different programs and found 75 percent of them to be unhappy with the results in their organizations.

What accounts for such disastrous results? We believe it is the failure of U.S. management to address its most serious problem: a lack of pragmatic judgment. The widespread adoption of trendy management techniques during the 1980s allowed managers to rely on ready-made answers instead of searching for creative solutions. Although some companies are starting to question this reliance on quick fixes, the adoption of off-the-shelf "innovations" continues at a disturbing rate.

If managers want to reverse this trend, they must start by reclaiming managerial responsibility. Instead of subscribing impulsively to fads, they must pick and choose carefully the managerial ideas that

Exhibit II.   The Competitive Decline of U.S. Businesses

U.S. Share as Percentage of Worldwide Sales of the 12 Largest Companies in Each Industry

Industry	1960	1970	1980	1990
Autos	83%	66%	42%	38%
Banking	61	67	26	0
Chemicals	68	40	31	23
Computers	95	90	86	70
Electricals	71	59	44	11
Iron and Steel	74	31	26	12
Textiles	58	44	41	21

Source: Lawrence G. Franko, "Global Corporate Competition: Is the Large American Firm an Endangered Species?" Business Horizons, November–December 1991.

promise to be useful. And they must adapt those ideas rigorously to the context of their companies. Managers will often profit most by resisting new ideas entirely and making do with the materials at hand. However unfashionable this may seem, it is precisely as it should be. The manager's job is not to seek out novelty; it is to make sure the company gets results. Pragmatism is the place to start.

Pragmatism in an Age of Ready-Made Answers

Management ideas should be:

• Adopted only after careful consideration
• Purged of unnecessary buzzwords and clichés
• Judged by their practical consequences
• Tied to the here and now
• Rooted in genuine problems
• Adapted to suit particular people and circumstances
• Adaptable to changing and unforeseen conditions
• Tested and refined through active experimentation
• Discarded when they are no longer useful

"Flavor of the Month" Managing

Given that managerial innovations disappoint with such regularity, we are surprised that companies continue to adopt them with such abandon. The lure of new management fads remains irresistible to managers looking for easy answers. And some companies seem particularly vulnerable to the gurus' hype.

We have identified three basic syndromes that perpetuate the adoption of ineffective, off-the-shelf solutions. The first might be called the "we didn't get it right the first time, let's do it better this time" syndrome. In this case, managers attribute the failure of an imported practice or concept to some missing element in how the idea was formulated and implemented. Old management consultants and champions are thrown out, and new ones are brought in. Eager to succeed where others have failed, the new pundits introduce variations on the original idea that promise to set things right.

Unfortunately, in most cases, this syndrome has led only to a proliferation of ideas, each one claiming—with little justification—to be the correct one. Consider, for example, today's increasingly fuzzy notion of total quality management (TQM). The Ernst & Young and American Quality Foundation study surveyed 584 companies and found they used a total of 945 standardized programs, each promoted by different "experts."[1] In such an environment, managers find themselves adrift in a sea of competing ideas, increasingly insecure about whether the right approach will ever be found.

Frustration with this all-too-common scenario leads to a second pattern, which we term the "flavor of the month" syndrome. In this scenario, managers cast aside old ideas as misguided and introduce new ones that will finally—this time—deliver the business to the promised land. Thus, for instance, TQM programs are derided for their incremental nature, while reengineering is championed as the key to achieving "breakthrough" performance. The half-life of such ideas is becoming so short that we find managers shifting abruptly from one idea to the next. Employees wise up to this syndrome very quickly. Experience teaches them not to get terribly enthused about any new idea. They learn to shrug it off, reasoning, "If we wait until Monday, this too shall pass."

Other companies fall into a third syndrome: they "go for it all." We know of one large U.S. bank where the vice president of HR proudly declared that his organization had implemented every new management program it could find. It had more than 1,000 self-managed teams, over 500 quality initiatives, more than 300 reengineering initiatives, and a host of other programs. Of course, if you probed a bit, you discovered that the majority of these initiatives addressed such crucial management issues as what color to paint the walls. Employees found all their time taken up participating in initiatives of varying importance. And this was happening in an organization where the core business was eroding at an alarming rate.

What happens when managers or their gurus are confronted with the situations we have been depicting? In our experience, they tend to respond with a few unchallengeable replies: "It's only natural to expect some failures—look at the great successes that other companies have had"; "It's not easy to change decades of existing practice"; or, "In time, we'll see results." By deflecting all possibility of judgment into the future like this, it is possible to sustain faith in a managerial promised land almost indefinitely.

But what about the success stories of the new management? Certainly, there have been some, but they have happened because managers used their ingenuity to adapt new ideas, such as TQM, to the particular contexts of their companies. When tailored to fit specific situations, and often changed beyond recognition, these new ideas can prove invaluable. This is pragmatic management at its best.

The Four Faces of Pragmatism

We are calling for a return to pragmatism as espoused by the nineteenth-century American pragmatists: to judge any idea by its practical consequences, by seeing what it allows you to do, rather than by chasing after an elusive notion of truth. Or as the pragmatist philosopher William James put it, "Theories are instruments, not answers to enigmas in which we can rest." Every managerial situation, we believe, demands a pragmatic attitude. For purposes of discussion, we can divide this approach into four general components: sensitivity to context, willingness to make do, focus on outcomes, and openness to uncertainty.

SENSITIVITY TO CONTEXT

We cannot stress enough that the central concept of pragmatic management is the need to adapt ideas to a given context. Being able to judge the parameters of a particular situation and decide what ideas and actions will work in that context is what distinguishes the truly effective manager.

Context includes both the macro and micro—from the cultural milieu of a host country, for example, to the personalities of employees on a management team. Managers who are sensitive to context have a keen sense of the company's history, including the successes and failures of past management programs. They know the company's resources intimately, from physical assets to human capital. And they understand the organization's and the employees' strengths and weaknesses, so they can discern what actions are possible and how much the organization can be stretched.

Pragmatic managers understand that a change initiative that worked in one context could just as easily fail in another and that programs must be continually reevaluated as circumstances evolve. Otherwise, change programs can get stuck at lofty levels of abstraction and ambiguity and have little relevance to the day-to-day workings of the corporation. Even when an overall program like TQM has been adopted, managers should make frequent pragmatic judgments about how best to implement it. Management gurus may peddle a glossary of rules that describe how to do this, but universal answers rarely meet particular needs.

Many of the most successful managerial innovations in recent years have come from companies that have adapted, rather than adopted, popular ideas. Consider an example that has been much in the news in recent years, GE's Work-Out program.[2] Before developing Work-Out in the late 1980s, GE tried to implement the popular Japanese quality circles, teams of employees dedicated to significant quality improvement, throughout the company.

In Japanese quality circles, people are isolated in small groups that often receive substantial direction from above. This approach, GE soon discovered, had limited value in an American context, however. CEO Jack Welch believed the top-down model would never foster the trust necessary to convince line employees to buy into major change. Nor would it sway many middle and upper level managers, whom he saw as "actively resistant to new ideas."

In 1989, Welch began replacing quality circles with the broader, homespun Work-Out program. Instead of gathering in small groups, workers and managers met in large forums dedicated to airing new ideas, the more radical the better. Frequency and duration of work-outs were flexible, according to need, and the town-meeting-like settings fostered a sense of community while ensuring the visibility of individual contributions. The public setting also forced reticent managers to face up to pressures for change. Welch insisted that manager give on-the-spot responses to employee proposals. Nothing was considered sacred in the Work-Out program. Even major changes like overhauling an existing business process (now hyped as reengineering) could be brought up and dealt with in less than a day. In sum, by following the pragmatic strategy of tailoring a program to fit the company, GE was able to avoid the pitfalls of generic quality management.

Homespun solutions are not always the answer, however. Sometimes it makes the most sense for companies to abandon ideas entirely, even those touted as "the next big thing." Some companies have discovered, for example, that just-in-time manufacturing, while beautiful theoretically, doesn't make sense in their manufacturing contexts. Even some Japanese companies that use JIT at home have found that American marketing methods and distribution systems make JIT less attractive in the United States.

In stressing the importance of sensitivity to context, however, we are not advocating a rejection of any idea that originates outside the company. We would hate to see managers conclude too quickly, "It won't work because our context is so different." That will stop the flow of ideas. We are urging only that innovative ideas, such as TQM, and basic management practices, such as strategic planning, be adopted with an acute sensitivity to the situation at hand. Careful forethought and monitoring should determine how practices are used and to what extent they are followed. Managers should also bear in mind that a solution that works today may fail tomorrow. After all, even the best management ideas, such as portfolio planning, have had a half-life of no more than ten to fifteen years.

WILLINGNESS TO MAKE DO

Pragmatic managers, we have found, are particularly adept at "making do." They know what resources are available and how to round up more on short notice; they seek pragmatic answers based on the materials at hand.

We call this aspect of pragmatism *bricolage,* a word French anthropologist Claude Lévi-Strauss used to describe the thought processes of primitive societies. Against prevailing stereotypes of these societies as intellectually inferior, Lévi-Strauss argued that they have ingenious, nonrational ways of thinking. They reason inductively, deriving principles from their daily experience to guide them. For example, these societies have developed elaborate systems of medicine by continually experimenting with local herbs and flowers until they discover the right mixtures to cure their ailments.

Effective managers are *bricoleurs* in this same sense. They play with possibilities and use available resources to find workable solutions. They tinker with systems and variables, constantly on the lookout for improved configurations.

One of our favorite examples of bricolage comes from a director we met a few years ago at a large telecommunications company. While most other people were focusing on the massive IT overhaul the company needed, she directed her attention to how it could use the existing computer resources more creatively.

The engineers who maintained the huge telecommunications network stored data on a trio of aging, overstuffed, and incompatible mainframes. Most people believed it was time to scrap them and install a new, cutting-edge information architecture that would integrate all the company's computer resources. The director concurred that the mainframes would eventually have to go, but she believed it didn't have to happen right away, and, given the time necessary for planning such a change, it couldn't. Why not get the most we can from the mainframes in the interim, she asked. Why not use computer workstations to simulate the multimillion-dollar information architecture that the company would have in the future? With little direction from above, she and her team developed a series of software applications that delayed the need for mainframe replacement while, at the same time, cutting the system-project time from months to weeks.

When a bricoleur is making do, solutions are never fixed or final. This innovative director's project evolved constantly from the day it was conceived until it was sent on-line. Indeed, being a bricoleur entails a willingness to take actions without a clear sense of how things are going to unfold in the future. This doesn't mean that bricoleurs don't care about results, but that they are willing to experiment to get there.

Motorola CEO Bob Galvin's skillful management of a change effort during the 1980s is another good example of bricolage. In 1983, Motorola had just come off a very good year, but Galvin was aware of rumblings throughout the company that the organizational structure wasn't working because it was too bureaucratic. A recent trip to Japan had also convinced him that Motorola was slow to respond to changes in the marketplace.

Rather than waiting for a crisis to erupt, postponing action until he could come up with the perfect strategy, or hiring outside consultants to implement a prepackaged program, Galvin plunged his managers into the change process. At a May meeting of more than 100 senior officers, he announced that the corporation would begin a large-scale change initiative. What he neglected to say was how.

Understandably, the officers were confused. No one was clear about the CEO's agenda or what anyone was expected to do. And this is precisely what Galvin was after. He wanted the officers to be creative and to experiment with different ways of addressing the problems they were confronting in their particular situations. While some managers became preoccupied with "not really knowing what Galvin wanted," others used his challenge as a jumping-off point for experimentation. They came up with numerous structural changes and product innovations, from more market-driven business units to a new line of cellular products, which enabled Motorola to weather an economic downturn and emerge as the most powerful player in the cellular industry. An intuitive pragmatist, Galvin had created a situation that allowed those closest to the problems to come up with solutions.

FOCUS ON OUTCOMES

Pragmatists are concerned with getting results. But they don't get overly hung up on how to get them. The telecommunications director didn't mind a Rube Goldberg approach to system design if it could make a positive contribution to the business. The managers who rejected just-in-time manufacturing realized that the most elegant theory would mean nothing if it couldn't improve delivery time.

Failure to focus on outcomes can spell disaster. Consider the case of the large bank we referred to earlier that had "gone for it all," adopting every change program in the book. Progress was defined in terms of the number of people who had received quality training and the number of quality and reengineering teams that had been established. This had created the illusion of progress. But the bank's performance continued to decline.

Allen-Bradley, a Rockwell-owned manufacturer of industrial controls, learned the hard way about the value of focusing on outcomes. The company's early experience with team-based management at its Industrial Computer and Communications Group had been successful because the teams had a clear mission: to deliver an innovative computer-integrated manufacturing product as quickly as possible. Their focus on outcomes made them flexible and pragmatic; when it was more reasonable for a few people to tackle a problem instead of a team, they went off on their own and did it.

When ICCG switched the whole organization to teams, however, the mission became more diffuse. Teams became a virtue unto themselves, and suddenly all problems had to be solved through teams, whether or not this was the most pragmatic solution. People became caught up in the novelty of teams, and the company took on a summer-camp atmosphere. "Whoever dies with the most teams wins," an employee joked.

Eventually, senior managers noticed that the proliferation of teams had led to a lack of discipline, while failing to get rid of the negative bureaucratic elements of the old system. Chastened by this experience, ICCG began using teams much more cautiously. Today senior managers decide when, where, and how teams are used. First, they ask three critical questions: Is a team necessary? What will we gain? How will we measure our gains? The emphasis is less on fostering camaraderie than on seeing concrete results.

An incident at a major computer company shows what happens when a manager focuses on the *wrong* outcome. After years of indifferent performance, the company's PC division was finally beginning to show some signs of life. The hardware group had developed a full line of PCs that could compete on price. A third-party software group had made promising alliances with major software vendors. And an internal software development group had produced a networking product that had great market potential.

To promote these new products, the managers of each group asked the division's marketing director to assign additional people to their marketing efforts. Had this director been thinking pragmatically, she might have assigned a couple of key staff members to each group. But she refused because she did not want to take the focus off her first priority, improving the performance of her overall marketing department.

With this goal in mind, she hired internal and external consultants to initiate a formal strategic planning exercise. To empower her people and maintain a spirit of participation, she solicited input at a series of off-site meetings and undertook team-building exercises. Of course, while all this was going on, the three managers felt like Nero was fiddling while Rome burned. Eventually, they appealed to the division's vice president, who intervened and broke up the marketing department. He assigned the director's star employees to the three groups and left her with only a skeletal staff. The marketing director had become so caught up in developing a trendy new strategy for her department that she had lost sight of the outcomes critical to her company's success. And she lost her employees in the process.

OPENNESS TO UNCERTAINTY

The last important component of a pragmatic attitude is a willingness to embrace uncertainty and surprise. We believe that most of today's off-the-shelf managerial innovations foster a regimentation that discourages managers from dealing effectively with the unexpected. The fashionable emphasis on being "proactive" can give a false sense that all circumstances can be anticipated. But more often than not, managers are thrown into situations in which they must act quickly and without certainty. To quote economist Kenneth Arrow, in many situations, "we must simply act, fully knowing our ignorance of possible consequences."

For those who associate pragmatism with conservatism or prudence, stressing an openness to uncertainty may seem counterintuitive. But the two concepts are linked. Pragmatists understand that it is unrealistic to try to avoid uncertainty. Attempts to deny or ignore it can blind managers to the real contexts in which they are working and prevent them from responding effectively. Instead of fearing sudden changes, pragmatic managers welcome them as unanticipated opportunities. They learn to capitalize on the unexpected, whether implementing a companywide change initiative or making a critical business decision.

Reebok CEO Paul Fireman is a manager who knows how to profit from uncertainty. At a shoe manufacturers' show in Europe in 1989, Fireman was unimpressed by the merchandise displayed on the floor. He noticed that members of the trade press, looking for a good story, seemed bored with the show as well. Fireman realized that this situation presented an opportunity for Reebok; if he could come up with something new and exciting, he could generate a lot of publicity. A

Reebok product that was still in development, THE PUMP, boasted an innovative, inflatable technology that could give the wearer a close personal fit. He knew it would make a great story. But the marketing plan for the shoe had not been completed, and many details had not been worked out, including the price. But Fireman decided to "just do it." He introduced THE PUMP at the show.

The early launch turned out to be a hit. These rave reviews, according to Fireman, not only created market anticipation for the shoe but also helped "light a fire inside the company to get the product developed and released quickly." It was produced in record time and turned out to be a huge success in the marketplace.

Fireman's boldness could have gotten the company in trouble had Reebok not been able to deliver on time. Many companies have been skewered in the press for making new product promises they couldn't keep. But Fireman's move was not quite as brash as it seemed. He based it on a quick but careful assessment of the state of the industry, his company's capabilities, and just how much Reebok could be stretched in a pinch. Because he understood the context in which he was operating, Fireman was able to seize the moment. No time-to-market program could have produced such positive results. No companywide initiative can ever be a substitute for the pragmatic judgment of an individual manager.

American management is at a crossroads. It must decide whether to continue on its present path, on the fruitless quest for managerial Holy Grails, or whether to face up to the challenge of pragmatism. It is worth noting that in many academic disciplines, this sort of pragmatism has witnessed something of a revival. American management may stand to gain the most from looking back to this indigenous style of thought, particularly to its pragmatic successes of the past.

A case in point is the long list of uncommon accomplishments of the United States during World War II. Planes were designed, built, and flown safely in combat in less than two years. Today it takes more than ten years to accomplish the same. During the war, ships were built in weeks; today it takes years. And one could go on and on with stories of achievements that now seem beyond the realm of possibility. A crisis like World War II focuses people on pragmatic action in an uncommon way. It unites national and personal interests. Of course, it may be nearly impossible to replicate such conditions, but creating this kind of urgency is exactly what effective managers have always known how to do. And they have always been able to create urgency with or without the invocation of a brand-new management paradigm.

We are by no means arguing that the new ideas hyped to managers are without worth or that managers should go back to focusing on the much-maligned bureaucratic practices of the past. Instead, we are saying that the time has come to reconsider the relative balance between management innovations and management fundamentals. If the eighties were the time for the flowering of new perspectives on managerial practice, the remainder of the nineties may be the time for a sober reevaluation of managerial responsibility.

Notes

1. "The International Quality Study—Best Practices Report" (Cleveland, Ohio: American Quality Foundation and Ernst & Young, 1992).
2. Work-Out is discussed in detail in Noel M. Tichy and Stratford Sherman, *Control Your Destiny or Someone Else Will: How Jack Welch Is Making G.E. the World's Most Competitive Corporation* (New York: Doubleday, 1993).

Double-Edged Pragmatist: An Interview with Shikhar Ghosh

Shikhar Ghosh was a partner at the Boston Consulting Group, specializing in creating responsive organizations, until 1988, when he became CEO of the Appex Corporation, a start-up cellular communications company. Now called EDS Personal Communications Corporation and a division of Electronic Data Systems, it is an $8 billion business and one of the fastest growing information management enterprises.

A self-avowed pragmatist, Ghosh speaks about his experience as an outsider who has recommended change strategies to corporations and as a CEO who implements change from within. He also discusses his role as a *bricoleur,* a pragmatic manager who constantly tinkers with systems and variables to create a stronger organization.

How would you define pragmatism as it relates to organizational change programs?

Being pragmatic is creating a balance between a company's objectives and constraints. The constraints may be its finances, history, relationships, or employees' ability to learn. You have to adjust constantly the objectives of any change program to conform to what a company can learn and absorb.

Do any organizational change fads you've seen live up to the hype?

Many have merit, but they often represent only particular truths. When you combine these change fads with the reality of a company, you get very mixed results. Quality and reengineering are not bad in themselves, but management gurus underplay the practical difficulty of implementing them in an organization. Gurus represent these programs as complete solutions, when most of them deal with only one facet of an organization's problems.

Most programs view companies as machines. But companies are more like organisms. If you do something to them, they react. And a program has to be fine-tuned constantly based on those reactions.

What kind of organizational problems did you encounter at Appex?

Appex had no structure. When I arrived, I called a meeting of the twenty-five employees to say that we needed some rules. I said that people had to be in by 10 A.M., or they had to call in. Someone got up and said, "What right do you have to tell us anything?"

So what did you do?

I implemented a Japanese circular structure to instill discipline without losing informality or building in too much hierarchy. I was in the center of the organizational chart, and groups were around me in concentric circles. People doing different functions were at the same level, and the boundaries between groups were blurred. For example, customer service flowed into engineering; engineering flowed into marketing.

The structure was based on Japanese principles of flat organizations, but we didn't just pull it out of a textbook. We designed the structure pragmatically to reflect the way people really worked.

How did it work?

We found that we could respond very quickly to changes in the market. And we were far more innovative than many competitors. But in a short while, we realized that we were growing too rapidly to allow for this level of informal communication. There was no standardized way of doing things. If work didn't get done, no one knew who was accountable.

What happened next?

Within six months, we went to the other extreme and opted for a functional organization. Department managers reported to me, and lower level managers reported to them. To some extent, this went against the grain. But by this time, employees saw the need for more structure. We were missing deadlines. Too much work was falling between the cracks.

Choosing a functional organization was initially a pragmatic move in that it addressed an urgent problem: the need for procedures and accountability. Within a few months, however, Appex developed the traditional symptoms of bureaucracy: lack of flexibility and responsiveness. There was no teamwork, and people started to align themselves more with their functions than with overall company goals.

And the next move?

Teams. People served on cross-functional teams that focused on one line of the business. This approach worked reasonably well for seven months, until we realized that we had too many products and not enough general management talent to direct all the teams.

So we restructured the company, tailoring the team concept to our own constraints. We consolidated the teams so that each one handled several lines of work. And we turned them into self-contained divisions. Traditional wisdom said we were too small to divide the company, but because of our needs and limitations, it was the pragmatic choice for us.

Were your employees starting to feel dizzy from all these changes?

In the beginning, employees would say, "Wait, not another structure!"

But then they got used to change and saw its value. After a while, an organizational structure becomes a tool you're using to create a balance between conflicting modes of organizational behavior, such as flexibility and consistency. Each structure emphasizes one type of behavior and deemphasizes another. By continuing to change, you can balance the needs of the organization.

Some of what is learned from an organizational change program stays with employees long after the program is replaced. People get to know one another; they understand other functions. And because the organization is constantly changing, people don't have time to develop a power base within a particular structure. They have to identify with the broader objectives of the company.

So, are you a bricoleur?

Yes, I guess I am. While it seems as if we implemented changes every six months, in reality, we were constantly changing. We weren't satisfied with off-the-shelf solutions. We were always tweaking the structure we had in place. And when we bumped against too many constraints, we would change the structure once again.

When you change often, you know that nothing is permanent. You don't have to have all the answers before you try something. You can afford to experiment because the current structure doesn't have to be "just right."

Managing is a matter of constantly looking at the way you do things and adjusting the process to reflect your goals and resources. That's pragmatism. You use the resources you have to get where you need to go.

—Julia Lieblich

2
Information Technology and Tomorrow's Manager

Lynda M. Applegate, James I. Cash, Jr.,
and D. Quinn Mills

The year is 1958. It's a time of prosperity, productivity, and industrial growth for U.S. corporations, which dominate the world economy. Organizations are growing bigger and more complex by the day. Transatlantic cable service, which has just been initiated, and advances in transportation are allowing companies to expand into international markets. To handle the growth, companies are decentralizing decision making. To keep track of these burgeoning operations, they are hiring middle managers in droves. In fact, for the first time ever, white-collar workers outnumber blue-collar workers. Large companies are installing their first computers to automate routine clerical and production tasks, and "participatory management" is the buzzword.

It's also the year Harold J. Leavitt and Thomas L. Whisler predicted what corporate life would be like 30 years later. Their article "Management in the 1980s" (*Harvard Business Review*, November–December 1958) and its predictions ran counter to the trends that were then underway. Leavitt and Whisler said, for instance, that by the late 1980s, the combination of management science and information technology would cause middle-management ranks to shrink, top management to take on more of the creative functions, and large organizations to centralize again. Through the 1960s, 1970s, and early 1980s, Leavitt and Whisler's predictions met strong criticism. But as the 1980s draw to a close, they don't seem so farfetched. Instead, they seem downright visionary. (See "Their Future, Our Present.")

Downsizing and "flattening" have been common in recent years. One estimate has it that organizations have shed more than one million managers and staff professionals since 1979. As companies have reduced the number of middle managers, senior managers have increased their span of control and assumed additional responsibilities. Consider these two examples:

- Within weeks after a comprehensive restructuring thinned management by 40 percent, the president of a large oil company requested an improved management control system for his newly appointed senior management team. In response, a sophisticated, online executive information system was developed. It did the work of scores of analysts and mid-level managers whose responsibilities had been to produce charts and graphs, communicate this information, and coordinate operations with others in the company. The president also mandated the use of electronic mail to streamline communication throughout the business.

- A large manufacturing company recently undertook a massive restructuring to cut the cost and time required to bring a new product to market. The effort included layoffs, divestitures, and early retirements, which thinned middle management by 30 percent. The company adopted a sophisticated telecommunications network, which linked all parts of the multinational company, and a centralized corporate data base, which integrated all aspects of the highly decentralized business. Senior managers used the data base and networks to summarize and display data from inside and outside the company and to signal to employees the kinds of things they should focus on.

Information technology, which had once been a tool for organizational expansion, has become a tool for downsizing and restructuring. Both these companies used technology to improve centralized control and to create new information channels. But this improved centralized control did not come at the expense of decentralized decision making. In fact, the need to be responsive led to even more decentralized decision making. The companies reduced the number of middle managers, and the computer systems assumed many of the communication, coordination, and control functions that middle managers previously performed. The line managers who remained were liberated from some routine tasks and had more responsibility.

These effects are similar to what Leavitt and Whisler predicted. Taking their clues from the management science and technology research of the 1950s, Leavitt and Whisler contemplated how technology would influence the shape and nature of the organization. They understood that technology would enable senior management to monitor and control large organizations more effectively and that fewer middle managers would be needed to analyze and relay information. They did not anticipate, however, that microcomputers would enable simultaneous improvement in decentralized decision making.

Their Future, Our Present

Harold J. Leavitt and Thomas L. Whisler's "Management in the 1980s" appeared in the November–December 1958 issue of the *Harvard Business Review*. In that article, the two authors hypothesized what the organization of the future would look like. They predicted that in the 1980s:

The role and scope of middle managers would change. Many of the existing middle management jobs would become more structured and would move downward in status and compensation. The number of middle managers would decrease, creating a flatter organization. Those middle-management positions that remained would be more technical and specialized. New mid-level positions with titles like "analyst" would be created.

Top management would take on more of the innovating, planning, and creating. The rate of obsolescence and change would quicken, and top management would have to continually focus on the horizon.

Large organizations would recentralize. New information technologies would give top managers more information and would extend top management's control over the decisions of subordinates. Top executives chose to decentralize only because they were unable to keep up with the changing size and complexity of their organizations. Given the chance, however, they would use information technology to take more control and recentralize.

In the past, managers had to choose between a centralized and a decentralized structure. Today there is a third option: technology-driven control systems that support the flexibility and responsiveness of a decentralized organization as well as the integration and control of a centralized organization.

What Next?

Now that this wave of information technology has worked its way into practice, it's time to think about where we're headed next. When we turn to research to see what technical breakthroughs are on the horizon, as Leavitt and Whisler did, we find that the horizon itself has changed. It's now much closer. Since the 1950s, development time has been cut in half. What once took thirty years to get from pure research to commercial application now takes only ten to fifteen.

Moreover, when earlier generations of technology were commercialized, managers tended to adopt the technology first and then try to figure out what to do with the new information and how to cope with the organizational implications. But for many companies, that approach is now grossly inadequate. The new technology is more powerful, more diverse, and increasingly entwined with the organization's critical business processes. Continuing to merely react to new technology and the organizational change it triggers could throw a business into a tailspin.

At the same time, the business environment is changing ever faster, and organizations must be more responsive to it. Yet certain facts of life restrain them from doing so. Companies want to be more flexible, yet job descriptions, compensation schemes, and control mechanisms are rigid. They want to use their resources effectively, yet it's not always clear who can contribute most to a project, especially among people in different functional areas. They want to be productive, but every time an employee goes to another company, a little bit of corporate history and experience walks out the door.

With the help of technology, managers will be able to overcome these problems and make their organizations far more responsive than they are today. We can look forward, in fact, to an era in which managers will do the shaping. Large organization or small, centralized or not—business leaders will have options they've never had before. The technology will be there to turn the vision into reality and to change it as circumstances evolve. With that in mind, making a next round of predictions and waiting to see if they come true seems too passive. It makes more sense to begin thinking about the kind of organization we want and taking the steps necessary to prepare for it.

We already see glimpses of the future in some progressive companies that have used technology creatively, but even they do not give us a complete picture of the kind of organization that will be possible—maybe even prevalent—in the twenty-first century. Some companies will choose to adopt a new organizational form that we call the "cluster organization."[1] By doing so, they will be able to run their large companies like small ones and achieve the benefits of both.

In the cluster organization, groups of people will work together to solve business problems or define a process and will then disband when the job is done. Team members may be geographically dispersed and unacquainted with each other, but information and communication systems will enable those with complementary skills to work together. The systems will help the teams carry out their activities and track the results of their decisions. Reporting relationships, control mechanisms, compensation schemes—all will be different in the cluster organization.

Technology will offer new options even to companies that don't wish to make all of the changes the cluster organization implies. The first step in understanding these options is to look, as Leavitt and Whisler did, at the technologies that will make them possible.

Tomorrow's Machines

Much of the technology that will give managers the freedom to shape their organizations is already being commercialized—expert systems, group and cooperative work systems, and executive information systems. Expert and knowledge-based systems (a subset of artificial intelligence technology) are rapidly appearing in commercial settings. Every large company we've polled expects to have at least one production system using this technology by late 1989. Group and cooperative work systems have sprung up in a number of companies, primarily for use by multidisciplinary teams. Executive information systems, which track both internal and external information, enable senior managers to monitor and control large, geographically dispersed and complex organizations.

By the turn of the century, these and other technologies will be widely available. Companies will be able to pick and choose applications that fit their requirements. Computers will be faster, smaller, more reliable, and easier to use. They'll store vast amounts of information, and they'll be flexible enough to allow companies to change their information and communication systems as the environment changes.

In the twenty-first century, desktop computers will be as powerful as today's supercomputers, and supercomputers will run at speeds over a thousand times faster than today's. Computer chips now with one million processing elements will have more than one billion, and parallel processing (the ability to share a task among a number of processing units) will boost power tremendously.

It will be possible to communicate voluminous amounts of information in a variety of forms over long distances within seconds. Standard telephone lines and advanced cellular radio technology will provide access to high-speed networks that will whisk data, text, graphics, voice, and video information from one part of the world and send it to another instantly. Improved reliability and security will accompany the significantly higher network speeds and the improved performance.

Plugging all shapes and sizes of computers into tomorrow's network will be as easy as plugging in a telephone today. Telephones, in fact, will be replaced by computer phones that can convert speech into machine-readable text and can simultaneously transmit video images, voice, and data. Storing messages, transferring documents, paying bills, and shopping at home will all be possible through the same connection.

Computers the size of a small book will have the information processing power and storage capabilities of today's desktop workstations, yet will fit in a briefcase. They'll enable us to create and revise documents, review and answer mail, and even hold video conference meetings from anyplace that has a phone jack. Cellular terminals will allow even more freedom, since they won't require a wired telephone connection. And we will no longer be a slave to the keyboard; voice recognition technology will allow us to dictate messages and create and revise text as easily as using a dictaphone.

As computers become faster at processing and communicating information, we'll need better ways of storing and managing it. Optical storage media, similar to the compact-disk technology that is used today to store music, will hold much more information than is possible today and will retrieve information much more quickly.

And no longer will it be necessary to store data in static data bases that must be reprogrammed every time the business changes. Flexible, dynamic information networks called associative networks will do away with these rigid systems. Associative networks will allow us to store and manipulate information in a manner similar to the way we think. They will store data, voice, video, text, and graphics—but beyond that, they will store the relationships between information elements. As needs change and the network is reconfigured, the relationships among the data remain intact. Primitive associative information systems, used primarily to process large-text data bases (e.g., hypertext), are currently on the market. We can expect significant enhancements to these associative information systems in the next several years.

Tomorrow's computers will truly be more intelligent. Today's computers are designed to process information sequentially, one command at a time. This capability works well if the problem or task is structured and can be broken down into a series of steps. It doesn't work well for complex, unstructured tasks involving insight, creativity, and judgment. "Neural network" computers will change that.

Rather than processing commands one at a time, a neural network computer uses associative reasoning to store information as patterns of connections among millions of tiny processors, all of which are linked together. These computers attempt to mimic the actions of the human brain. When faced with a new pattern, the computer follows rules of logic to ask questions that help it figure out what to do with the anomaly.

Prototypes of neural network computers already exist. One group of researchers developed a neural network computer that contained the logic to understand English phonetics. The researchers gave the computer typed transcripts, containing 1,024 words, from a child in first grade, and it proceeded to read out loud. A human instructor "told" the computer each time it made a mistake, and within ten tries, the computer was reading the text in an understandable way. Within fifty tries, the computer was reading at 95 percent accuracy. No software programming was ever done.[2] The computer learned to read in much the same way that humans do.

We can also expect that by the twenty-first century there will be many companies that routinely use expert systems and other artificial intelligence applications. Knowledge bases, in which expertise is stored along with information, will become as commonplace as data bases are today. Technology will increasingly help people perform tasks requiring judgment and expert knowledge. Already, fighter aircraft technology is moving toward having the plane respond to what the pilot is thinking rather than his physical movements.

This type of technology will no longer simply make things more efficient; instead, the computer will become a tool for creativity, discovery, and education. Interactive technology based on optical storage is currently used in flight simulators to help pilots learn to make decisions. Some companies are experimenting with similar systems, described as digital video interactive, to help planners, analysts, researchers, functional specialists, and managers learn to make decisions without the risk and time associated with traditional experiential learning. These should help managers learn to be effective much more quickly.

Technologies will be well developed to meet the needs of senior executives. Sophisticated analytical, graphical, and computer interface capabilities will be able to aggregate, integrate, and present data in flexible and easy-to-use formats. Computers and special software will support executive planning, decision making, communication, and control activities. Some executives already use these applications to manage their businesses.

While in the past computers primarily supported individual work, the computer systems of the future will also be geared toward groups. Research on computer support for cooperative work has gained momentum over the past five years, and many companies are developing promising new technologies. Several companies are installing automated meeting rooms, and a number of vendors are working on software to support group activities. Researchers are now testing electronic brainstorming, group consensus, and negotiation software, and general meeting support systems. To help geographically dispersed group members work together, some companies are developing electronic communication software and applications that make communication and the exchange of documents and ideas faster and easier. These applications will allow skills to be better allocated.

The Structure, the Process, and the People

These and other advanced technologies will give managers a whole new set of options for structuring and operating their businesses. In the twenty-first century, like today, some companies will be small, some will be large; some will be decentralized, others will not. But technology will enable new organizational structures and management processes to spring up around the familiar ones, and the business world will be a very different place as a result. Here we describe the organizational structures, management processes, and human resource management strategies associated with the cluster organization and how the technology will make them possible in years to come.

Organizational structure:

Companies will have the benefits of small scale and large scale simultaneously.

Even large organizations will be able to adopt more flexible and dynamic structures.

The distinctions between centralized and decentralized control will blur.

The focus will be on projects and processes rather than on tasks and standard procedures.

The hierarchy and the matrix are the most common formal organization designs for large companies today. They structure communication, responsibility, and accountability to help reduce complexity and provide stability. But, as implemented today, they also tend to stifle innovation. With the environment changing as quickly as it does, the challenge has been to make large companies, with their economies of scale and other size advantages, as responsive as small ones.

Small companies, of course, have fewer layers of management and less bureaucracy, so the organization is less rigid. They adapt more easily to change and allow for creativity. Leadership and control are generally easier in small businesses because top management can communicate directly with workers and can readily trace the contribution individuals make. Information is also easier to track. Much of the knowledge is in people's heads, and everyone knows who to go to for expertise on a particular subject. People often have a chance to get involved with a broad range of responsibilities and therefore have a better understanding of the business as a whole.

These small organizations, especially those that are information-intensive and have a large percentage of professional employees, tend to be structured differently. We have termed the most fluid and flexible forms "cluster." Other authors talk of a network organization or an adhocracy.[3] In the network organization, rigid hierarchies are replaced by formal and informal communication networks that connect all parts of the company. In the adhocracy, a set of project-oriented work groups replace the hierarchy. Both of these forms are well known for their flexibility and adaptiveness. The Manned Space Flight Center strategies of NASA, an example of an adhocracy, changed its organization structure seventeen times in the first eight years of its existence.[4]

In what will be an even faster changing world than the one we now know, businesses of all sizes will need the ability to adapt to the dynamics of the external environment. Automated information and communication networks will support the sharing of information throughout a large, widely dispersed, complex company. The systems will form the organization's infrastructure and change the role of formal reporting procedures. Even in large corporations, each individual will be able to communicate with any other—just as if he or she worked in a small company.

Management processes:

Decision making will be better understood.

Control will be separate from reporting relationships.

Computers will support creativity at all organizational levels.

Information and communication systems will retain corporate history, experience, and expertise.

The technologies that will allow these more fluid organizational forms are already coming into use in the form of electronic mail, voice mail, fax, data networks, and computer and video conferencing. Speed and performance improvements will collapse the time and distance that now separate people who could benefit from working together. The large organizations of the future will seem as tightly connected as small ones.

Computers will also help identify who in the company has the expertise needed to work on a particular problem. Data bases of employees' skills and backgrounds will ensure that the mix of talent can be tailor-made for every task that arises. The systems will keep track of who knows what, and how to prepare an individual for the next project.

Managers in large companies will also have technological help in keeping track of where information resides and how to analyze it. Associative information networks and neural network computers will preserve the relationships among data elements and will store and manage information in a manner similar to the way we think. They will provide concise snapshots of the vast activities and resources of a large corporation. This will prevent managers from being overwhelmed by the scale and complexity.

Executives and senior managers will be less insulated from operations because executive information systems will help them get the information they need to monitor, coordinate, and control their businesses. Rather than waiting for the analysts and middle managers to prepare reports at the end of a prolonged reporting period, executives will have immediate access to information. Software will help do the analysis and present it in a usable format. With such immediate feedback, managers will be able to adjust their strategy and tactics as circumstances evolve rather than at fixed time intervals. And if a change in tactics or strategy is warranted, advanced communication technology will send the message to employees promptly.

Top management's ability to know what is going on throughout the organization won't automatically lead to centralization. With feedback on operations readily available at the top, the rigid policies and procedures that now aim to keep line managers on track can be relaxed. The systems will also liberate business managers by giving them the information and analytic support they need to make decisions and control their operations. Individuals and project teams will be able to operate fairly autonomously while senior management monitors the overall effects of their actions by the hour or day.

Most of the day-to-day activity will be project oriented. Because circumstances will change even faster than they do now, no two situations will be exactly alike or call for the same set of experts or procedures. The employees' skills and the approach will vary with the task at hand, so teams of people will form around particular projects and subsequently dissolve. Most responsibilities, then, will be handed over to project managers. Associative information networks will help those managers deploy resources, and software specially designed to support group work will aid communication, decision making, and consensus reaching. People who work together only infrequently will have the tools they need to be at least as effective as the permanent management team in a small company.

Decision making is not well understood in most organizations. Managers often make choices based on thought processes they themselves cannot explain. They gather the information they think is relevant and reach what seems like the best conclusion. In the future, sophisticated expert systems and knowledge bases will help to capture those decision-making processes. Companies can then analyze and improve them.

As the decision processes become more explicit and well-defined and as companies learn what information is required, the level of the person making the decision becomes less important. It will still be important to monitor the outcome and to make sure the circumstances surrounding the decision haven't completely changed.

Management control is now exerted through the formal organizational chart. A manager at a given level in the organization is responsible for everything that happens below that level. That same person channels information up through the organization to the person he or she reports to.

But when technology allows top management to monitor data at the lowest organizational level without the help of intermediaries and when employees at all levels and in all functions can communicate directly, formal control systems do not have to be embedded in organizational reporting relationships. The ability to separate control from reporting relationships means that both systems can be handled most effectively. For instance, top management can exercise control directly by monitoring results at all levels, while a different set of relationships exists for reporting purposes. These reporting relationships would focus on employee motivation, creativity, and socialization.

By doing a lot of the analytical work, expert systems and artificial intelligence tools will free up workers at all levels to be more creative. Up to now, only top management jobs have been structured to allow as much time as possible for creative thinking. As technology helps managers with coordination, control, decision making, and communication, they too will have the time and encouragement to make discoveries and use the new resources innovatively.

The transience of even specialized workers won't be nearly the problem in the twenty-first century that it is today. Information systems will maintain the corporate history, experience, and expertise that long-time employees now hold. The information systems themselves—not the people—can become the stable structure of the organization. People will be free to come and go, but the value of their experience will be incorporated in the systems that will help them and their successors run the business.

In this environment, companies will need fewer managers. Those managers that do assume executive positions, however, will lack the experiential learning acquired through years as a middle manager. Their career paths will not take them through positions of increasing responsibility where they oversee the work of others. Executive information systems will enable them to "get up to speed" quickly on all parts of the business. Sophisticated business analysis and simulation models will help them analyze business situations and recognize the consequences, thereby decreasing and managing risk.

In the 1950s and 1960s, computers took on many operational and routine tasks. In the 1970s and 1980s, they assumed some middle-management decision making, coordinating, and controlling tasks. As the technology affects even more aspects of the business, work itself will change and require a different set of skills. People will need to be technically sophisticated and better educated in order to cope with the demands on them. Employees must be capable of leading—rather than being led by—the technology, capable of using technology as a lever against the increased complexity and pace of change in their business environments.

Human resources:

> Workers will be better trained, more autonomous, and more transient.
>
> The work environment will be exciting and engaging.
>
> Management will be for some people a part-time activity that is shared and rotated.
>
> Job descriptions tied to narrowly defined tasks will become obsolete.
>
> Compensation will be tied more directly to contribution.

As top management seizes on its ability to monitor without restricting freedom, employees will have more control over their own work. There will be fewer rigid policies from a less visible headquarters. Also, as the nature of the work changes from implementing a particular company's standard operating procedures to participating in a series of projects that call on one's expertise, workers will be less tied to any one organization, and building loyalty to a company will be harder than it is today. In some companies, loyalty may be less critical than having access to the skills a given employee has to offer. As companies pull together the resources they need on a project-by-project basis and as information and communication networks extend beyond the organization, company boundaries will be harder to define. Organizations may draw on expertise that lies in a supplier or an independent consultant if appropriate.

Because workers will be highly skilled and the organization will offer fewer opportunities for advancement, employees will expect the work environment to be rewarding. If they are not stimulated or if their independence is threatened, they will go elsewhere.

In these ways, companies of the future will closely resemble professional service firms today. The most successful firms attract and retain employees by providing an environment that is intellectually engaging. The work is challenging, the projects diverse, and the relationships with clients fairly independent. Some professionals work with more than one firm—like doctors who admit patients to several hospitals.

Management will be a part-time job as group members share responsibility and rotate leadership. Except at the top of the organization, there will be few jobs that consist solely of overseeing the work of others—and then primarily for measurement and control purposes. Each work group may have a different leader. In addition, the leadership of a single group may rotate among members, depending on what the business problem requires. Employees will take on a management role for short periods, and as a result, will have a better understanding of the entire business.

Detailed, task-oriented job descriptions will be less important because the job will be changing all the time. In a sense, everyone will be doing the same job—lending their special skills and expertise to one project after another. In another sense, every job will be unique—people with different kinds of expertise will work on different sets of projects. Information systems will be able to account for the work each person does and the skills and experience he or she possesses.

The ability to track each individual's skill and participation in the company outside the traditional organizational forms creates a whole new freedom: the ability to pay each person for his or her actual contribution to the organization without upsetting an entire pay scale or hierarchical structure. Currently, if the company wants to create an incentive for a particular person, it is often constrained by the compensation system itself. To raise one person's salary requires boosting everyone else above that point in the hierarchy.

Flexible, dynamic compensation packages will allow companies to treat individuals as unique contributors and to reward them based on their particular skills. In some companies, an employee's compensation may follow the pattern of a normal distribution curve, matching the employee's desired work pattern and contribution to the company. Salaries would increase and peak between ages forty and fifty, and then decline.

Be Creative But Be Careful

The new technologies hold great promise that our large, rigid hierarchies will become more adaptive, responsive, and better suited to the fast-paced world of the twenty-first century. But these technologies do not come without risk. Processing information faster may seem like a good idea, but it is possible to process information too fast. As speed increases, efficiency of a process improves only to a point. That point is reached when it is no longer possible to monitor and control the results of the process. Beyond that point, the process of collecting information, making decisions, monitoring feedback, and evaluating performance breaks down. The experience of some companies during the stock market crash of October 19, 1987, shows what can happen when information is processed faster than we can monitor and control it.

There are also risks associated with integrating data from diverse sources. For one thing, we run the risk of data overload, in which case people unable to understand or use the information and the tools that convert data into information may fail. Also, the creation of integrated data bases may lead to unintended liabilities. For example, when an elevator manufacturer created a centralized service and repair center, it also created a legal liability. A large, centralized data base containing the maintenance and repair records of all of their elevators in North America provided an attractive target for subpoena by any suitor.

Computerization of critical business processes may also create security risks. Sabotage, fraud, record falsification, and theft become more threatening than ever. And with more information stored electronically, privacy issues become more acute.

Leavitt and Whisler were wise to believe that information technology would influence the structure of organizations, their management processes, and the nature of managerial work. Our 30-year history of information technology use in organizations suggests that in the future managers must be much more actively involved in directing technology and managing its influence on organizations.

Technology will not be an easy solution to serious problems and it won't guarantee competitiveness. As always, it will require thoughtful planning and responsible management. But as never before, it will tax the creative powers of the business leaders who must decide when to use it—and to what end.

Conversations with Leavitt and Whisler

In January 1988, Lynda Applegate, Mark Cannon (a research associate), and James Cash visited with professors Leavitt and Whisler and asked them to reflect on their 1958 article. Here are excerpts from those conversations.

What prompted you to write the article "Management in the 1980s"?

Leavitt: As a graduate student at MIT in the late 1940s, I was exposed to all kinds of new ideas about machines that might be able to learn and even think. It was an expansive and optimistic time of very rapid technical change. Management theory was also changing to a much more human approach. The emphasis was shifting away from hierarchical formalism toward decentralization and participative management. Tom and I wanted to shake people up and get them to look at not only the human side, but also the technical and social sides. We wanted to stimulate debate—and we did.

Whisler: Hal and I shared an office at the University of Chicago. I was interested in organization structure and technology's influence on it. Hal was a social scientist interested in organization and management theory. We had a number of lively discussions on how computers would change organizations. We believed the trend toward decentralization was a response to increasing complexity. We were convinced that given the right tools to deal with the complexity, managers would recentralize. We saw the computer as one of those tools.

How would you evaluate your predictions today?

Leavitt: One thing we didn't anticipate was the tremendous impact of miniaturization. We thought of computers as massive, centralized machines. We couldn't even imagine modern PCs sitting on our desks. The whole question of centralization versus decentralization becomes almost irrelevant when you consider the potential of decentralizing computer processing.

Whisler: In our 1958 predictions, we focused on the influence of information technology, although we knew that other factors also affected organization structure. A major development to which we did not pay sufficient attention was the rapidly expanding economy of the 1960s and the consequent explosive growth of companies. These companies needed more middle managers to keep them under control, which had a decentralizing effect. For a while, growth upstaged the special kind of "downsizing" of middle management we foresaw. As growth slowed in the late 1970s and 1980s, and competition became intense, the effect of information technology became evident. The timing of events was fortunate for us.

You were among the first, if not the first, to use the term information technology. What did you mean by it?

Leavitt: We were influenced by the early research on artificial intelligence, heuristic programming, and quantitative modeling by people like Norbert Wiener and Herbert Simon. So we were looking at the computer from a human and managerial—not a data processing—point of view. We were thinking about computers that might influence human learning and decision making—not computers that would automate routine work.

Whisler: The mid-1950s were a time of intense interest in management science. The computer was seen as a tool to support complex, quantitative modeling. We used the term *information technology* because we wanted to stress the use of the computer to support decision making and organizational information processing. Many people misinterpreted our perspective.

Notes

1. See D. Quinn Mills, *The Cluster Organization: A New Alternative to the Hierarchy* (forthcoming, 1989).
2. Terrence Sejnowski and Charles Rosenberg, "Parallel Networks That Learn to Pronounce English Text," *Complex Systems,* vol. 1, 1987, p. 145.
3. See Robert G. Eccles and Dwight B. Crane, "Managing Through Networks in Investment Banking," *California Management Review,* Fall 1987, p. 176; and Henry Mintzberg, "The Adhocracy," in *The Strategy Process,* ed. James Brian Quinn, Henry Mintzberg, and Robert M. James (Englewood Cliffs, N.J.: Prentice-Hall, 1988), p. 607.
4. As reported in Henry Mintzberg, *Structuring in Fives: Designing Effective Organizations* (Englewood Cliffs, N.J.: Prentice-Hall, 1983).

3
Prepare Your Organization to Fight Fires

Karl Weick

Young Men and Fire
Norman Maclean
Chicago: University of
Chicago Press, 1992

What should the structure of a small group be when its business is to meet sudden danger and prevent disaster? That question was not posed by an arbitrage unit leader, a turnaround artist, or an aircraft dispatcher coping with the blizzard of the century. Instead, it was asked by a former professor of English literature at the University of Chicago who studied a forest fire that killed thirteen young men.

The professor, Norman Maclean (1902-1990), is best known for his novella *A River Runs Through It* (1976). *Young Men and Fire,* which Maclean spent more than a decade researching and writing, was published posthumously in 1992. It chronicles the attempt to extinguish a deadly forest fire that raged in the mountains of Montana in August 1949. Maclean combines interviews with the survivors and other U.S. Forest Service veterans, personal observations of the remote Mann Gulch site, documents from Forest Service archives, and mathematical models of the blaze to reconstruct the events of that tragic day nearly half a century ago.

On August 5, 1949, at about 4 P.M., fifteen smoke jumpers—trained firefighters but new to one another as a group—parachuted into Mann Gulch. The crew's leaders originally believed that the blaze was a basic "ten o'clock fire," meaning that the crew would have it under control by ten the next morning. Instead, the fire exploded and forced the men into a race for their lives.

The Mann Gulch fire may seem to be a distant tragedy, but Maclean's exploration of the event touches on many questions of deep significance for readers today. For those of us concerned about leadership in organizations, the episode illuminates problems facing corporate leaders. Increasingly, corporate work unfolds in small, temporary outfits where the stakes are high, turnover is chronic, foul-ups can spread, and the unexpected is common. As we will see from what follows, minimal organizations, exemplified by the crew at Mann Gulch and found at a growing number of businesses, are susceptible to sudden and dangerous losses of meaning.

Fight Fire with Fire

The fire at Mann Gulch probably began on August 4 when lightning set a small fire in a dead tree. The temperature reached 97 degrees the next day and produced a fire danger rating of seventy-four out of a possible one hundred, indicating the potential for the fire to spread uncontrollably. When the fire was spotted by a lookout on a mountain thirty miles away, sixteen smoke jumpers were sent at 2:30 from Missoula, Montana, in a C-47 transport plane. (One man became ill and didn't make the jump.) A forest ranger posted in the next canyon, Jim Harrison, was already on the scene trying to fight the fire on his own.

Wind conditions that day were turbulent, so the smoke jumpers and their cargo were dropped from 2,000 feet rather than the usual 1,200. The parachute connected to their radio failed to open, and the radio was pulverized as it hit the ground. But the remaining crew and supplies landed safely in Mann Gulch by 4:10. The smoke jumpers then collected their supplies, which had scattered widely, and grabbed a quick bite to eat.

While the crew ate, foreman Wagner Dodge met up with ranger Harrison. They scouted the fire and came back concerned that the thick forest near which they had landed could become a "death trap." Dodge told the second-in-command, William Hellman, to take the crew across to the north side of the gulch, away from the fire, and march along its flank toward the river at the bottom of the gulch. While Hellman did this, Dodge and Harrison ate a quick meal. Dodge rejoined the crew at 5:40 and took his position at the head of the line moving toward the river. He could see flames flapping back and forth on the south slope as he looked to his left. Then Dodge saw that the fire had suddenly crossed the gulch about 200 yards ahead and was moving toward them. He yelled at the crew to run from the fire and began angling up the steep hill toward the bare ridge of rock.

The crew was soon moving through slippery grasses two and a half feet high but was quickly losing ground to the flames—eventually towering at a height of thirty feet—rushing toward them at a rate that probably reached a speed of 660 feet per minute. Sensing that the crew was in serious danger, Dodge yelled at them to drop their tools. Two minutes later, to everyone's astonishment, he lit a fire in front of the men and motioned to them to lie down in the area it had burned. No one did. Instead, they ran for the ridge and what they hoped would be safety.

Two firefighters, Robert Sallee and Walter Rumsey, made it through a crevice in the ridge unburned. Dodge survived by lying down in the ashes of his escape fire. The other thirteen perished. The fire caught up with them at 5:56—the time at which the hands on Harrison's watch melted in place.

Sense Making and Structure

It is easy to read about this fire and conclude that it was a tragedy caused by bad luck or poor decision making. In fact, the problems at Mann Gulch cannot be attributed solely to those factors; the reader must also consider the issues of "sense making" and structure. In retrospect, Maclean knew that the smoke jumpers were meeting sudden danger. But the firefighters themselves didn't know that. And that very uncertainty is the core issue in this disaster, and one that has lessons for executives.

When the noise created by wind, flames, and exploding trees is deafening and the temperature is approaching a lethal 140 degrees, and when relative strangers who "love the universe but are not intimidated by it" are strung out in a line, people can neither confer with a trusted neighbor nor pay close attention to a boss who is unknown and whose commands make no sense whatsoever. As if these obstacles were not enough, it is hard to make common sense when each person sees something different—or nothing at all—because of the smoke.

But the level of disorganization at Mann Gulch is not all that different from what companies face today. People are often thrust into unfamiliar roles to fulfill difficult tasks, and small mistakes can combine into something monstrous. Faced with sudden crises, organizations that seem quite sturdy can collapse.

We often attribute such collapses to a company's wrongheaded strategy or to a failed move into an unstable product market. We presume that business problems arise from bad decisions. The problem with this diagnosis is that the world of decision making is about *strategic* rationality and is built from clear questions and answers that attempt to remove ignorance.

The world of sense making, however, is different. Sense making is about *contextual* rationality. It is built out of vague questions, muddy answers, and negotiated agreements that attempt to reduce confusion. The men at Mann Gulch did not face clear questions such as: Where should we go? When do we take a stand? What should our strategy be? Instead, they faced the more basic, frightening feeling that their roles as firefighters no longer worked. They were outrunning their past experience and were not sure about what was happening or who they were.

As the events unfolded on that August afternoon, the smoke-jumper crew at Mann Gulch began to unravel and lose its structure. As it did so, the firefighters became anxious and found it harder to make sense of what was happening. Finally, they were unable to understand the one thing that would have saved their lives, the escape fire.

At least two key events destroyed the tenuous organization that held the firefighters together. The first occurred when Dodge told his second-in-command, Hellman, to take the crew to the north side of the gulch. During the twenty-minute period of Dodge's absence, the crew became confused and ended up in two groups 500 feet apart; each had its own leader, one of whom was making up his own rules as he went along. Hellman was more familiar with implementing orders than with constructing them or plotting possible escape routes. As a result, the crew was left for a crucial period with unclear orders that were apparently challenged by at least one crew member.

When Dodge reappeared on the scene, he began to reunite the crew. About five minutes later, he realized that the fire had jumped the gulch and was now proceeding toward the men. At that point, Dodge was probably the only one to have seen the fire. He yelled at the crew to reverse direction, which alarmed the firefighters; they could not see the fire yet but began to suspect that they were running from one.

Eight minutes later, with disaster only three minutes away, Dodge instructed the retreating crew to drop their heavy tools. That was the second—and in some ways more unsettling—threat to the role system. A fire crew that retreats from a fire rather than face it will necessarily find its identity and morale strained. But if retreating firefighters are then told to discard the very tools that are their reason for being there, the moment quickly turns existential. If I am no longer a firefighter, then who am I? With the fire bearing down, the only possible answer is, an endangered person in a world where it is every man for himself.

It was under such circumstances that the firefighters encountered Dodge's escape fire. The foreman pointed to it and yelled, "this way, this way." But he could not persuade the men; he overheard one of them—probably Hellman—say, "to hell with that, I'm getting out of here."

Because clear communication, familiarity, and trust were missing, the firefighters failed to understand that Dodge was actually setting the fire to clear an area in which they would be safe. With no structure in place and an absence of clear sense, it is not surprising that the crew would refuse to escape one fire by walking into another one that had been set intentionally.

Resilience and Wisdom

There are larger lessons in this tragedy for those whose job it is to make sense of environments that suddenly change from the expected to the unexpected, the inconceivable, or the incomprehensible. To point the way to safety in the face of surprise, leaders today need to develop resilient groups that are capable of four things: improvisation, wisdom, respectful interaction, and communication.

The collapse of role systems need not result in disaster if people develop skills in improvisation. By *improvisation*, I mean bringing to the surface, testing, and restructuring one's intuitive understandings of phenomena on the spot, at a time when action can still make a difference.[1] Improvisers remain creative under pressure precisely because they have the ability to bring order out of chaos. Thus, when situations unravel, they can proceed with whatever materials are at hand.

Dodge knew how to use the things at his disposal, fire and brush, to create a safe area where none existed.

If organizations paid more attention to improvisation, it would be possible, when one organizational order collapsed, to invent a substitute immediately. Swift replacement of a traditional order with an improvised one can forestall the confusion that follows a command such as "drop your tools" or "jump into this fire."

Wisdom is the second source of resilience. To understand its role in this case, we need to remind ourselves of the crew's belief that most fires could be extinguished by 10 the next morning. That was consistent with the general experience of smoke jumpers in 1949 and with their belief in their ability to control any fire they landed on. Their major purpose was to put out fires so fast that they didn't become big ones. The "tragic corollary," as Maclean calls it, is that the smoke jumpers could not learn much about big fires by fighting small ones.

To state the point more generally, what most organizations miss—and what explains why most fail to learn—is that ignorance and knowledge grow together. The more people learn about a particular domain, the more questions they raise about other areas in that same domain.

The organizational culture best able to accept that ignorance and knowledge grow together is one that values wisdom. In a fluid world, wise people know that they don't fully understand what is happening at a given moment, because what is happening is unique to that time. They avoid extreme confidence and extreme caution, knowing that either can destroy what organizations need most in changing times, namely, curiosity, openness, and the ability to sense complex problems. The overconfident shun curiosity because they think they know what they need to know. The overcautious shun curiosity for fear it will only deepen their uncertainties. Both the cautious and the confident are closed-minded, which means that neither make good judgments. In this sense, wisdom, understood as simultaneous belief and doubt, improves adaptability.

Wise behavior is easier to display in a setting where people are respectful of the interactions that hold the group together. Respectful interactions have three imperatives: Respect the reports of others and be willing to base beliefs and actions on them (trust); report so that others may use your observations in coming to valid beliefs (honesty); and respect your own perceptions and beliefs and integrate them with the reports of others without depreciating them or yourself (self-respect).[2]

If a role system collapses among people for whom trust, honesty, and self-respect are underdeveloped, then they are on their own. And fear often swamps their resourcefulness. If, however, a role system collapses among people for whom trust, honesty, and self-respect are developed, then new options, such as mutual adaptation, blind imitation of creative solutions, and trusting compliance are created. When a formal structure collapses, there are no leaders, roles, or routines; the situation no longer makes sense. That is what seems to have happened in Mann Gulch. Dodge couldn't lead, because the role system in which he was the leader disappeared. Worse, he couldn't rely on his crew members to trust him, question him, or pay attention to him, because they didn't have time to get to know him. The key question is, When formal structure collapses, what is left? The answer is communication, but only if there is trust and time.

It is striking how little communication occurred during the three and a half hours that the crew was together. There was apparently little discussion during the noisy, bumpy plane ride or while the men retrieved equipment scattered on the ground. After a meal together, people began hiking toward the river but quickly got separated. They were suddenly turned around and told to run for the ridge, and they quickly ran out of breath scaling the steep north slope. The point is an important one: Evidence is growing that nonstop talk is a crucial source of coordination in complex systems that are susceptible to disasters.

Readers may conclude that the world they face is simply not as threatening or explosive as the one faced by the men at Mann Gulch. Remember, however, that in the beginning the Mann Gulch fire seemed safe and small. And when events are increasingly interdependent—as they are in today's world—small, unrelated flaws can interact to produce a forest fire blowup or a currency market meltdown. Maclean tells us that the fire at Mann Gulch was shaped by "little screw-ups that fitted together tighter and tighter until all became one and the same thing—the fateful blowup."

Maclean's book helps us talk more candidly about little mistakes that escalate. Talking about Mann Gulch at a distance of nearly fifty years enables us to glimpse vulnerabilities that lie much closer at hand. To grapple with those vulnerabilities and design our way around them is not an exercise in rationality and decision making. Instead, it is a task that requires a closer look at the social context in which sense making creates the decisions that people think are so crucial.

Mann Gulch teaches us that the real action occurs long before decisions ever become visible. By the time a decision needs to be made, sense-making processes have already determined its outcome. That's why, in answer to Maclean's question about the need for better structures to meet disaster, we need to design structures that are resilient sources of collective sense making. If, instead, we design for better decision making, then we improve a minor portion of organizational life that occurs too late to make much difference. Sense making is where the action—and the tragedy—live.

Notes

1. See D. A. Schön, *Educating the Reflective Practitioner* (San Francisco: Jossey-Bass, 1987).
2. See Donald T. Campbell, "Asch's Moral Epistemology for Socially Shared Knowledge," in *The Legacy of Solomon Asch: Essays in Cognition and Social Psychology,* ed. Irwin Rock (Hillsdale, N.J.: Erlbaum, 1990), pp. 39–52.

4
Informal Networks:
The Company Behind the Chart

David Krackhardt and Jeffrey R. Hanson

Many executives invest considerable resources in restructuring their companies, drawing and redrawing organizational charts only to be disappointed by the results. That's because much of the real work of companies happens despite the formal organization. Often what needs attention is the *informal* organization, the networks of relationships that employees form across functions and divisions to accomplish tasks fast. These informal networks can cut through formal reporting procedures to jump start stalled initiatives and meet extraordinary deadlines. But informal networks can just as easily sabotage companies' best laid plans by blocking communication and fomenting opposition to change unless managers know how to identify and direct them. Learning how to map these social links can help managers harness the real power in their companies and revamp their formal organizations to let the informal ones thrive.

If the formal organization is the skeleton of a company, the informal is the central nervous system driving the collective thought processes, actions, and reactions of its business units. Designed to facilitate standard modes of production, the formal organization is set up to handle easily anticipated problems. But when unexpected problems arise, the informal organization kicks in. Its complex webs of social ties form every time colleagues communicate and solidify over time into surprisingly stable networks. Highly adaptive, informal networks move diagonally and elliptically, skipping entire functions to get work done.

Managers often pride themselves on understanding how these networks operate. They will readily tell you who confers on technical matters and who discusses office politics over lunch. What's startling is how often they are wrong. Although they may be able to diagram accurately the social links of the five or six people closest to them, their assumptions about employees outside their immediate circle are usually off the mark. Even the most psychologically shrewd managers lack critical information about how employees spend their days and how they feel about their peers. Managers simply can't be everywhere at once, nor can they read people's minds. So they're left to draw conclusions based on superficial observations, without the tools to test their perceptions.

Armed with faulty information, managers often rely on traditional techniques to control these networks. Some managers hope that the authority inherent in their titles will override the power of informal links. Fearful of any groups they can't command, they create rigid rules that will hamper the work of the informal networks. Other managers try to recruit "moles" to provide intelligence. More enlightened managers run focus groups and host retreats to "get in touch" with their employees. But such approaches won't rein in these freewheeling networks, nor will they give managers an accurate picture of what they look like.

Using network analysis, however, managers can translate a myriad of relationship ties into maps that show how the informal organization gets work done. Managers can get a good overall picture by diagramming three types of relationship networks:

- The advice network shows the prominent players in an organization on whom others depend to solve problems and provide technical information.
- The trust network tells which employees share delicate political information and back one another in a crisis.
- The communication network reveals the employees who talk about work-related matters on a regular basis.

Maps of these relationships can help managers understand the networks that once eluded them and leverage these networks to solve organizational problems. Case studies using fictional names, based on companies with which we have worked, show how managers can bring out the strengths in their networks, restructure their formal organizations to complement the informal, and "rewire" faulty networks to work with company goals.

The Steps of Network Analysis

We learned the significance of the informal network twelve years ago while conducting research at a bank that had an 80 percent turnover rate among its tellers. Interviews revealed that the tellers' reasons for leaving had less to do with the bank's formal organization than with the tellers' relationships to key players in their trust networks. When these players left, others followed in droves.

Much research had already established the influence of central figures in informal networks. Our subsequent studies of public and private companies showed that understanding these networks could increase the influence of managers outside the inner circle. If they learned who wielded power in networks and how various coalitions functioned, they could work with the informal organization to solve problems and improve performance.

Mapping advice networks, our research showed, can uncover the source of political conflicts and failure to achieve strategic objectives. Because these networks show the most influential players in the day-to-day operations of a company, they are useful to examine when a company is considering routine changes. Trust networks often reveal the causes of nonroutine problems such as poor performance by temporary teams. Companies should examine trust networks when implementing a major change or experiencing a crisis. The communication network can help identify gaps in information flow, the inefficient use of resources, and the failure to generate new ideas. They should be examined when productivity is low.

Managers can analyze informal networks in three steps. Step one is conducting a network survey using employee questionnaires. The survey is designed to solicit responses about who talks to whom about work, who trusts whom, and who advises whom on technical matters. It is important to pretest the survey on a small group of employees to see if any questions are ambiguous or meet with resistance. In some companies, for example, employees are comfortable answering questions about friendship; in others, they deem such questions too personal and intrusive. The following are among the questions often asked:

• Whom do you talk to every day?
• Whom do you go to for help or advice at least once a week?
• With one day of training, whose job could you step into?

- Whom would you recruit to support a proposal of yours that could be unpopular?
- Whom would you trust to keep in confidence your concerns about a work-related issue?

Some companies also find it useful to conduct surveys to determine managers' *impressions* of informal networks so that these can be compared with the actual networks revealed by the employee questionnaires. In such surveys, questions are posed like this:

- Whom do you think Steve goes to for work-related advice?
- Whom would Susan trust to keep her confidence about work-related concerns?

The key to eliciting honest answers from employees is to earn their trust. They must be assured that managers will not use their answers against them or the employees mentioned in their responses and that their immediate colleagues will not have access to the information. In general, respondents are comfortable if upper-level managers not mentioned in the surveys see the results.

After questionnaires are completed, the second step is cross-checking the answers. Some employees, worried about offending their colleagues, say they talk to *everyone* in the department on a daily basis. If Judy Smith says she regularly talks to Bill Johnson about work, make sure that Johnson says he talks to Smith. Managers should discount any answers not confirmed by both parties. The final map should not be based on the impressions of one employee but on the consensus of the group.

The third step is processing the information using one of several commercially available computer programs that generate detailed network maps. (Drawing maps is a laborious process that tends to result in curved lines that are difficult to read.) Maps in hand, a skilled manager can devise a strategy that plays on the strengths of the informal organization, as David Leers, the founder and CEO of a California-based computer company, found out.

Whom Do You Trust?

David Leers thought he knew his employees well. In fifteen years, the company had trained a cadre of loyal professionals who had built a strong regional reputation for delivering customized office informa-

Exhibit I.   The Formal Chart Shows Who's on Top

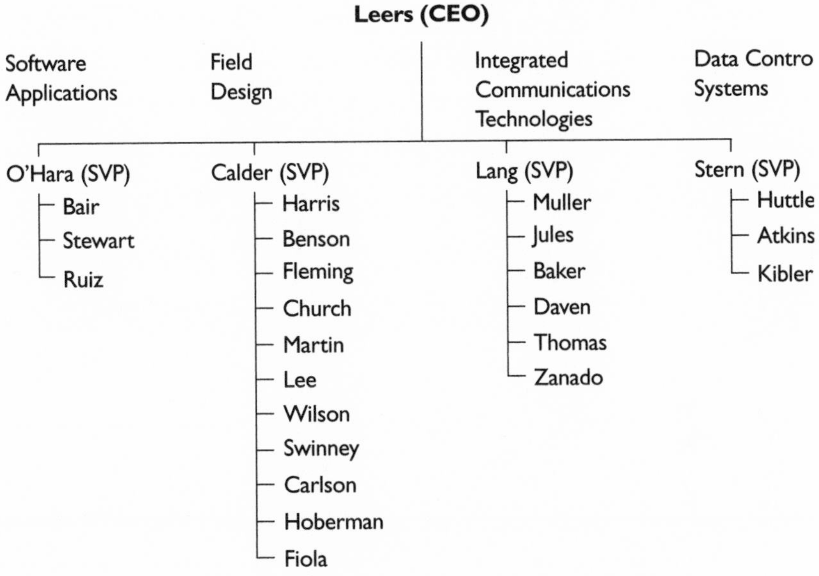

Leers (CEO)

Software Applications	Field Design	Integrated Communications Technologies	Data Contro Systems
O'Hara (SVP)	Calder (SVP)	Lang (SVP)	Stern (SVP)
├ Bair	├ Harris	├ Muller	├ Huttle
├ Stewart	├ Benson	├ Jules	├ Atkins
└ Ruiz	├ Fleming	├ Baker	└ Kibler
	├ Church	├ Daven	
	├ Martin	├ Thomas	
	├ Lee	└ Zanado	
	├ Wilson		
	├ Swinney		
	├ Carlson		
	├ Hoberman		
	└ Fiola		

tion systems (see Exhibit I). The field design group, responsible for designing and installing the systems, generated the largest block of revenues. For years it had been the linchpin of the operation, led by the company's technical superstars, with whom Leers kept in close contact.

But Leers feared that the company was losing its competitive edge by shortchanging its other divisions, such as software applications and integrated communications technologies. When members of field design saw Leers start pumping more money into these divisions, they worried about losing their privileged position. Key employees started voicing dissatisfaction about their compensation, and Leers knew he had the makings of a morale problem that could result in defections.

To persuade employees to support a new direction for the company, Leers decided to involve them in the planning process. He formed a strategic task force composed of members of all divisions and led by a member of field design to signal his continuing commitment to the group. He wanted a leader who had credibility with his peers and was a proven performer. Eight-year company veteran Tom Harris seemed obvious for the job.

Leers was optimistic after the first meeting. Members generated

Exhibit II.   *The Advice Network Reveals the Experts*

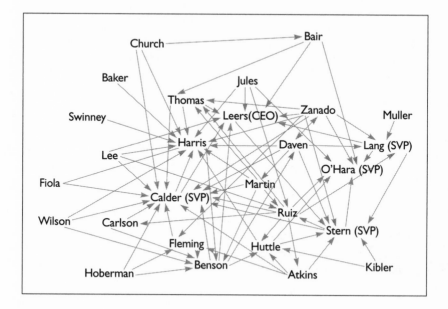

good discussion about key competitive dilemmas. A month later, however, he found that the group had made little progress. Within two months, the group was completely deadlocked by members championing their own agendas. Although a highly effective manager, Leers lacked the necessary distance to identify the source of his problem.

An analysis of the company's trust and advice networks helped him get a clearer picture of the dynamics at work in the task force. The trust map turned out to be most revealing. Task force leader Tom Harris held a central position in the advice network—meaning that many employees relied on him for technical advice (see Exhibit II). But he had only *one* trust link with a colleague (see Exhibit III). Leers concluded that Harris's weak position in the trust network was a main reason for the task force's inability to produce results.

In his job, Harris was able to leverage his position in the advice network to get work done quickly. As a task force leader, however, his technical expertise was less important than his ability to moderate conflicting views, focus the group's thinking, and win the commitment of task force members to mutually agreed-upon strategies. Because he was a loner who took more interest in computer games than

Exhibit III.   But When It Comes to Trust . . .

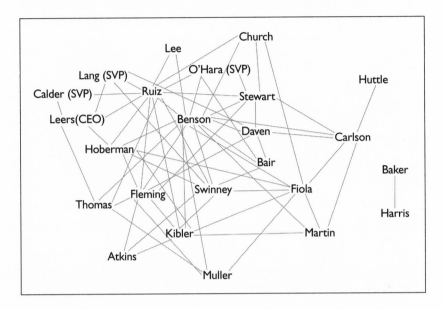

in colleagues' opinions, task force members didn't trust him to take their ideas seriously or look out for their interests. So they focused instead on defending their turf.

With this critical piece of information, the CEO crafted a solution. He did not want to undermine the original rationale of the task force by declaring it a failure. Nor did he want to embarrass a valued employee by summarily removing him as task force head. Any response, he concluded, had to run with the natural grain of the informal organization. He decided to redesign the team to reflect the inherent strengths of the trust network.

Referring to the map, Leers looked for someone in the trust network who could share responsibilities with Harris. He chose Bill Benson, a warm, amiable person who occupied a central position in the network and with whom Harris had already established a solid working relationship. He publicly justified his decision to name two task force heads as necessary, given the time pressures and scope of the problem.

Within three weeks, Leers could see changes in the group's dynamics. Because task force members trusted Benson to act in the best interest of the entire group, people talked more openly and let go of their fixed positions. During the next two months, the task force made significant progress in proposing a strategic direction for the company. And in the process of working together, the task force helped integrate the company's divisions.

A further look at the company's advice and trust networks uncovered another serious problem, this time with the head of field design, Jim Calder.

The CEO had appointed Calder manager because his colleagues respected him as the most technically accomplished person in the division. Leers thought Calder would have the professional credibility to lead a diverse group of very specialized design consultants. This is a common practice in professional service organizations: make your best producer the manager. Calder, however, turned out to be a very marginal figure in the trust network. His managerial ability and skills were sorely lacking, which proved to be a deficit that outweighed the positive effects derived from his technical expertise. He regularly told people they were stupid and paid little attention to their professional concerns.

Leers knew that Calder was no diplomat, but he had no idea to what extent the performance and morale of the group were suffering as a result of Calder's tyrannical management style. In fact, a map based on Leers's initial perceptions of the trust network put Calder in a central position (see Exhibit IV). Leers took for granted that Calder had good personal relationships with the people on his team. His assumption was not unusual. Frequently, senior managers presume that formal work ties will yield good relationship ties over time, and they assume that if *they* trust someone, others will too.

The map of Calder's perceptions was also surprising (see Exhibit V, on page 148). He saw almost no trust links in his group at all. Calder was oblivious to *any* of the trust dependencies emerging around him—a worrisome characteristic for a manager.

The information in these maps helped Leers formulate a solution. Again, he concluded that he needed to change the formal organization to reflect the structure of the informal network. Rather than promoting or demoting Calder, Leers cross-promoted him to an elite "special situations team," reporting directly to the CEO. His job involved working with highly sophisticated clients on specialized problems. The position took better advantage of Calder's technical skills and turned out to be good for him socially as well. Calder, Leers learned, hated dealing with formal management responsibilities and the pressure of running a large group.

Exhibit IV. How the CEO Views the Trust Network

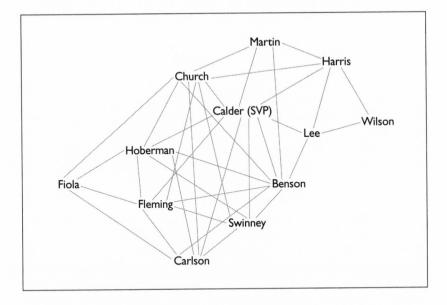

Leers was now free to promote John Fleming, a tactful, even-tempered employee, to the head of field design. A central player in the trust network, Fleming was also influential in the advice network. The field group's performance improved significantly over the next quarter, and the company was able to create a highly profitable revenue stream through the activities of Calder's new team.

Whom Do You Talk To?

When it comes to communication, more is not always better, as the top management of a large East Coast bank discovered. A survey showed that customers were dissatisfied with the information they were receiving about banking services. Branch managers, top managers realized, were not communicating critical information about available services to tellers. As a result, customers' questions were not answered in a timely fashion.

Management was convinced that more talking among parties would improve customer service and increase profits. A memo was

Exhibit V.   The Trust Network According to Calder

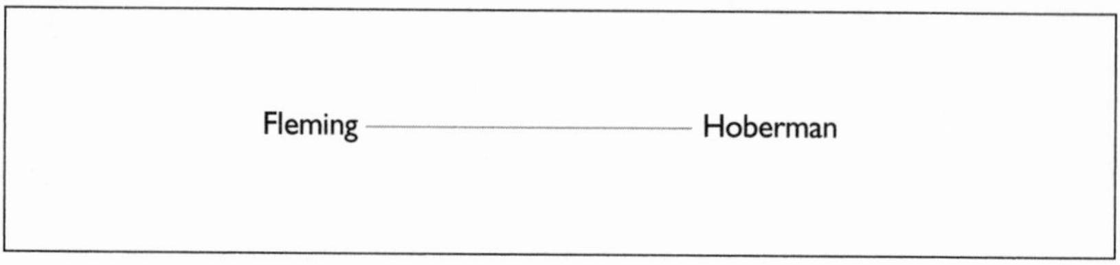

Fleming ——————————————— Hoberman

circulated ordering branch managers to "increase communication flow and coordination within and across branches and to make a personal effort to increase the amount and effectiveness of their own interpersonal communications with their staffs."

A study of the communication networks of twenty-four branches, however, showed the error of this thinking. *More* communication ties did not distinguish the most profitable branches; the *quality* of communication determined their success. Nonhierarchical branches, those with two-way communication between people of all levels, were 70 percent more profitable than branches with one-way communication patterns between "superiors" and staff.

The communication networks of two branches located in the same city illustrated this point. Branch One had a central figure, a supervisor, with whom many tellers reported communicating about their work on a daily basis. The supervisor confirmed that employees talked to her, but she reported communicating with only half of these tellers about work-related matters by the end of the day. The tellers, we later learned, resented this one-way communication flow. Information they viewed as critical to their success flowed up the organization but not down. They complained that the supervisor was cold and remote and failed to keep them informed. As a result, productivity suffered.

In contrast, Branch Two had very few one-way communication lines but many mutual, two-way lines. Tellers in this branch said they were well-informed about the normal course of work flow and reported greater satisfaction with their jobs.

After viewing the communication map, top management abandoned the more-is-better strategy and began exploring ways of fostering mutual communication in all the branches. In this case, management did not recast the formal structure of the branches. Instead, it opted to improve relationships within the established framework.

The bank sponsored mini-seminars in the branches, in which the problems revealed by the maps were openly discussed. These consciousness-raising sessions spurred many supervisors to communicate more substantive information to tellers. District managers were charged with coming up with their own strategies for improving communication. The bank surveyed employees at regular intervals to see if their supervisors were communicating effectively, and supervisors were informed of the results.

The communication network of a third branch surfaced another management challenge: the branch had divided itself into two distinct groups, each with its own culture and mode of operation. The network map showed that one group had evolved into the "main branch," consisting of tellers, loan officers, and administrative staff. The other group was a kind of "sub-branch," made up primarily of tellers and administrators. It turned out that the sub-branch staff worked during non-peak and Saturday hours, while main-branch employees worked during peak and weekday hours. The two cultures never clashed because they rarely interacted.

The groups might have coexisted peacefully if customers had not begun complaining about the sub-branch. The main-branch staff, they reported, was responsive to their needs, while the sub-branch staff was often indifferent and even rude. Sub-branch employees, it turned out, felt little loyalty to the bank because they didn't feel part of the organization. They were excluded from staff meetings, which were scheduled in the morning, and they had little contact with the branch manager, who worked a normal weekday shift.

The manager, who was embedded in the main branch, was not even aware that this distinct culture existed until he saw the communication network map. His challenge was to unify the two groups. He decided not to revamp the formal structure, nor did he mount a major public-relations campaign to integrate the two cultures, fearing that each group would reject the other because the existing ties among its members were so strong. Instead, he opted for a stealth approach. He exposed people from one group to people from the other in the hopes of expanding the informal network. Although such forced interaction does not guarantee the emergence of stable networks, more contact increases the likelihood that some new ties will stick.

Previously planned technical training programs for tellers presented the opportunity to initiate change. The manager altered his original plans for on-site training and opted instead for an off-site facility, even though it was more expensive. He sent mixed groups of sub-branch and main-branch employees to programs to promote gradual, neutral interaction and communication. Then he followed up with a series of selective "staff swaps" whereby he shifted work schedules temporarily. When someone from the main branch called in sick or was about to go on vacation, he elected a substitute from the sub-branch. And he rescheduled staff meetings so that all employees could attend.

This approach helped unify the two cultures, which improved levels of customer satisfaction with the branch as a whole over a six-month period. By increasing his own interaction with the sub-branch, the manager discovered critical information about customers, procedures, and data systems. Without even realizing it, he had been making key decisions based on incomplete data.

Network Holes and Other Problems

As managers become more sophisticated in analyzing their communication networks, they can use them to spot five common configurations. None of these are inherently good or bad, functional or dysfunctional. What matters is the *fit*, whether networks are in sync with company goals. When the two are at odds, managers can attempt to broaden or reshape the informal networks using a variety of tactics.

IMPLODED RELATIONSHIPS

Communication maps often show departments that have few links to other groups. In these situations, employees in a department spend all their time talking among themselves and neglect to cultivate relationships with the rest of their colleagues. Frequently, in such cases, only the most senior employees have ties with people outside their areas. And they may hoard these contacts by failing to introduce these people to junior colleagues.

To counter this behavior, one manager implemented a mentor system in which senior employees were responsible for introducing their apprentices to people in other groups who could help them do their jobs. Another manager instituted a policy of picking up the tab for "power breakfasts," as long as the employees were from different departments.

IRREGULAR COMMUNICATION PATTERNS

The opposite pattern can be just as troubling. Sometimes employees communicate only with members of other groups and not among themselves. To foster camaraderie, one manager sponsored seasonal sporting events with members of the "problem group" assigned to the same team. Staff meetings can also be helpful if they're really used to share resources and exchange important information about work.

A lack of cohesion resulting in factionalism suggests a more serious underlying problem that requires bridge building. Initiating discussions among peripheral players in each faction can help uncover the root of the problem and suggest solutions. These parties will be much less resistant to compromise than the faction leaders, who will feel more impassioned about their positions.

FRAGILE STRUCTURES

Sometimes group members communicate only among themselves and with employees in one other division. This can be problematic when the contribution of several areas is necessary to accomplish work quickly and spawn creativity. One insurance company manager, a naturally gregarious fellow, tried to broaden employees' contacts by organizing meetings and cocktail parties for members of several divisions. Whenever possible, he introduced employees he thought should be cultivating working relationships. Because of his warm, easygoing manner, they didn't find his methods intrusive. In fact, they appreciated his personal interest in their careers.

HOLES IN THE NETWORK

A map may reveal obvious network holes, places you would expect to find relationship ties but don't. In a large corporate law firm, for example, a group of litigators was not talking to the firm's criminal lawyers, a state of affairs that startled the senior partner. To begin tackling the problem, the partner posed complex problems to criminal lawyers that only regular consultations with litigators could solve. Again, arranging such interactions will not ensure the formation of enduring relationships, but continuous exposure increases the possibility.

"BOW TIES"

Another common trouble spot is the bow tie, a network in which many players are dependent on a single employee but not on each other. Individuals at the center knot of a bow tie have tremendous power and control within the network, much more than would be granted them on a formal organizational chart. If the person at the knot leaves, connections between isolated groups can collapse. If the person remains, organizational processes tend to become rigid and slow, and the individual is often torn between the demands of several groups. To undo such a knot, one manager self-consciously cultivated a stronger relationship with the person at the center. It took the pressure off the employee, who was no longer a lone operative, and it helped to diffuse some of his power.

In general, managers should help employees develop relationships within the informal structure that will enable them to make valuable contributions to the company. Managers need to guide employees to cultivate the right mix of relationships. Employees can leverage the power of informal relationships by building both strong ties, relationships with a high frequency of interaction, and weak ties, those with a lower frequency. They can call on the latter at key junctures to solve organizational problems and generate new ideas.

TESTING THE SOLUTION

Managers can anticipate how a strategic decision will affect the informal organization by simulating network maps. This is particularly valuable when a company wants to anticipate reactions to change. A company that wants to form a strategic SWAT team that would remove key employees from the day-to-day operations of a division, for example, can design a map of the area without those players. If removing the central advice person from the network leaves the division with a group of isolates, the manager should reconsider the strategy.

Failure to test solutions can lead to unfortunate results. When the trust network map of a bank showed a loan officer to be an isolate, the manager jumped to the conclusion that the officer was expendable. The manager was convinced that he could replace the employee, a veteran of the company, with a younger, less expensive person who was more of a team player.

What the manager had neglected to consider was how important this officer was to the company's day-to-day operations. He might not have been a prime candidate for a high-level strategy team that demanded excellent social skills, but his expertise, honed by years of experience, would have been impossible to replace. In addition, he had cultivated a close relationship with the bank's largest client—something an in-house network map would never have revealed. Pictures don't tell the whole story; network maps are just one tool among many.

The most important change for a company to anticipate is a complete overhaul of its formal structure. Too many companies fail to consider how such a restructuring will affect their informal organizations. Managers assume that if a company eliminates layers of bureaucracy, the informal organization will simply adjust. It will adjust all right, but there's no guarantee that it will benefit the company. Managers would do well to consider what type of redesign will play on the inherent strengths of key players and give them the freedom to thrive. Policies should allow all employees easy access to colleagues who can help them carry out tasks quickly and efficiently, regardless of their status or area of jurisdiction.

Experienced network managers who can use maps to identify, leverage, and revamp informal networks will become increasingly valuable as companies continue to flatten and rely on teams. As organizations abandon hierarchical structures, managers will have to rely less on the authority inherent in their title and more on their relationships with players in their informal networks. They will need to focus less on overseeing employees "below" them and more on managing people across functions and disciplines. Understanding relationships will be the key to managerial success.

5

How to Integrate Work *and* Deepen Expertise

Dorothy Leonard-Barton, H. Kent Bowen,
Kim B. Clark, Charles A. Holloway,
and Steven C. Wheelwright

To be a leader in global manufacturing in the 1990s, a company must excel in two seemingly contradictory ways. First, it must constantly build and refresh its individual areas of expertise so it has the critical capabilities needed to stay ahead of the pack. And second, it must get its ever-changing mix of disciplines to work together in the ever-changing way needed to prevail in the ever-changing competitive environment. In other words, a company must find the way that best enables it at a given point in time both to come up with a product that meets customer needs better than the competition's *and* to create that product faster and more efficiently than competitors.

Most manufacturers, especially those companies that have reorganized themselves by cross-functional processes, have already discovered how difficult it is to integrate various disciplines and still maintain functional excellence. "Is it even possible to achieve both things?" executive after executive laments. There is a solution. It lies in the creative use of development projects.

As the critical juncture where functional groups meet, development projects are the true test of an organization's integrative abilities. More important, development projects can be used as a tool for strengthening the relationship among functions, while still giving them the room they need to advance their own expertise. To attain this leverage, though, executives must approach development projects with those goals in mind and must take into account how their company's strengths and weaknesses will help or hinder the project in try-ing to attain those goals.

Eastman Kodak learned this lesson when it developed its Fun-Saver camera in the late 1980s. Although the project was not all smooth sailing, it had a happy ending and, overall, superbly illus-trates how a company can get functions to work together effec-tively, enhance functional expertise, and create a winning product to boot.

Looking to expand the company's product line, Kodak's technical-development group in the mid-1980s proposed an intriguing new product: a disposable camera. Film would be packaged in a simple, in-expensive, sealed plastic camera. Once the pictures had been taken, the consumer would hand the camera to a photofinisher, who would extract the film and discard the camera. (Later on, the company de-veloped a system to recycle the used cameras.) Marketing would tar-get this "single-use" camera at people who suddenly found them-selves without their camera or who needed a camera for outdoor activities like boating or a beach outing, where they might be nervous about bringing an expensive camera. The disposable camera would be sold at convenience outlets and at major tourist attractions such as Disney World.

Initially, senior managers placed the project under the direction of the film division because they envisioned the FunSaver more as a pre-mium film product than as a camera, but that proved to be a mistake. The project languished for months because the film division thought the camera would be a low-margin business that would cannibalize sales of film, a very high-margin business.

In the meantime, the camera division lobbied Kodak executives to take over the project, pointing out that Fuji intended to market a single-use camera in the United States that it had already introduced in Japan. The camera division also promised to structure the camera's costs and pricing so that its per-unit profit margin would match or ex-ceed the company's current margin on a roll of film. Management gave the nod.

The project then took off. In a bid to streamline decision making, design the camera rapidly and efficiently, and ensure that its design would make it easy to manufacture, the camera division's develop-ment team decided to take several steps. It placed design and manu-facturing, which traditionally were separate functional groups at Ko-dak, under one project leader. And it created a small, dedicated team of engineering, manufacturing, and marketing people, who shared the same work space. While this approach was new for Kodak, the team members believed it was essential to complete the project rapidly.

The project leader also strongly believed that computer-aided design and computer-aided manufacturing (CAD/CAM) could make a huge difference in designing the camera and optimizing its manufacturability. Kodak had used CAD/CAM systems in other projects, but they had been technical engineering systems used by specialists. The project leader wanted a CAD/CAM system that could do more—one that could help integrate the work of the entire team—and persuaded senior managers to buy into his vision of using the project to create this new capability. So, at the outset of the project, the team had three explicit goals: to produce the camera quickly; to create new methods for integration; and to develop new CAD/CAM technology that would enable Kodak to develop high-quality, easy-to-manufacture products faster and more efficiently.

Team members customized the new CAD/CAM system to make it easy for them to share information and get immediate feedback from one another. Each designer of a component, system, mold, or manufacturing subsystem would work on his or her part, then insert an updated drawing into the master schematic for the whole camera and/or the manufacturing process. Then each morning, a new composite design would be downloaded so that all engineers could see the effects of their combined efforts. Although only the original designer could alter the drawing of his or her part, anyone could critique any drawing and request changes. In addition, manufacturing engineers used the system to generate simulations of prototypes of the manufacturing process, which enabled them to work out kinks that would have shown up in the actual manufacturing system. As a result, they were able to reach full production much faster when actual manufacturing began.

Kodak introduced the FunSaver in 1988, just as Fuji's camera was hitting the U.S. market. But, aided by aggressive advertising, the FunSaver immediately grabbed the lead, and it has held on to it. Kodak quickly introduced two follow-on products, the Weekend, a waterproof camera, and the Panoramic, a camera with a wide-angle lens. These products contributed greatly to the overall success of the FunSaver: more than 100 million have been sold. Kodak was able to develop the Weekend and the Panoramic in record time by using not only the same basic product design and manufacturing process but also the same people, the same project-management procedures, and the same CAD/CAM system.

Besides creating a successful product, the FunSaver project proved to the company that integrating functions was possible and highly advantageous. In this case, the CAD/CAM technology fostered a significant degree of interaction among the design, tooling, and manufacturing engineers within engineering as well as between engineering and marketing. In addition, the CAD/CAM system provided discipline and a common set of principles for achieving the desired integration. Subsequent development teams at Kodak organized their work in a similar manner, and leaders of the FunSaver project implemented the new principles for achieving integration elsewhere, when they moved on to other projects.

The FunSaver project also gave Kodak a new technical capability: CAD/CAM. Rather than try to introduce this emerging technology on a companywide or divisional scale, Kodak—thanks to the inspiration of the project manager—gave it a test run on a manageable scale. Afterward, the company went on to widen its use of the CAD/CAM system, again by means of development projects, charging each team with customizing the system to best serve its needs.

The project also provided Kodak with a path leading away from a tradition that had become a major problem for the company: the autonomy of each functional group. Before the FunSaver, development projects had proceeded in sequential fashion, with one functional department completing its work and passing the results to the next in the chain. While this approach resulted in high performance and quality, it slowed decision making and meant that an extensive amount of rework typically had to be conducted during the development process in order to get all the components and subsystems of a product or process to mesh. In the new time-sensitive competitive environment, Kodak's design-engineering process, once a core capability, had become a rigidity.

Finally, the shaky beginning of the project provided a valuable lesson about development teams. It demonstrated that a project must fit the objectives of the organization that is responsible for carrying it out. The film division did not fully support the project. The camera division, however, got right behind it and refined its definition so that it would meet Kodak's profitability goals, advance companywide learning, and develop new capabilities.

Leveraging Capabilities, Breaking Rigidities

Core capabilities are not just technologies and workforce skills. They are a capacity for action. They are the essence of what makes an organization unique in its ability to provide value to customers over a long period of time. But this is hardly a revelation.

What many managers do not yet understand about capabilities, however, is that each consists of four elements whose interaction determines how effectively the organization can exploit it. Those elements are: *knowledge and skills*—technical know-how and personal "know-who," including ties to important groups such as government regulatory bodies or the scientific community; *managerial systems*—tailored incentive systems, in-house educational programs, or methodologies that embody procedural knowledge; *physical systems*—plant, equipment, tooling, and engineering work systems that have been developed over the years, and production lines and information systems that constitute compilations of knowledge; and *values*—the attitudes, behaviors, and norms that dominate in a corporation.

An interesting example of a core capability that encompasses several of these elements is networking at Digital Equipment. Workstations or terminals are on virtually everyone's desk and are connected with sophisticated software so that any employee around the world can reach any other. The physical system supports a very horizontal, networked style of management. Because individual freedom and responsibility are the values that DEC employees prize the most, any requests for action are more likely to be met, and met more quickly, if they are sent through the horizontal chain of the informal network than if they are passed through the vertical chain of command. This networking approach permeates the company's routines and culture and fosters a task-force approach to most issues.

Take DEC's CDA software project to develop a computer architecture for linking desktop-publishing products. During this project, which started in late 1986, DEC employees were asked to field-test prototype software sent to them over the network. Some 150 reviewers provided their feedback in an electronic notes file. The on-line file provided "living specs" that enabled the team to perfect the software code continually. Later, the team members estimated that 90 percent of the bugs in the software were found by this method. DEC's networking capability clearly enhanced the project's success.

DEC's networking system is also a reason why project ideas often originate in the ranks. Development teams are authorized to initiate projects off-line, which give rise to multiple, ongoing experiments, some of which became full-fledged projects. Corporate strategy evolves as much from these projects as from top-management direction. Such empowerment of employees engenders a tremendous sense of project ownership and spurs team members to make remarkable achievements, often in the face of great odds. Development teams charge ahead with little supervision, believing they will be able to alter the direction of their group significantly and turn the course of their mammoth corporation a critical degree or two.

The downside of a core capability, as we have pointed out, is that it can become a rigidity. A strength can become a weakness. The very reason for a company's traditional success can become an obstacle to developing new capabilities or maintaining the right balance of capabilities. This was most obvious in the technology-intensive companies that the Manufacturing Vision Group studied.

Consider the DECstation 3100 effort, which was undertaken in 1988 to develop DEC's first workstation based on reduced-instruction-set computing (RISC) technology. In this project, the internal field-testing capability that had served DEC so well in the past proved to be a liability. The project team recruited an internal "wrecking crew" of DEC volunteers to evaluate the prototype product and rewarded employees who found the most bugs with prototype workstations.

But both the DEC engineers designing the workstation and the volunteers who tested it focused almost exclusively on the machine's performance—on building a "hot box" of excellent hardware—rather than on the amount of applications software that could run on it. In hindsight, that is not surprising. DEC had become a giant in the computer industry as a result of its machines that shared DEC's proprietary VAX architecture and VMS operating system. A plethora of applications software was available for these machines. As a result, DEC engineers designing new machines typically did not worry about software availability. But the DECstation 3100 was aimed at giving DEC a foothold in the market dominated by RISC-based machines with UNIX operating systems.

Though the workstation was a technical gem and benefited from the wrecking crew's suggestions, it had difficulty penetrating the market because only twenty application programs had been developed by the time DEC introduced the product. Potential customers chose competing workstations, even though they were less advanced, because they had many more application programs (more than 500 in some cases). The team members naïvely believed that the DEC volunteers provided a good test market, that a hot box would sell simply on its performance, and that users would develop their own applications. DEC's engineers might have been happy to do so, but potential customers clearly were not.

THE DARK SIDE OF VALUES

Of the four elements that determine the effectiveness of a core capability, the one most overlooked and most misunderstood—and most difficult to change—is also the one that is the most powerful when aligned with the other three. This element is values.

A project undertaken in the early 1980s at Hewlett-Packard to develop the company's first personal computer illustrates how values can trip up a project. In this case, HP consciously pitted the project against one of its core values, the fierce autonomy of its divisions, but underestimated how hard it would be to change that core value. Each HP division traditionally focused on specific product lines and had its own marketing, manufacturing, engineering, finance, and personnel functions. Division managers were expected to make a profit, and if one division developed a component for another, it would "sell" it at full price. This approach made a lot of sense when the challenge was attacking several distinctly separate, fast-growing markets at the same time and the key to success was to be able to respond quickly to the demands of disparate customers. HP's phenomenal growth was proof of that. But in the PC project, it certainly was not a plus.

HP senior managers decided to attack the fledgling PC market by coordinating the efforts of four divisions. While integrating the technologies of several divisions seemed logical, the company had virtually no mechanism for getting them to work closely together. HP senior managers also did not make integration an explicit project goal; they, like the division leaders, assumed that the traditional practice of divisions selling components to one another would suffice.

HP assigned the main responsibility for the PC to a team that had just started work on a new terminal for the HP 3000 minicomputer at HP's minicomputer division in Cupertino, California. Corporate executives reasoned that the team could squeeze enough computing power into the terminal, known as the HP 150, to enable it to perform as a PC.

The job of developing the keyboard was originally given to the desktop computers division in Fort Collins, Colorado. The HP 150 team required that the keyboard cost only $25. The existing Fort Collins keyboard, designed for big computers, cost $100, and the general manager of the division did not believe that the team's request for a $25 keyboard was a high priority. Keyboard design rapidly became a bottleneck. Finally, the work was brought back to the team in Cupertino for a "crash" effort that ended up taking six months.

The responsibility for the HP 150's disk drive fell to the disk-drive division in Greeley, Colorado. Rather than developing a new cost-effective drive, it simply modified an existing one. And following HP custom, the division's leaders priced the drive so that they could make a profit on the "contract." This made it harder for the team to achieve the targeted margins. In retrospect, the team would have been much better off had it turned to outside suppliers to develop the keyboard and disk drive.

As a terminal, the HP 150 did well. Customers liked it, and the division made a profit on the sales. As a personal computer, however, the HP 150 never became profitable and was unable to gain significant market share.

One value that often affects development projects is the status that companies accord different disciplines. The dominance of a given discipline can create powerful capabilities, but it can also result in dangerous rigidities. That was particularly evident at DEC and at Hewlett-Packard, where the belief that design engineering was the most critical function caused design engineers to become the elite. This status enabled both companies to grow very strong in design, which became a strategic core capability and led to the creation of a stream of sophisticated products. But it also led to an arrogance in that group that eventually turned this capability into a rigidity. The attitude at HP and at DEC was that marketing and manufacturing were less valuable than design. As a result, designers began to assume that they knew better than customers what product features and attributes were best.

The pervasive perception that manufacturing people and their concerns were relatively less important eventually became a significant problem at both companies. As a result, manufacturing problems were tackled only late in projects, causing delays, rework, and higher expenses. And because of manufacturing's perceived lower status, fewer skilled people were attracted to the function. That left manufacturing less able to solve difficult problems, which further convinced everyone that the lower status was deserved. In the United States, this problem persists in many industries, which helps explain this country's persistent weakness in manufacturing engineering and process-equipment development.

This problem was a big one in HP's Hornet project, which developed an inexpensive spectrum-analyzer instrument for testing and analyzing radio-frequency and microwave signals, that HP introduced in the mid-1980s. The manufacturing engineers on the project were assigned to it only part-time and were not added to the team until the testing phase had already begun. As a result, there was almost no thought given to manufacturability in designing the product, and the ramp-up to full production was long, complicated, and stressful for the people working in the plant.

OVERCOMING RIGIDITIES

HP's DeskJet project for developing a low-cost computer printer shows how a company can use a development project to overcome a rigidity. HP executives purposely designed the project to break the negative cycle that had sapped its strength in manufacturing and to get the company to start looking to other functions besides design engineering for creative solutions. Manufacturing was strongly represented from the beginning because the project involved—for HP—novel products, markets, and customers and, as a result, novel manufacturing cost and volume requirements. Once the project team was established, managers moved the manufacturing engineers to the R&D site and insisted that the R&D engineers consult with them continually regarding the design. Eventually, the manufacturing engineers became such valuable team members that the designers even lobbied for more of them.

Sure, the chief motive for initiating this new approach was to benefit the DeskJet project. But HP executives also wanted it to signal to the rest of the company that their view of the traditional status of design and manufacturing was changing. The project was a model for teamwork, and subsequent projects were organized along similar lines. Moreover, as the status of manufacturing engineers rose, the company began to attract stronger, broader, and more senior people to manufacturing.

Managing Development to Build Capabilities

In the wide range of products it studied, the Manufacturing Vision Group discovered several essential principles that can help companies correct conflicts and imbalances and build core capabilities. They are: an incremental approach to improving and expanding capabilities; a focus on process as well as product; innovative ways to challenge conventional thinking; and coherent vision, leadership, and organization.

INCREMENTAL ADVANCES

Companies must strive to "push the envelope" steadily and avoid reliance on great leaps. And to avoid overwhelming their development teams, they also must be careful not to push on too many fronts at the same time. The Kodak team that sought to develop the "factory of the future" failed in part because it tried to push the envelope on too many fronts.

Chaparral Steel's failure to develop an electric-arc saw for cutting steel in 1985 to 1987 shows that even the best can succumb to the temptation to try to make a leap that is just too far. Chaparral wanted to find a faster and more efficient way to cut the steel it produced and discovered that the aerospace industry was using an intensely hot electric arc to cut stainless steel. But the aerospace industry had tried neither to cut sections thicker than eight inches nor to cut through high volumes of material with this process, which is what Chaparral wanted it to do. But Chaparral employees, who time and again had figured out how to get equipment to perform in ways never intended, were undeterred. They discovered, however, that they lacked the knowledge of physics and electromagnetics necessary for the project to succeed. Even with the help of an outside consultant versed in the required physics, the project was beyond Chaparral's ken.

FOCUS ON MANUFACTURING PROCESS

U.S. companies have tended to push new products but not manufacturing processes. The conventional wisdom is that efforts to develop superior product features, functionality, and ease of use, and to lower costs will create demand for new processes. But in this paradigm, process will always lag product, which can severely handicap a company because the lead time needed to develop a new process typically exceeds that for a new product.

As a company in a process industry, Chaparral naturally focuses on production processes. But the internal capability that it has developed, which enables it to obtain feedback on processes from customers, suppliers, and competitors, and to revise processes continually in almost real time is nonetheless extraordinary. Furthermore, Chaparral does this frequently *in advance of* specific product requirements, thereby creating additional new-product opportunities. With the exception of Kodak and Chaparral, the other companies that the Manufacturing Vision Group studied rarely made processes the primary target of a development project. And in those handful of instances when they did, it was virtually always in response to a desire to create specific new products.

DEC's RA90 project to develop a high-density disk drive in the 1980s is a good example. While the project did not achieve many of the original product goals, DEC viewed it as a success because it achieved a major strategic goal set at the beginning: to lay a strong foundation for future high-density storage products. DEC executives were willing to invest heavily—to the tune of $1 billion, including a new manufacturing plant—in the development of skills, market position, and critical manufacturing processes. Team members were inspired to redefine the state of the art, which would put DEC in a strong competitive position in the long run.

This view may constitute a bit of Monday-morning quarterbacking on the part of DEC managers. But, as we discussed, it is important to realize that a development project can result in a less-than-successful product and still create a strategically crucial new process.

Something similar happened with Chaparral's Microtuff 10 steel project to develop new high-quality forging steels. Although sales of the end product were limited, hardly yielding enough revenues to justify the investment, the Microtuff 10 extended the company's product line. And the fact that Chaparral, a minimill, could even produce the kind of high-quality product that only large, integrated steel companies previously could make, burnished Chaparral's reputation as a high-tech company and gave it a big advantage over other minimills.

Of course, the best projects to improve processes are those that also result in product successes, which was the case with Kodak's efforts to improve its antistatic coating process. For years, Kodak had been a leading manufacturer of micrographic films, which include the film used in microfiche machines in libraries. Studies showed that some users—the main customers are banks and insurance companies—thought that the images on Kodak films were less sharp than those on competitors' films. Kodak determined that the problem wasn't clarity; it was darkness. The images on its films appeared a bit darker because of a coating placed on the film to reduce the buildup of static electricity, which attracts dust.

The project team charged with developing a clearer antistatic coating spotted a recent process invention made by a Kodak unit in France and used it to develop quickly a new manufacturing process. New films reached the streets within a year—a feat that enabled Kodak not merely to maintain its market share but also to increase it.

"OUT-OF-THE-BOX" THINKING

A third ingredient for building capabilities and breaking rigidities is an ability to challenge conventional thinking. The Manufacturing Vision Group found several effective ways to create the out-of-the-box thinking needed to do this.

One method is the clever use of benchmarking. Most companies benchmark products or processes to find out what competitors are doing so that they can match the best or go them one better. But there are creative ways a company can use benchmarking to attain a sustainable leadership position. Chaparral demonstrated such creative thinking when it looked at practices outside its industry to develop the horizontal caster, a project we described in the first article.

Another way to challenge conventional thinking—and stay ahead of competitors—is to be more resourceful and industrious in tapping the best minds in the field. When Chaparral began the Microtuff 10 project, it approached the Colorado School of Mines about cosponsoring a technical conference on forging steel, and the school agreed. The conference attracted technical papers and brought together experts who otherwise would not have convened. Chaparral employees learned enough to create new formulas for forging steel as well as related production processes.

Breaking the conventional flow of information is yet another way to challenge conventional thinking. Often, this can help a company alter its basic values so they help rather than hinder it in adapting to changes in its competitive environment. During HP's DeskJet printer project, marketing people conducted studies in shopping malls and brought back twenty-four suggestions for changes that they believed would ensure market acceptance. But design engineers heeded only five, discounting the others largely as a "marketing wish list." The people from marketing and the project leaders were so convinced of the important nature of the information, however, that they insisted that the design engineers go to the malls to hear for themselves what test customers were saying. Grudgingly, the engineers went, listened, and then did an about-face and made seventeen more changes.

In DEC's LAN Bridge 200 project to develop a communications product for linking computer networks, the marketing people discovered early on several important features that users wanted. However, they lacked the stature and self-confidence to persuade the design engineers to include the features. Not until two senior DEC technologists gathered the same information from customers was it actually used. By the time the new information had been incorporated into the design, however, the project schedule had slipped four months.

In subsequent projects at both HP and DEC, development teams made greater efforts to ensure that designers heard what customers were demanding and heeded it. In other words, the companies had learned.

VISION, LEADERSHIP, AND ORGANIZATION

While constantly striving to make incremental advances, focusing on process, and generating creative thinking are important, three things are even more crucial. More than anything, a project's success—and the success of a company's range of projects—in enhancing competitiveness and generating knowledge depends on a coherent vision, strong leadership, and organization. A clear vision enables projects to take off from the start. Then, when a project faces seemingly impossible odds or hits a point where failure seems inevitable, the right kind of leadership can pull it through.

There is no one right way to organize and lead a project. Companies that master the art of picking the best for each project will end up with more than a system for managing development projects effectively. They will end up with a system that cultivates leaders who excel in getting functions to work together and advance their knowledge. Such managers will enable manufacturers not merely to attain the lead but to keep it.

Prototypes: Tools for Learning and Integrating

Effective development teams build prototypes often and early to learn rapidly, minimize mistakes, and successfully integrate the work of the many functions and support groups involved in the project. Prototypes can provide a common language and a focal point for people from a wide variety of disciplines. They help each group understand how its work affects the work of other groups and enable the team to spot problems that require cross-functional solutions. By doing so, prototypes not only enable products to be developed and launched more quickly but also result in products that are both higher-quality and more effective in fulfilling their intended purpose in the marketplace.

By prototypes, we do not mean merely the physical embodiments of the nearly final products made by craftspeople before production begins. We mean a series of representations, including early mock-ups, computer simulations, subsystem models, and models featuring system-level engineering, as well as production prototypes. The most successful teams studied by the Manufacturing Vision Group frequently and regularly built a variety of prototypes; started creating prototypes of the entire system very early in the development process; and made each successive model more closely approach the desired final product in terms of form, content, and the customer experience it provoked. This process provided each team with an invaluable progress report on its success in dealing with unresolved issues and in meeting its schedule. The most successful teams also built multiple copies of each prototype so that everyone involved in the development and eventual production, sale, use, and servicing of the product (including suppliers, prospective customers, and dealers) could rapidly evaluate it and offer feedback. Indeed, the best use of prototypes enabled companies to test regularly during the development process:

- the degree to which the decisions made about factors like design specifications, and materials were executing faithfully *the intent* of the design;
- the cost and ease with which the manufacturing system—including production processes, purchasing, and test routines—could deliver the product;
- the extent to which the critical aspects of the unfolding product—including the functionality of individual subsystems and the way the subsystems work

together—were satisfying the targeted customers' stated desires and latent needs (qualities or features they seem to want but have trouble articulating).

But the projects that exploited prototypes in this manner were the exception. Indeed, most of the projects studied by the Manufacturing Vision Group failed to create enough prototypes. And often the prototypes they did build (1) were not created early enough to solve problems that took more time and resources to solve later; (2) focused on only one or two components and not on the entire system; (3) were not used to test the manufacturing processes that would produce the final product; and (4) were not widely tested in the field, meaning that an opportunity to glean potentially invaluable reactions from customers was missed.

Building prototypes early is critical for companies because decisions affecting about 85 percent of the ultimate total cost of the product (including its manufacture, use, maintenance, and disposal) are typically made during the first 15 percent of a development project. Changes that are made late in the project invariably upset the sought-after balance among product features, cost, and quality, and therefore cause subsequent delays and suboptimal solutions. Conversely, if needed changes in, say, one subsystem can be spotted early or proposed changes for improving performance can be tested and acted on early, the ripple effect—the impact on and changes that need to be made in other subsystems—can be minimized.

For example, when Ford was developing its 1991 Crown Victoria/ Grand Marquis in the late 1980s, it had its plant in St. Thomas, Ontario, build full-scale prototypes of the car on the same line producing the current model. As a result, line workers could suggest numerous ways to improve the manufacturability of the car relatively early in the project. This not only enabled the development team to alter designs without greatly disrupting the project but also gave plant employees in-depth information about the product that enabled them to move to full production relatively quickly when actual manufacturing began.

A process of building prototypes, testing and evaluating them internally and in the field, and then incorporating what is learned into the next prototype is a powerful mechanism for focusing a development team's efforts. These cycles also provide milestones, when management can review progress, assess what remains to be done, and consider whether alternative paths should be taken to complete the effort.

Companies can and should use prototypes in this way for the development of processes as well as products. At Chaparral Steel, for example, a team developing a new process will typically make small batches of steel using a prototype of the process, then refine the process, make more batches, refine the process more, and so on, gradually increasing the scale until the process reaches full-production levels. Chaparral also typically puts prototypes on the shop floor from the outset of a project. That approach has enabled the company to push a given new process's performance level 15 percent to 20 percent beyond what would have been possible had it taken the traditional approach of conducting most of the development work off-site.

All in all, the extensive use of prototypes provides a structure, discipline, and approach that significantly enhance the rate of learning and integration in development projects. It gives both the project team and senior managers a powerful tool for effectively monitoring, guiding, and improving the development effort.

6
Getting It Done: New Roles for Senior Executives

Thomas M. Hout and John C. Carter

A decade of process improvement has transformed the way corporations operate. With such change has come an equally broad transformation in the job of the senior executive. Top-down autocrats are out and bottom-up teams are in. The CEO as hero is giving way to Team Xerox and Team Taurus. To hear some executives tell it, the traditional hands-on role of the senior manager is disappearing. The message seems to be: Get the processes right, and the company will manage itself.

But this message belies a simple truth: Managers, not processes, run companies. In fact, process-focused companies need *more* top-down management, not less. That's why at some of the most successful companies, senior executives are becoming more activist and interventionist. They are designing bigger, more powerful roles for themselves, often managing dimensions that go far beyond their formal job descriptions. They are not just enablers or coaches; they are *doers*.

However, today's active CEOs operate very differently from executives in the past. The CEO as hero really *is* dead. Given the complexities of modern business competition, no single individual—or even the top two or three people—can do all that it takes to achieve success for a company. Success depends on the willingness and ability of the entire senior executive group to address not just their individual functional or divisional responsibilities but also their collective responsibility for the company as a whole. Only senior managers can rise above the details of the business, recognize emerging patterns, make unexpected connections, and identify the points of maximum leverage for action.

Senior executives must be activists for three important reasons:

- First, only senior executives can finish the work that reengineering starts by managing the political conflicts that process improvement inevitably stimulates and by removing the managerial obstacles that are the biggest barrier to successful reengineering efforts.
- Second, senior executives can use their authority to go to the heart of a problem—and therefore provide superior solutions—in ways that no midlevel team can, no matter how empowered it is. Thus it often pays for senior managers to play a hands-on role in improving operations and redesigning work.
- Third, only senior executives can create competitive breakthroughs by linking process improvements to strategy. On its own, process excellence rarely leads to sustainable competitive advantage. And yet frequently, a company's strategy (what it intends to do) is disconnected from its capability (what it is able to do). The ultimate responsibility of activist senior executives is to make the connection between strategy and capability.

When a company's senior executives are in sync, actively managing political issues and removing obstacles, they can make an impact that no one else can. We became interested in senior executive activism after conducting a study on innovation practices at some 550 American, European, and Japanese companies across a wide variety of industries. (See "How Activist Executives Spur Innovation.") Our goal was to identify the management characteristics and organizational capabilities in those companies that innovate faster than their competitors and increase their market share on the strength of that innovation. We discovered that none of the best-known programs—total quality management, reengineering, the formation of self-managing teams, or the institution of cross-functional processes—are enough to produce faster and more effective product development. In fact, the best performers in our study tended, if anything, to have fewer of these programs than the less innovative companies. We found that what really separates the best performers from the rest is the role that senior executives play.

How Activist Executives Spur Innovation

We studied innovation practices at some 550 American, European, and Japanese companies across a wide variety of industries to identify the management characteristics and organizational capabilities of the most nimble innovators. We found that the executives at the best companies take responsibility for creating a supportive and urgent environment for new product development, even though most of them have no formal accountability for the development process. For example, they guarantee effective staffing by insisting on the release of all members of a new team in time for a project's start-up. They also enforce a total business perspective by working with one another to make sure that teams have a critical mass of marketing and sales people so that engineering and manufacturing don't dominate the process. And they guarantee that people coming off lengthy projects have a soft landing when they return to their functional organizations.

Senior executives at the fastest innovators also insist on seeing early prototypes of prospective new products. Often, the problems that a development team is having with a new product are indications of organizational obstacles in their way—obstacles that the team needs senior-level intervention to overcome.

Finally, activist executives help drive innovation by frequently going into the field and watching and listening to their customers. They are not content just to coach the development process and check milestones. Through the intimate knowledge that comes from direct contact with customers, they can decisively shape the specs for new products early in the process—then step back and let teams do their work.

Managers as Barons

Despite the best intentions, it is difficult for the senior management group at any big company to function effectively as a team. In principle, each executive wants to do what's best for the company. In practice, powerful forces keep managers from doing so. Why? For starters, each player on a senior-level team has a different view of the business. The vice president of purchasing, the head of Asian operations, and the group leader responsible for the company's U.S. cash-cow product line all have different perspectives. It's hard for them to develop a shared understanding of the business that transcends those perspectives. Besides holding divergent views of the business, top-level managers also have real conflicts of interest. However much they may need to cooperate, they also *compete* with one another—for resources, for recognition, and ultimately for the top job.

Senior managers frequently respond to such pressures by engaging in self-interested behavior. In effect, they act like feudal barons seeking favor from the king. Acutely aware of the potential for head-to-head conflict, they protect their own turf and avoid attacking anyone's sacred cows. The result: Major issues are left unaddressed.

In a competitive environment marked by continuous process improvement, baronial management is a recipe for disaster. Consider, for example, what happened at a well-regarded U.S. manufacturing company that had recently reengineered its product-development process. The company did all the right things: It benchmarked itself against industry best practices and empowered cross-functional development teams. Early results were strong, particularly in terms of streamlined work flow and shortened cycle times. After a period of steady progress, however, improvement ground to a halt.

What went wrong? The problems weren't with the reengineering team that designed the new process or with the cross-functional product-development teams themselves. Improvement stopped because senior managers did not recognize the myriad ways in which *they* were hindering the reengineering effort. Put simply, they were good at championing change but poor at changing themselves. For instance, many of the top function heads did not assign their best people to the reengineering team because they feared that the work of their own departments would suffer. Lacking the best possible staff members, the team had neither the authority nor the political firepower to push for changes opposed by powerful function heads.

In addition, top-level managers avoided making decisions that might lead to conflict within the senior executive group. For example, the company had a long-standing policy of rotating up-and-coming young managers through new assignments every two years to broaden their experience. But the development teams needed leaders to stay with them for at least three or four years in order to make a strong impact. The design team pointed out the contradiction, but the executives ignored it. They didn't want to interfere with career-track policies that affected the entire company. As a result, the teams lost their effectiveness when leaders rotated off too early. Moreover, these problems in staffing teams sent a powerful message to other employees: Here is another change effort you don't have to take seriously.

Senior executives also failed to address the implications of the reengineered process for their own work. For example, unless the vice presidents of marketing, engineering, purchasing, and sales approved promising new concepts for products early in the development cycle, the best ideas couldn't get the priority they deserved. However, instead of actively reaching back into the pipeline and asking themselves what they needed to learn to make an informed decision, the executives waited for the formal presentation of new ideas. As a result, many promising ideas never made it to market in time. Finally, the executives took a self-interested approach to sharing the political costs of reengineering. On paper, reengineering the product-development process had taken considerable non-value-added work out of the company. In practice, few employees had actually been reassigned. As is often the case, the biggest potential savings could be found in the largest business units and functions. But because the senior-level group had never discussed how they might share reductions in personnel equitably, the powerful managers who ran the largest units were able to protect their own people.

In this particular case, senior managers' preoccupation with their own routines and their respect for one another's turf led them to neglect the crucial issues that they could resolve only as a team. In fact, what passed for respect was really irresponsibility and ultimately undermined the entire reengineering effort.

In a big company, senior executives will always have their own independent authority and power base. Divergences of perspective, differences of opinion, and conflicts of interest won't magically disappear—nor should they. At the same time, senior executives need to recognize and manage the tension between their individual responsibilities for discrete parts of the business and the collective needs of the business as a whole. They must learn new roles and take on challenging new responsibilities, even for parts of the business that they don't directly control.

Finishing What Reengineering Starts

How might a well-functioning executive group have handled the problems faced by the manufacturing company? To begin with, it would have recognized that process improvement tends to expose the political fissures in a company, uncovering organizational and personal conflicts of interest over who will bear the costs of change and how the benefits will be distributed. And it would have understood that the biggest source of managerial conflict in process-improvement initiatives involves the staffing of teams. Although individual executives do not want to lose their top performers to cross-functional teams, they have a collective interest in contributing them to the effort. Reengineering works only if the company's best people develop the new process designs and then sell them to their respective parts of the organization.

The executive group at an electronics manufacturer developed a simple rule to avoid problems in creating reengineering teams. The rule stipulated that every team member proposed by a function head would have to be accepted by all the other function heads. What's more, team members could not be shifted off without the executive group's unanimous consent. That way, the executive team as a whole controlled the makeup of the reengineering teams; in the process, senior executives forced themselves to learn more about the strengths and weaknesses of middle managers throughout the company.

The senior team at a major telephone operating company faced a different kind of problem. In order to clear the way for new investments in information technology, the company needed a massive retraining of employees and a write-off of existing systems. However, major disincentives kept senior managers from carrying out their own write-offs and investing in new technology: In particular, doing so would have hurt their individual P&Ls, the chief metric against which their performance was evaluated. To avoid potentially destructive political fights, the group collectively agreed to take a $1.1 billion write-off and thus paved the way for the company's reengineering effort.

In some cases, removing obstacles to reengineering requires senior executives to change not just company policies but also their own managerial practices. At Medrad, an $85 million medical diagnostic imaging company in Pittsburgh, Pennsylvania, the product-development process was too slow for a niche leader that must reach market quickly with the right product. The company's executive vice presidents and function heads decided to rethink the process. For several months, nine senior managers devoted one day a week to investigating how the company developed new products. To their surprise, they discovered that the working cycles of the development teams were pretty tight.

Frustrated with their inability to shed light on the problem, the executives found themselves discussing the pressures and frustrations that they often felt as function heads responsible for developing new products. For example, departments did not share decreases in operating budgets equally; as a result, the development teams were not balanced by an equal mix of talent, and some teams were much smaller than others. Moreover, executive vice presidents often impeded progress by delaying the assignment of someone to a cross-functional development team. The more the senior managers talked, the more they realized that delays in product development had little to do with the work of development teams and much to do with their own management practices and behavior.

Having met the proverbial enemy, the executives moved quickly. They drafted, signed, and published a set of principles that would govern all product-development efforts. One rule specified the makeup of the ideal cross-functional team and declared that every team would be staffed at the scheduled start of a project (a change from the usual practice of starting a project and assuming that the right resources would "turn up" later). As with the electronics manufacturer, senior managers were prohibited from pulling members off teams without the agreement of their peers. Another principle encouraged product-development teams to think of themselves as customers of the senior management group and to offer feedback on its performance. These principles have allowed Medrad to cut the front end of product-development time in half.

Systems such as capital budgeting, career planning and job rotation, and compensation constitute a kind of permanent backstage in any large corporation. But unless those systems are adapted to new ways of working, they become, at best, a built-in drag on the effectiveness of process-improvement initiatives. At worst, they can completely undermine them. Reengineering teams or cross-functional working teams can rethink the mechanics of processes, but long-held inflexible corporate policies concerning such areas as career-track management or acceptable test procedures in new product development can get in the way of newly improved processes. Only the senior executives at a company can address such obstacles. If they don't take on these tough issues, empowerment can start to look a lot like abandonment.

Redesigning Executive Roles to Solve Business Problems

Many champions of reengineering assume that the most radical solutions to business problems are likely to come from deep in the organization because top-level management is too distant from the real action. But as the Medrad example proves, activist senior executives can often devise innovative solutions that would elude a midlevel team. By redesigning their own roles, senior managers can bring their power and expertise to bear on a company's key business problems.

For example, because of deregulation, another telephone operating company faced new competitive pressures; in particular, it needed to step up the pace of day-to-day decision making and respond to customers better. Other companies in similar circumstances have immediately turned to reengineering, but the CEO and three executive vice presidents at this $4 billion company resisted that course of action. They had seen earlier process-improvement efforts produce disappointing results. It wasn't that the executives didn't recognize that the company's processes needed fixing; rather, they understood that slow, inefficient processes were only symptoms of a more fundamental problem: poorly designed roles at the very top of the company.

For instance, operating responsibility was fragmented across too many narrowly defined senior positions. The second tier of managers in the company—twenty vice presidents and directors—had too many opportunities to veto decisions and obstruct action. One vice president determined prices, another ensured that the company was in compliance with regulations, and a third estimated the financial implications of different pricing strategies. Until the company could untangle its problems at the top, it would never be able to resolve its problems with slow processes.

The top four senior managers began to redesign the executive structure for the level immediately below them. They ended up with a list of fourteen new positions, each with broad responsibilities and all of them closely integrated with one another. The redesigned roster included a diagram of the informal communication and interaction patterns expected to evolve across the fourteen positions. After announcing the jobs, the senior managers invited the twenty vice presidents and directors to apply for them.

During interviews for the positions, the CEO and the executive vice presidents asked the applicants how they would approach problems in the new system. What kind of collaboration would be needed to accomplish the company's goals? Who would they have to influence across the network of senior executives in order to fulfill their own responsibilities, and how would they gain that influence? The interviews turned into an important learning process. Not only did they allow the top-level managers to identify which vice presidents could thrive in the new organization, they also helped the entire senior executive group develop a shared understanding of the business.

The payoff was immediate. The company greatly improved the operation of key management processes such as the preparation of the capital budget. In the past, the engineering and financial executives who ran this process were isolated from the company's actual business; thus they had no way to factor new patterns of customers' needs into their capital budgets. Now that the senior financial people have much broader operating responsibilities, they can make sure that capital spending relates to the changing needs of the market.

The new roles have also allowed the company's senior managers to respond quickly to new competitive threats. In particular, the company has rapidly unbundled the old regulated pricing structure, a change that provides more freedom to create customized packages of telephone service. Because activist executives *led* these moves—rather than simply reviewing recommendations for change from middle management—senior managers came to a consensus on the new approaches much faster than they would have in the past.

A Double-Barreled Response

Trade-offs are necessary in any business. Whether the need is to balance long-term performance against short-term results or to settle feuds between marketing and manufacturing, choices must be made every day in one part of an organization that may lead to unforeseen and unintended consequences in other parts. In the past, people in the middle ranks settled many of these trade-offs. Today activist senior executives are embedding this complexity into their own roles.

Consider the premier process-improvement story of the 1990s: Chrysler Corporation. The company has received well-deserved credit for its cross-functional product-development teams and for its fast time-to-market with new cars. What observers have missed, however, is how Chrysler's success also depends on a major change in the way the company's senior executives define their own roles.

Most members of the senior management group at Chrysler occupy two formal positions that combine functional and product-line responsibilities. For instance, the company's vice president of procurement and supply is also in charge of the large-car platform; the vice president for strategy and regulatory affairs is also responsible for the small-car platform. These dual responsibilities not only embody the tension between product lines and functions, they are also the chief mechanism for managing such tension. All the senior executives know that they have to accomplish two conflicting tasks. One is to develop and build new cars, which requires their colleagues' cooperation; the other is to deliver functional services needed by their colleagues. As a result, function heads and product-line heads are no longer pitted against each other—they *are* each other.

This division of responsibility dramatically changes behavior at the top. For one thing, it keeps political problems manageable so they can't slow down the work of the company. Even more important, the structure of dual responsibilities forces senior executives to balance trade-offs, make tough choices, and think ahead continuously as they identify competing imperatives.

Chrysler's approach is not a return to the matrix organization. The problem with most matrix structures is that they push complexity down into the organization, thus forcing middle managers to make difficult trade-offs between the competing goals of two bosses. At Chrysler, by contrast, the complexity of dealing with competing interests is pushed upward to senior executives. That allows them to work through and contain the complexity, thus simplifying and clarifying subordinates' roles.

Put another way, the matrix is in the minds of the executives. The senior people work face-to-face to settle the difficult political questions (Who is going to give up staff for this project?) and the risky priority issues (Which investment program are we going to do first?). Such clarity makes life easier for middle managers and the employees working under them and has helped Chrysler significantly outperform its competitors in new product development. For example, Chrysler's new large-car platform, the LH, was introduced in 1992 after just 39 months of development—a full 25 percent faster (and at 20 percent lower cost) than any of Chrysler's previous development programs. In 1994, the company introduced its Neon economy car in even less time, thirty-one months.

Dual roles for senior managers have helped Chrysler resolve another internal conflict that has traditionally bedeviled carmakers. In the automobile industry, there has been a systemic tendency to overproduce popular new cars as powerful function heads in manufacturing strive to maximize utilization of their plants and finance managers push for short-term returns. Excess inventory, however, often leads to steep discounts and rebates in the showroom. The result: Many cars are sold but at a poor price realization per car. Because Chrysler's dual roles combine profit-center responsibility for a particular car platform with functional responsibility, it has been easier for the senior executive group to address the inevitable conflict between short-term and long-term goals. The combination of rapid development of popular new products and restraint on overproduction has allowed the company to command premium prices, a key factor in making Chrysler the most profitable U.S. automaker in recent years.

Another big company that has embraced dual executive roles is Whirlpool. For example, the company's chief technology officer is also responsible for worldwide purchasing. Why? As globalization pushes Whirlpool to coordinate multiple product lines across geographic regions, and as component makers increasingly drive technological innovation, Whirlpool's relationship with its suppliers becomes more and more important. In such an environment, putting technology and supply management together makes a lot of sense.

In this instance, Whirlpool is trying to avoid the usual situation in which the two tasks are organized as separate functions. Although executives in charge of separate functions may coordinate their activities, their different perspectives on the business slow the process down. The purchaser's mind-set is "steady as she goes." People in purchasing tend to favor current suppliers who have demonstrated that they can deliver on both cost and quality. Technologists are more experimental. They focus on capabilities that go beyond delivery and may want to put new suppliers in business. An executive wearing two hats can develop and test new ideas quickly, make trade-offs between the two perspectives, and intervene when necessary without invading someone else's turf.

Creating Competitive Breakthroughs by Linking Process and Strategy

Recently, a great deal of attention has been devoted to the relatively high percentage of reengineering projects that fail. What rarely gets discussed, however, is that even in those initiatives that succeed in cutting cycle times and reducing costs, the ultimate result is frequently disappointing. Typically, a company finds that reengineering improves processes, saves the company money, and perhaps even provides better service to customers. But those changes, however welcome in their own right, never quite add up to a significant difference in the company's competitive position.

Why not? Too often, process improvement is disconnected from a company's strategy. As a result, strategy and capability are out of sync. In some cases, strategy leads capability: A company develops a coherent plan to create new value and build competitive advantage but doesn't have the operations in place to make the plan a reality. In other cases, strategy lags behind capability: Process improvements make new ways of competing possible, but the company's strategy has yet to take these new possibilities into account.

Managers can't assume that strategy and capability will come together automatically. Rather, they have to pull them together and then continuously calibrate them over time. By far the most important role of activist senior executives is to identify the mismatches between a company's processes and its strategy and then to integrate them in ways that lead to major competitive breakthroughs.

In the early 1990s, a company that we'll call the Southland Furniture Company, one of the largest in the United States, found itself in a situation that many successfully reengineered companies face. For more than a year, a midlevel team had been studying the company's main sequence of processes: order taking, production scheduling, inventory management, and the like. The team had found many opportunities to reduce cost, inventory, and cycle times. It had designed new processes to get customers' orders scheduled and produced faster. It had also developed a way for the manufacturing unit to produce a greater variety of furniture shapes and styles in smaller lot sizes and without as much work-in-process inventory. Both the reengineering team and the company's senior executives assumed that these changes would make a significant difference in the company's profitability and in its competitive position.

To their surprise, however, they discovered that the new capabilities weren't relevant to the company's traditional customers—large, owner-operated retail furniture stores that had grown over the years through aggressive merchandising. The stores were mass-market, promotion-driven businesses in which sales were volatile and hard to predict. As a result, they tended to order a few standard styles of furniture in large quantities (either to replenish their inventories or to stock up for big promotions) but at highly irregular intervals. Often there were last-minute changes as the stores tried to respond to abrupt shifts in sales.

To serve these customers, Southland had to keep large stocks of raw materials on hand. The fact that the new processes reduced work-in-process inventory didn't really address the high costs of the inventory of raw materials. What's more, the company had to be prepared to dedicate its capacity to unanticipated large production orders, which meant that its newfound capability to make a greater variety of shapes and styles in smaller lot sizes couldn't really be exploited.

Put simply, the new processes were useless without a new strategy, and only Southland's senior executives could provide that. As they met to discuss the situation, there was little agreement on what to do. The head of manufacturing argued for faster, more up-to-date equipment that would get large orders through the plant with less labor and machine time, thus freeing up capacity for smaller orders. The chief financial officer disagreed, arguing that the investment would be so large that it would not be recouped for years. Instead, he wanted cuts in the marketing and engineering budgets. New designs were only a small portion of sales, he pointed out, and yet they represented a large chunk of discretionary costs. But the new designs were critical for growth, countered the vice president for marketing and sales, especially for a small but important new class of customers—small, regional furniture chains that were trying to appeal to more sophisticated consumers. How can we abandon our core customers? wondered the head of purchasing. After all, they are Southland's bread and butter.

To break this impasse, Southland's CEO ordered a detailed review of the company's business strategy and set a few simple ground rules for the effort. First, the executives couldn't charter a group of subordinates to develop a new strategy. They had to do it themselves. Second, they had to carry out the project not as individuals or as representatives of particular functions but as a group. That prohibited them from tacking on the strategy review as one more agenda item in their regular round of meetings; they had to set aside time exclusively for the review. Third, the CEO announced that he would participate in the group but he wouldn't chair it. Whatever strategy they developed would reflect all of their input, not just his alone.

To begin, the executive group organized field trips to some current customers and to some noncompeting furniture producers overseas. They traveled in pairs to ensure that one partner would pick up information that the other missed and to encourage a dialogue between executives that might not happen otherwise.

For the most part, the visits didn't bring new information to the surface. But the pair that visited one of the new regional chains did report on an interesting discussion with the chain's top-level managers, who praised Southland's new styles but complained that its prices were too high. The Southland executives had explained that high prices were a function of the large inventories of raw materials and the extra capacity they needed to fill the large, hard-to-schedule orders of their core customers.

The retailers were puzzled. *Their* orders weren't large or irregular. Although they selected a large variety of styles, they ordered by the week and with only modest variations in volume. In fact, their pattern of orders was part of their entire merchandising philosophy, which applied just-in-time inventory techniques to retail sales. They minimized promotions and used sophisticated information systems to track sales and ordering.

The conversation with the regional chain's managers made the furniture company executives think twice. They had known that the regional chains sold a broader variety of products than the independent retail stores, but they had never realized that there was such a stark difference in the way the chains actually did business. The executives analyzed incoming orders and discovered that many of the new regional chains followed a similar pattern: weekly or biweekly orders of a large variety of styles in stable volume and with few last-minute changes. They began to understand that these characteristics weren't coincidental: They represented a whole new business model in the industry.

Armed with this insight, Southland's managers looked at their traditional customers differently. The chief financial officer, who had always thought that large orders of traditional shapes and styles were the most profitable, grasped that such orders were also responsible for hidden costs in inventory and processing. Perhaps the company's core customers weren't low-cost to serve after all. And despite their low-volume, high-variety orders, perhaps the regional chains weren't really such high-cost customers.

As the executive group's learning continued, the managers began to question their commitment to the company's core business. They realized that they had become so close to their traditional customers that they were blind to the costs of serving them. In effect, the large retail stores, hard-pressed by giant furniture discounters and still committed to old-fashioned "push" merchandising, were shifting more and more of the costs of inventory and sales-cycle variations back onto Southland. Meanwhile, a more sophisticated set of fast-growing new customers—the regional chains—wanted something different, something that the reengineering team's process changes were well suited to provide. But the company couldn't just shift its target group of customers: The great majority of its sales were with the traditional retail stores.

The executive group needed to define a step-by-step trajectory for changing from the old way of doing business to the new.

The group decided to break down the ordering patterns of the traditional furniture-store customers, and it discovered that some core accounts behaved differently from others. In effect, there was a modernizing segment of traditional customers that, much like the new regional chains, was ordering more regularly because it used up-to-date methods of tracking sales, placing orders, and merchandising. The modernizers were winning local battles for market share, whereas Southland's tradition-bound customers were losing. Clearly, Southland had to increase its sales to the modernizing group.

Based on a better understanding of how its customers operated, Southland pursued a new strategy. Members of the executive group began visiting their core customers to announce that they wanted to change the way they did business with them. They asked for more regular orders and for more advance notice of promotions to allow for planning of raw materials inventory. In return, Southland offered to share its new process expertise to help the retailers reengineer their own processes. And it promised lower prices to retailers willing to change the way they ordered. Meanwhile, the company actively pursued the new regional chains, using its reengineered processes to supply them with the variety they wanted.

As a result of this shift in strategy, Southland was able to expand the business of the modernizing segment, gain new business from the regional chains, and influence some of its less advanced customers to change their ordering patterns. By the second year of the new strategy, the company felt confident enough to change its request into a demand, saying, This is the way we do business. If you cannot work this way, we can no longer serve you. Southland ended up losing about 15 percent of its old customer list, but the loss was more than made up for by new business. As the number of undesirable orders declined, the company's new processes were working on the business for which they had been designed.

Today the turnover of raw materials inventory at Southland is up by 40 percent. Profit margins have improved, and the company is growing at a rate 3 percent faster than the industry as a whole. Implementation of the new strategy has also had a major impact on the way Southland's executive group operates. Senior managers interact more and participate actively in decision making. Roles are broader; issues get on the table faster. Put simply, Southland is a much better managed company.

Could an empowered midlevel team have done the analysis and developed the same breakthrough strategy that Southland's executive team did? Probably. Could it have moved quickly to make the trade-offs and take the action that would transform those insights into reality? Almost certainly not. As Southland's CEO put it, "We were the only people who could say, 'We're going to dump this group of customers.'" Such strategic choices are the essence of executive activism.

Unleashing Executive Activism: The Role of the CEO

Southland Furniture's CEO did not put himself at the center of the company's strategic redirection. He did not set "the vision" around which the senior executives rallied to work out the details. Nor did he dictate every step in the strategic review process. Rather, he encouraged the executive group to walk down a path of mutual discovery, participating in but not controlling the decision-making process.

Does this example mean that when a company has activist executives, it doesn't need an activist CEO? It depends on what one means by activism. Traditional hands-on CEOs are unlikely to create the kind of integrated senior executive group that we have been describing, precisely because they take the lead far too often. As a result, they prevent the collective leadership of the entire senior executive group from emerging. At the same time, activist executives cannot exist without a CEO who can create the conditions that allow a senior-level group to cohere as an effective unit. In those terms, Southland's CEO played an extremely active role as he unleashed and then channeled the energies of his senior managers.

Put simply, the chief responsibility of activist CEOs is to encourage interaction among the senior executive group. How do they accomplish this task? They take away the traditional excuses that have kept senior managers from working well together by aggressively reducing the number of senior line and staff assistants who prepare the briefing books that make it easy for senior managers not to engage with one another.

Better communication and teamwork is the real advantage, far beyond that of cost reduction, of all the downsizing of the past decade. There are no layers left to filter; no one remains to cook the plans and fudge the numbers; and there is no place to hide. Senior executives are forced to deal with one another, face-to-face, with their strengths and weaknesses equally on display. This increased interaction has its benign side: The opportunities for executives to talk and learn from one another are greater. And by definition, fewer senior executives in broader roles means more opportunities to exercise influence on the business. But for the individual manager, it also has its severe side—it's a lot easier to see who is competent and who is not, whose views hold sway and whose do not. While they are learning, senior managers are also being evaluated, not only by the CEO but also by their peers.

Some people aren't cut out for the new environment. Others want to change but don't know how. The second task for activist CEOs is to create situations that will test and broaden their senior executives. Sometimes the CEO will design a learning situation for an individual executive—for example, giving a traditional baron a special assignment that requires the reconciliation of competing goals. Those who do not want to or cannot perform will eventually be moved aside by the CEO, and those who are able to learn will become more valuable. In such cases, the CEO is helping executives find ways to try out new behavior, to put themselves in situations in which they must draw on unfamiliar networks of people and sources of support.

The most powerful experiences are those the CEO designs for the entire executive group. We are not talking about popular off-site team-building exercises like Outward Bound. The best learning comes from real situations with a direct impact on the business, such as the senior reengineering project at Medrad or the strategic review at Southland. Often, activist CEOs will hold key meetings not at corporate headquarters or at some plush off-site resort but out in the field—at a business unit dealing with a thorny problem or on the shop floor of a new customer half a world away. The goal is to get executives out of their comfort zone. They won't all understand the experience in the same way, but it will likely create enough of a shared ·framework to make for constructive dialogue, healthy disagreement and debate, and eventually a collective sense of direction.

Activist CEOs use all the traditional levers available to them—organizational design, evaluation and feedback, compensation, and new appointments—but to a new end. They strive to make their subordinates dependent on one another rather than exclusively on the CEO. For instance, they design dual roles, like those at Chrysler, that force executives to look toward one another to resolve problems or to make connections that trigger insights.

They also make sure that executives get performance feedback from as many sources as possible. Increasingly, that means evaluations by peers, upward feedback from one's own subordinates, and periodic systematic responses from customers. People simply work better with one another when they are sure of their strengths and aware of their weaknesses. Some CEOs even take the time to sit down with each of their executives to develop a personal development plan to identify new opportunities for activism.

Sooner or later, leaders have to align compensation systems with their aspirations for their executives' behavior. Activist CEOs go beyond formal incentive systems that pay people for reaching targets contained in plans and budgets. They compensate managers for doing the unexpected, like stepping up to an especially difficult new role or creating value in unusual ways. They know that often the most valuable contributions are those that are off the map of the company's annual plan—and that when managers are rewarded for making such contributions, it encourages others to step forward.

Finally, and perhaps most important, activist CEOs expand the criteria that they use to bring people into the senior management ranks. Specifically, they supplement the traditional skill requirements for particular jobs with broader cognitive and behavioral requirements. Activist CEOs want people who have technical skills and get results but who also have the intuitive capacity to make connections, strong communication skills, an ability to collaborate with peers, and an orientation to action—especially in situations where the right thing to do isn't always clear. Such leaders will often pass over someone who, from a purely technical point of view, is the logical candidate for a job; instead, they will appoint someone with a broader range of behavioral skills.

But even when activist CEOs have done all these things, their job is not really finished. Genuine collaboration is always fragile. Therefore, executive activism requires continuous fine-tuning. CEOs must constantly monitor the dynamics of executive interaction, making allowances for the varying strengths and weaknesses of the senior team's members and modeling the frankness and respect on which successful group interactions depend.

Executive Activism at Krupp

At many companies, the shift to executive activism is a pragmatic response to the harsh realities of a tougher competitive environment. Consider Krupp, one of the largest companies in Germany with DM 24 billion in sales, some 70,000 employees, and six operating divisions including units in steel, engineering, and automotive components.

In December 1992, Krupp, then Germany's second-largest steel manufacturer, acquired its smaller rival Hoesch in what was the first (and to this date, still the only) hostile takeover in the history of German industry. Before the merger, Krupp was a venerable but stagnating company. Hard hit by the global turndown in steel of the early 1990s, it also had an insular managerial culture in which powerful unit heads often kept the company's management board from getting too close to the business. The combination of economic decline in its core business and bureaucratic management resulted in heavy losses. In 1992, Krupp lost DM 250 million on roughly DM 23 billion in sales.

As part of the merger, the combined company appointed a new executive committee, which currently consists of five members, four from Krupp's original management team and one from Hoesch. The group has embarked on a massive turnaround effort. Currently, there are 240 different projects in reengineering, process improvement, customer service, customer discovery, joint ventures, and globalization. The company has set out to reposition the core activities of its six lead companies, reduce the labor force by roughly 20 percent, and reduce costs by about DM 500 million per year.

At the center of this effort is Krupp's executive committee. For this group, executive activism is a competitive necessity. Managing director (the equivalent of CEO) Gerhard Cromme is the group's liaison to the world of German and international business and politics. Chief controller (the equivalent of COO) Ulrich Middelmann is responsible for the internal execution of the group's decisions. CFO Gerhard Jooss, a former politician from Bavaria, is the company's link to Germany's big banks. Head of personnel Jürgen Rossberg has long-standing ties with the unions that are crucial in German industrial relations. And Friedrich Clever, the sole remaining board member from Hoesch, is responsible for organizational development at the six operating divisions. These individual roles with their ties to key constituencies are critical in the turnaround battle.

But the Krupp executive committee is something more than a collection of strong individual managers. The group has also worked hard to balance individual strengths with a highly integrated perspective on the long-term needs of the business. To leverage their own learning and extend their reach down into the company, for example, key executive committee members occupy multiple roles. Cromme, Middelmann, and Jooss, for instance, each take charge of one of Krupp's three regions—Europe,

North America, and Asia. In addition, Jooss also has responsibility for sales and marketing, and Middelmann takes the lead in technology and innovation. Rossberg and Clever have a similar level of regional and functional responsibility.

In the old Krupp, senior managers played classic functional or regional roles, and different points of view were never fully reconciled. The company's various parts did not reinforce one another. The current group of five executives brings all the pieces of the business together among themselves, arguing out the points and pressing one another to see if they have enough knowledge to act. They are continuously rethinking the company's course based on the flow of input from their external constituencies and their internal areas of responsibility.

The group's small size allows them to spend a major part of their time in face-to-face interactions; their offices are all on the same floor of Krupp's headquarters in the city of Essen. It has become a common practice of the group to attend all meetings and events, both inside and outside the company, in rotating pairs. Since the merger, for example, pairs of executive committee members have visited each of Krupp's 240 project teams at least twice. The visits not only maximize the sharing of knowledge among the senior group, they also convey a powerful message that the senior management group has a shared understanding of the business and a common purpose.

This interaction helps the committee make decisions without slowing down the change process. Such decisions are already reshaping the company's culture and business mix.

Krupp's executive activism—pragmatic, highly interactive, and with special attention paid to senior executive roles—appears to be effective. The integration of Krupp and Hoesch has come about more quickly and smoothly than most observers expected, and so have positive business results. In 1993, one year after the merger, the new company had losses of DM 397 million. In 1994, through a combination of growing demand and massive cost reduction, it returned to profitability with DM 77 million in profits. This year, Krupp's profits are estimated to range between DM 500 million and DM 1 billion. Even more impressive is the increase in the company's market value. In the two years since its introduction on the German stock market in January 1993, Krupp's stock has risen 56 percent.

7
Real Work

Abraham Zaleznik

Many executives do not clearly understand that guiding an organization is not synonymous with leadership. We may recognize leadership when we see it, but its true nature is hidden by common misconceptions about organizations, human nature, and the substance of executive work. Worse, those misconceptions keep many able people from developing as leaders. And they subordinate real work—the work of thinking about and acting on ideas relating to products, markets, and customers—to psychopolitics.

To understand how we got into this mess, let's start not in the executive suite but in the Trobriand Islands in New Guinea, where for generations the natives engaged in a ritual called *Kula,* the exchange of beads while bartering for food and other valuables.

The natives' barter, as Fritz Roethlisberger long ago pointed out in his widely read classic, *Management and Morale* (Harvard University Press, 1941), was the group's purposeful, logical work, while the exchange of beads was its social, nonlogical activity. But the natives themselves made no distinction between the two and gave equal weight to both activities. They worked hard, building canoes and harvesting crops to have the goods to barter. At the same time, they saved beads and exchanged them with their partners according to strict yet implicit rules of social conduct.

This article was originally published in the January–February 1989 issue of *HBR.* For its republication as an *HBR* Classic, Abraham Zaleznik has written the commentary "Hard Thinking Constitutes the Executive's Real Work" (which appears at the end of the article) to update his observations.

The beads were not a medium of exchange. Nor did the natives hoard them or use them as ornaments to display their rank within the group. The rules of the Kula established well-understood expectations about social standing. The mode of exchange ensured that the beads acquired in one transaction would be held and admired for a short time only, then passed along in the course of more giving and receiving. Thus from a purely functional perspective, exchanging beads merely facilitated the real work of the society, which was the production and barter of goods. In fact, the beads were the way the natives expressed their allegiance to the tribe and their willingness to go along with its rules and expectations.

Like the Trobrianders, we too have tribal rituals, ways in which we symbolically express our membership in organizations and our willingness to meet the expectations of others. And, like them, we are capable of doing real work, work that is equivalent to making canoes and raising crops. But unlike our primitive cousins, we often subordinate the challenges of real work to the demands of psychopolitics—to balancing the rational and irrational expectations that others place on us. Social relations and psychopolitics get more attention than customers and clients. Managers are measured by how well they get people to go along with the company's expectations, not by how well the company performs. Executives are preoccupied with coordination and control.

The subordination of real work to psychopolitics is the understandable—but unintended—outgrowth of two phenomena. One is the evolution of large, complex organizations in which executives must play many roles and cooperation is truly hard to foster. The other is the great success the human relations school of management has had in uncovering the social aspects of organizations and educating executives to their importance.

During the 1930s, researchers, academics, and consultants began to look at business organizations not simply as technical or economic systems but as social systems—systems built on the expectations that individuals have about their place in the organization, their rights and obligations, and their mutual dependencies. Social systems are not the result of conscious planning (as, for example, a decentralized organizational structure would be) but rather exist as a result of human proclivities, of all the unwritten contracts that grow up between a company and its employees. Hence every organization has nonlogical underpinnings as well as logical ones—an informal pecking order, for instance, as well as the formal organization chart.

To sharpen this conception of organizations, human relations researchers focused next on teaching the conditions of cooperation—the things managers could do to enhance workplace harmony. Under their tutelage, managers learned to diagnose breakdowns in cooperation by looking for ways in which the formal, logical system was violating important requirements of the informal social organization. A change in the organization's formal structure might trigger a rebellion, for example, not because subordinates objected to the actual content or purpose of the change but because it upset the informal hierarchy of the workplace. And this analysis would hold, the experts taught, whether the subordinates were managers and professionals in corporate offices or workers on the factory floor.

The sensitivity of managers to social relations in the workplace was further heightened by the growing difficulty of achieving cooperation in ever larger corporations. Much of the problem was simply a function of size. But investigators of modern managerial work and its discontents paid less attention to that than to technology and hierarchy, which, they argued, isolate people in their work. Such isolation creates problems of cooperation because it keeps people from developing normal social relations. Workers become more alienated from managers. Managers become more alienated from their peers. For many, work becomes stressful; for some, downright unbearable. Pathological outcomes multiply to include absenteeism, turnover, and, perhaps even worse, apathy, indifference, and the reluctance to exert any more energy or effort than the bare minimum needed to get by.

From diagnoses such as these, the human relations school gradually shaped a new definition of managerial work: developing and maintaining a system of cooperation. This definition comprised all those activities concerned with fostering communication, placing people in a coherent organizational structure, and maintaining an informal executive organization. It also required managers to motivate employees and to formulate the organization's purpose and objectives.

In *The Functions of the Executive* (Harvard University Press, 1938), Chester I. Barnard called this array of activities "executive work." Conversely, what I call "real work"—specialized activities such as marketing, research, and production—fell into the category of nonexecutive work because it did not *directly* address those elements in the workplace that specifically affect cooperation. From the perspective of Barnard and his followers, therefore, technical and substantive activity came to look more and more like mere mechanics.

In my view, this conception of executive work led to an unhealthy preoccupation with process at the expense of productivity. Of course, process and procedures are important: they establish the conditions

for organizational cooperation and determine whether that cooperation will actually be achieved. In addition, they also influence deeply
how effective executives will be in coordinating and controlling the
work of others in the organization. But process and procedures are
not the substance of business, and they should not get as much attention as—or more attention than—the work of business itself.

Nevertheless, the human relations school was right about this basic
point: organizations are indeed social systems and are arenas for in-
ducing cooperative behavior. As such, they are quintessentially human and fraught with all the frailties and imperfections associated
with the human condition. So much so, in fact, that one especially
wise chief executive officer once commented, "Anyone in charge of
an organization with more than two people is running a clinic."

The truth of this wry comment comes from the fact that while people want to cooperate, they also want to control their own destiny.
And it is this universal desire to control our own destiny that creates
conflicts of interest within organizations. At the same time, of course,
it also stirs up conflict on a smaller, more personal scale.

Because people come together to satisfy a wide array of psychological needs, social relations in general are awash with conflict. In the
course of their interactions, people must deal with differences as well
as similarities, with aversions as well as affinities. Indeed, in social relations, Sigmund Freud's parallel of humans and porcupines is apt:
like porcupines, people will prick and injure one another if they get
too close, but they will feel cold if they get too far apart.

This complexity in human nature—especially our conflicting ten-
dencies to cooperate and to go it alone—leads managers to spend their
time smoothing over conflict, greasing the wheels of human interaction, and unconsciously avoiding aggression. The result is a seemingly
permanent cleavage between substance and process in organizations,
as managers struggle to maintain both peace and a balance of power.
Moreover, that cleavage imposes a Gresham-like law on organizations: Just as bad money drives out good, psychopolitics drives out
real work. People can focus their attention on only so many things.
The more their attention lands on politics, the less emotional and intellectual energy they have for attending to the problems that fall under the heading of real work.

To complicate matters further, another basic fact about the human
condition also enters into all considerations about work—that is, the
sensitive relationship within individuals between anxiety and self-
esteem. Anxiety is that awful feeling in the pit of your stomach when

uncertainty reigns and fear of the future abounds. People don't tolerate anxiety well. Its appearance is a signal to do something to protect
our integrity and to preserve our identity.

The need to act in the face of anxiety is as prevalent in a modern organization as in a primitive tribe, although the causes of anxiety and
the way people experience it differ in both. In a tribal ritual such as
the Kula, primitive people exchange gifts as a way of dealing with
anxiety about the future. The fear is a basic one: What if one group
goes after another and seeks to conquer? To relieve this anxiety, the
groups exchange beads and thereby signify their intention to respect
the peaceful alliance. More energy can go into real work, and less
needs to go into defense from the threat of danger.

For individuals in preliterate societies, danger is always external: a
bad storm during a fishing expedition or warfare among neighbors is
punishment from the gods for some transgression or failure in obei-
sance. People in modern societies are more or less conscious of the
distinction between internal and external danger. Indeed, the more
educated people are, the less they tend to project their ills onto the
outside world. They are more inclined to blame themselves for their
anxiety, experiencing guilt and shame in reaction to perceived shortcomings, and often requiring considerable support to rebuild diminished self-esteem. In this cycle of self-blame, they seek support from
authority, and whether they get it or not, they frequently suffer a reduced capacity for real work.

Being able to recognize people's struggles with anxiety—and dealing with the morale problems that inevitably ensue—can test a manager's capacity for empathy. It also challenges his or her social skills,
particularly the ability to reduce tensions in groups. Management
practice today recognizes those needs. Consequently, few managers
now behave as autocrats. As a group, they are exceedingly polite, con-
siderate of others, egalitarian in their behavior, and sincerely interested in making others comfortable with the differences in power that
exist in every organization. But this style of management poses at
least two kinds of problems in the interaction between real work and
psychopolitics.

The first problem appears in the doubts that frequently arise about
the nature of managerial competence. While no hard data exist, ob-
servation tells me that too many managers put interpersonal matters,
power relations, and peacekeeping ahead of real work. While generally active in their jobs, they avoid aggression (to use the Freudian
term) like the plague. They don't go on the offensive themselves, even

if that means suppressing their desire to give constructive criticism. Nor do they encourage conflict among subordinates or peers.

On the surface, this propensity for maintaining cordial relationships appears to be a useful way to ensure cooperation. But it has unintended consequences for the managers themselves and for their organizations. Followers tend to take their cues from authority figures. So if the leader's style is low-key, followers also will suppress aggression. Before long, group norms will foster the appearance of getting along and will discourage individuality. Process will take precedence over substance. Attention will turn inward to the organization's politics rather than outward to the real work of making and marketing goods and services.

For individuals, the costs are equally high because aggressive energy channeled into real work is the one sure route to a sense of mastery, to the pleasure that comes from using one's talents to accomplish things. In fact, without the application of aggression, little real work would ever get done. Of course, aggression can be misdirected. It can be turned inward and experienced as depression, with accompanying feelings of guilt and low self-worth. Or it can be turned on people with whom one should ostensibly be allied. But aggression is too valuable an emotion—and too basic a human drive—to suppress merely because it can be misdirected.

The second problem that arises from a disproportionate emphasis on social relations also relates to the reactions of subordinates. In the 1930s, the Austrian-born psychiatrist J. L. Moreno uncovered the simple yet profound fact that followers differentiate between task leaders and social leaders. Given a choice, followers would prefer to be friends with social leaders, who characteristically ease the tensions that arise in group relations. But they would not choose to work with them. Instead, they would choose to work with task leaders, whom they identify as being very proficient. But they would not choose to have them as friends.

Experiments in social psychology and observations of so-called natural groups have since corroborated Moreno's discovery. In primitive cultures that transfer authority patrilineally, for example, the young male will respect but maintain a distance from his father, who is responsible for providing food and shelter. For an easier relationship with an adult male, he will often choose his mother's brother, who provides a more nurturing and comforting relationship than his own father does.

These observations suggest that the ideal solution—one that promotes real work and provides for the expressive and supportive components of group relations—would be to foster two kinds of leadership in two different individuals: a task leader and a social leader. Not surprisingly, such splits often occur spontaneously. Often the chair of a company acts as the organization's social leader, while the president serves as the organization's task leader, who focuses attention on real work. But cultivating dual leadership leads to questionable results, because it reflects—and amplifies—the emphasis that is placed on seeking and maintaining cooperation even at the expense of superior performance in real work. Nothing will kill a middle manager's chances for promotion faster, for example, than a reputation for being aggressive (or worse, abrasive). But doesn't "aggressive" often really mean energetic, persistent, and goal oriented?

The end point of this analysis is not to encourage conflict and disharmony. It does suggest the need to look carefully at why real work generates respect and support from colleagues and subordinates, and also overcomes the anxiety people frequently experience in hard-driving situations. I believe that executives who are superior in performing real work overcome this anxiety, not because someone else drains off any tension or hostility but because there is something inherently humanizing about the use of talent to get things done.

Humankind does not live by bread alone but also by catchphrases. Thus the definition of management as "getting things done through other people" is often refined by the popular old saw that "the best salesperson doesn't make the best sales manager." Now, it's certainly true that managing is more than applying technical proficiency. But it also makes simple good sense to suppose that substantive talent is an invaluable asset—perhaps even the crucial building block—in developing managers who will become leaders.

Without attributing too much to Japan's current industrial ascendancy, it is worth asking why leading Japanese companies recruit and train their frontline factory supervisors from the ranks of graduate engineers. The answer, I believe, is self-confidence—the self-confidence of managers who have demonstrated mastery in the substance of their work. That self-confidence induces confidence in others, which by itself builds cohesion and morale. A feeling of optimism accompanies the knowledge, gained from firsthand experience, that the person in charge knows what he or she is doing. Indeed, the demise of conglomerates illustrates the point in reverse: it never takes a division head more than a step or two up the ladder of authority before he or she encounters a boss who has little idea about—and even less concern for—the substance of the division's work.

Making substance the leading edge of executive work means applying one or more talents, or business imaginations. Imaginations differ within a business. The marketing imagination relies on empathy with the customer and on the capacity to visualize what products and services will make life better for the customer. The manufacturing imagination is driven by the proposition that there is a better way to apply energies in the relationship between people and machines, and searches constantly for the better way. The financial imagination is impelled by the idea that market disjunctions create opportunities and seeks to take advantage of them.

An underlying aggressiveness drives all business imaginations. Typically, the executive takes a position: "We will cut prices, promote to increase market share, build a direct distribution network, and end our reliance on independent distributors." Or "We're going to get out of this business because it's a commodity." Or "We're in a business that depends on being cost-effective. So we're going to spend money on research to improve our manufacturing techniques, increase productivity, and deliver a top-quality product." This is the language of substance. It has content and direction. It also stimulates controversy. People will disagree, particularly if the position taken affects their own power and place. So leading with substance requires maturity not only to tolerate others' aggressiveness but also to direct it toward substantive issues.

Given the need for substance, it is particularly unfortunate that many executives have been misled by experts who say that managing by ambiguity and indirection is the wave of the future. Indirection suggests what the speaker wants but veils it with polite and even deferential language. The result is that it encourages the acting out of psychodramas. Often the drama goes something like this: A subordinate is giving a report and going in a direction the boss really doesn't like. Instead of saying, "Those are terrible ideas; here's what we should be doing," the well-trained manager asks courteously, "Have you considered the possibility of promoting the product with a premium instead of directly?" The question hardly invites the subordinate to get excited, defend his or her ideas, and tell the boss why the suggestion is a lousy idea. Instead, it just breeds more circumlocution, since the counterdefense in dealing with indirection is more indirection: "We gave that idea a lot of thought, and it has a lot going for it. But some new research suggests that premium promotion may fall a little short in getting the message across."

When a boss who is deeply (and probably unconsciously) angry manages by indirection, the effect can be really insidious—the kind of stuff that sets stomachs churning. For example, such managers often manipulate others by playing on their limited tolerance for anxiety. The psychodrama begins when the boss distances himself or herself from a subordinate. The subordinate, worried that something is wrong, tries to find out if he or she has caused some problem. The boss responds with reassuring words—and body language that says quite plainly, "You're in deep trouble!" Anxiety mounting, the subordinate begins to withdraw, until the boss, with exquisite timing, reverses behavior and becomes genuinely supportive. As for the poor victim? Instead of feeling angry over this subtle oppression, he or she is grateful to the boss for relieving the awful burden of anxiety and diminished self-esteem. The end product is a subordinate who is less autonomous, more psychologically dependent, and more concerned with avoiding another identity-threatening episode than with engaging in real work.

If this scenario were the whole story, organizations would produce a great deal more stress than they do. The fact that it is not attests to how well men and women in organizations are able to defend themselves—not least by using their street smarts to play psychopolitical games themselves. Their gambit is to reverse the flow of dependency, to make the boss need them more than they need the boss.

Playing that game means learning to be an organizational performer. Performers are adept at controlling the information they pass on to their bosses so that they're never faced with expectations they cannot meet. As long as their performance meets or exceeds the targets that have been set for them, the boss has little cause for scrutiny. But by the same token, the boss is also likely to understand little about what these subordinates are doing. The cost of this game is the demise of learning as well as the loss of any hope for organizational creativity. Short-term results look good; the long term is in jeopardy.

That analysis provokes a question: Is psychopolitics, or the victory of process over substance, the inevitable consequence of human nature, compounded by the complexity of living in a large, hierarchical organization? I think not. It's true that human beings learn political behavior as children, in their competition for love and standing from powerful parents and in their rivalries at school. But the politicization of work and human relationships is not an inevitable consequence of people being people. Rather, it goes hand in hand with defensive behavior.

And here, managers who want to stimulate real work and dampen political preoccupations can take a leaf from the book that sensible parents apply in raising their children. Such parents know that they cannot overcome the anxiety their children will inevitably feel as they develop and mature. Time cannot be made to stand still, nor can earlier satisfactions be sustained in the face of important developmental changes. So while these parents empathize with the children for whom they are responsible, they do not encourage them to wage an impossible war, a war that cannot be won on its own terms. Instead, like leaders, they learn to help the less powerful deal with life in different terms. They teach the lesson that substance is all, that the cultivation of talent is the route to independence and maturity. They also teach their children that good human relations depend on what a person gives to the work at hand, not on what he or she takes.

Superior business performance requires senior executives who have overcome their own political anxieties and the need for total control. It also requires cadres of managers who are learning to do the same. For if managers continue to rise in organizations by playing psychopolitical games, and if their deepest propensities continue to lead them away from substance and toward politics and process, then there is little hope for real work and real competitiveness.

Real work is the sure and sane way to enhance morale in organizations. The rituals of process are merely expressive reminders that those who contribute to the real work are the legitimate participants in the social satisfaction that accompanies true achievement.

Hard Thinking Constitutes the Executive's Real Work

The thrust of "Real Work" was to bring to readers' attention the differences and the tensions between ritualistic and substantive behavior in the organization. While acknowledging that ritual serves important and complex purposes in large business organizations—such as suppressing inwardly directed aggression and strengthening the individual's social ties to the organization—I was also trying to make the point that, uncontrolled, ritual can come to displace or substitute for the real work of a company. One of the chief executive's responsibilities as organizational leader is to manage the tension—to keep the ritualistic and substantive work of the company in proper balance and to determine on a continual basis what that balance should be.

Yet another one of the executive's responsibilities—and the more difficult one—is to be sure that this kind of balance exists in his or her own behavior. My view in 1989 was that too many senior executives were spending too much of their time tending to the inward psychopolitical rituals of their companies and not enough time dealing with the outward real work of serving customers and clients.

Since voicing those concerns eight years ago, I have noticed a change. During the 1990s, senior executives seem to have reestablished a balance between real work and ritual. I could cite as evidence the great variety and intensity of the activity executives have undertaken to maximize the shareholder value of their organizations. To serve that end, they have led their companies in the real work of cutting costs, creating products, pleasing customers, and developing markets. Even the leaders of AT&T, which was once called Ma Bell because of the security it afforded its managers, staff, and workers, seem to have done real work in slimming down and sharpening the organization so that it could survive and thrive in a deregulated and competitive environment.

But if ritual once overwhelmed real work in business organizations, it could happen again—and probably will. Today's real work will not necessarily remain tomorrow's real work as the external environment—and thus the challenges to the organization and its leaders—changes. Activities that for a time constitute real work have a way of becoming ritualized and thus perpetuated long after they've ceased to have value. Activity performed for its own sake becomes empty ritual.

Once a company has downsized, acquired, divested, and spread itself around the globe, what then? The easy answer is to do more of the same, which allows a company's senior executives to avoid the difficult work of crafting options and choosing among them. Executives also can duck their real work by invoking another kind of ritual—the substitution of process for substance. I see that happening today under the guise of empowerment when senior executives draft their subordinates into task forces that are led by consultants and charged with finding answers to questions that the executives themselves should be addressing.

Thus I am inclined to affirm my view about what constitutes the real work of the executive. Whatever else it involves—and the real work of the executive is continually changing—it always involves one crucial component. That component is thinking—the thinking that must precede action in order to inform and direct it. When leaders substitute ritual for thought, they are not performing the whole of their jobs.

PART

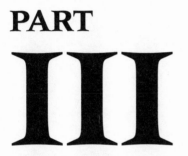

III

An Integrated Leadership Approach

1
Entrepreneurship Reconsidered: The Team as Hero

Robert B. Reich

"Wake up there, youngster," said a rough voice.

Ragged Dick opened his eyes slowly and stared stupidly in the face of the speaker, but did not offer to get up.

"Wake up, you young vagabond!" said the man a little impatiently; "I suppose you'd lay there all day, if I hadn't called you."

So begins the story of *Ragged Dick, or Street Life in New York*, Horatio Alger's first book—the first of 135 tales written in the late 1800s that together sold close to 20 million copies. Like all the books that followed, *Ragged Dick* told the story of a young man who, by pluck and luck, rises from his lowly station to earn a respectable job and the promise of a better life.

Nearly a century later, another best-selling American business story offered a different concept of heroism and a different description of the route to success. This story begins:

All the way to the horizon in the last light, the sea was just degrees of gray, rolling and frothy on the surface. From the cockpit of a small white sloop—she was thirty-five feet long—the waves looked like hills coming up from behind, and most of the crew preferred not to glance at them. . . . Running under shortened sails in front of the northeaster, the boat rocked one way, gave a thump, and then it rolled the other. The pots and pans in the galley clanged. A six-pack of beer, which someone had forgotten to stow away, slid back and forth across the cabin floor, over and over again. Sometime late that night, one of the crew raised a voice against the wind and asked, "What are we trying to prove?"

The book is Tracy Kidder's *The Soul of a New Machine,* a 1981 tale of how a team—a crew—of hardworking inventors built a computer by pooling their efforts. The opening scene is a metaphor for the team's treacherous journey.

Separated by 100 years, totally different in their explanations of what propels the American economy, these two stories symbolize the choice that Americans will face in the 1990s; each celebrates a fundamentally different version of American entrepreneurship. Which version we choose to embrace will help determine how quickly and how well the United States adapts to the challenge of global competition.

Horatio Alger's notion of success is the traditional one: the familiar tale of triumphant individuals, of enterprising heroes who win riches and rewards through a combination of Dale Carnegie-esque self-improvement, Norman Vincent Peale-esque faith, Sylvester Stallone-esque assertiveness, and plain old-fashioned good luck. Tracy Kidder's story, by contrast, teaches that economic success comes through the talent, energy, and commitment of a team—through *collective* entrepreneurship.

Stories like these do more than merely entertain or divert us. Like ancient myths that captured and contained an essential truth, they shape how we see and understand our lives, how we make sense of our experience. Stories can mobilize us to action and affect our behavior—more powerfully than simple and straightforward information ever can.

To the extent that we continue to celebrate the traditional myth of the entrepreneurial hero, we will slow the progress of change and adaptation that is essential to our economic success. If we are to compete effectively in today's world, we must begin to celebrate collective entrepreneurship, endeavors in which the whole of the effort is greater than the sum of individual contributions. We need to honor our teams more, our aggressive leaders and maverick geniuses less.

Heroes and Drones

The older and still dominant American myth involves two kinds of actors: entrepreneurial heroes and industrial drones—the inspired and the perspired.

In this myth, entrepreneurial heroes personify freedom and creativity. They come up with the Big Ideas and build the organizations—the Big Machines—that turn them into reality. They take the initiative, come up with technological and organizational innovations, devise new solutions to old problems. They are the men and women who start vibrant new companies, turn around failing companies, and shake up staid ones. To all endeavors they apply daring and imagination.

The myth of the entrepreneurial hero is as old as America and has served us well in a number of ways. We like to see ourselves as born mavericks and fixers. Our entrepreneurial drive has long been our distinguishing trait. Generations of inventors and investors have kept us on the technological frontier. In a world of naysayers and traditionalists, the American character has always stood out—cheerfully optimistic, willing to run risks, ready to try anything. During World War II, it was the rough-and-ready American GI who could fix the stalled jeep in Normandy while the French regiment only looked on.

Horatio Alger captured this spirit in hundreds of stories. With titles like *Bound to Rise, Luck and Pluck,* and *Sink or Swim,* they inspired millions of readers with a gloriously simple message: in America you can go from rags to riches. The plots were essentially the same; like any successful entrepreneur, Alger knew when he was onto a good thing. A fatherless, penniless boy—possessed of great determination, faith, and courage—seeks his fortune. All manner of villains try to tempt him, divert him, or separate him from his small savings. But in the end, our hero prevails—not just through pluck; luck plays a part too—and by the end of the story he is launched on his way to fame and fortune.

At the turn of the century, Americans saw fiction and reality sometimes converging. Edward Harriman began as a $5-a-week office boy and came to head a mighty railroad empire. John D. Rockefeller rose from a clerk in a commission merchant's house to become one of the world's richest men. Andrew Carnegie started as a $1.20-a-week bobbin boy in a Pittsburgh cotton mill and became the nation's foremost steel magnate. In the early 1900s, when boys were still reading the Alger tales, Henry Ford made his fortune mass-producing the Model T, and in the process became both a national folk hero and a potential presidential candidate.

Alger's stories gave the country a noble ideal—a society in which imagination and effort summoned their just reward. The key virtue was self-reliance; the admirable man was the self-made man; the goal was to be your own boss. Andrew Carnegie articulated the prevailing view: "Is any would-be businessman . . . content in forecasting his future, to figure himself as labouring all his life for a fixed salary? Not one, I am sure. In this you have the dividing line between business and non-business; the one is master and depends on profits, the other is servant and depends on salary."[1]

The entrepreneurial hero still captures the American imagination. Inspired by the words of his immigrant father, who told him, "You could be anything you want to be, if you wanted it bad enough and were willing to work for it," Lido Iacocca worked his way up to the presidency of Ford Motor Company, from which he was abruptly fired by Henry Ford II, only to go on to rescue Chrysler from bankruptcy, thumb his nose at Ford in a best-selling autobiography, renovate the Statue of Liberty, and gain mention as a possible presidential candidate.[2] Could Horatio Alger's heroes have done any better?

Peter Ueberroth, son of a traveling aluminum salesman, worked his way through college, single-handedly built a $300-million business, went on to organize the 1984 Olympics, became *Time* magazine's Man of the Year and the commissioner of baseball. Steven Jobs built his own computer company from scratch and became a multimillionaire before his thirtieth birthday. Stories of entrepreneurial heroism come from across the economy and across the country: professors who create whole new industries and become instant millionaires when their inventions go from the laboratory to the marketplace; youthful engineers who quit their jobs, strike out on their own, and strike it rich.

In the American economic mythology, these heroes occupy center stage: "Fighters, fanatics, men with a lust for contest, a gleam of creation, and a drive to justify their break from the mother company."[3] Prosperity for all depends on the entrepreneurial vision of a few rugged individuals.

If the entrepreneurial heroes hold center stage in this drama, the rest of the vast work force plays a supporting role—supporting and unheralded. Average workers in this myth are drones—cogs in the Big Machines, so many interchangeable parts, unable to perform without direction from above. They are put to work for their hands, not for their minds or imaginations. Their jobs typically appear by the dozens in the help-wanted sections of daily newspapers. Their routines are unvaried. They have little opportunity to use judgment or creativity. To the entrepreneurial hero belongs all the inspiration; the drones are governed by the rules and valued for their reliability and pliability.

These average workers are no villains—but they are certainly no heroes. Uninteresting and uninterested, goes the myth, they lack creative spark and entrepreneurial vision. These are, for example, the nameless and faceless workers who lined up for work in response to

Henry Ford's visionary offer of a $5-per-day paycheck. At best, they put in a decent effort in executing the entrepreneurial hero's grand design. At worst, they demand more wages and benefits for less work, do the minimum expected of them, or function as bland bureaucrats mired in standard operating procedures.

The entrepreneurial hero and the worker drone together personify the mythic version of how the American economic system works. The system needs both types. But rewards and treatment for the two are as different as the roles themselves: the entrepreneurs should be rewarded with fame and fortune; drones should be disciplined through clear rules and punishments. Considering the overwhelming importance attached to the entrepreneur in this paradigm, the difference seems appropriate. For, as George Gilder has written, "All of us are dependent for our livelihood and progress not on a vast and predictable machine, but on the creativity and courage of the particular men who accept the risks which generate our riches."[4]

Why Horatio Alger Can't Help Us Anymore

There is just one fatal problem with this dominant myth: it is obsolete. The economy that it describes no longer exists. By clinging to the myth, we subscribe to an outmoded view of how to win economic success—a view that, on a number of counts, endangers our economic future:

- In today's global economy, the Big Ideas pioneered by American entrepreneurs travel quickly to foreign lands. In the hands of global competitors, these ideas can undergo continuous adaptation and improvement and reemerge as new Big Ideas or as a series of incrementally improved small ideas.

- The machines that American entrepreneurs have always set up so efficiently to execute their Big Ideas are equally footloose. Process technology moves around the globe to find the cheapest labor and the friendliest markets. As ideas migrate overseas, the economic and technological resources needed to implement the ideas migrate too.

- Workers in other parts of the world are apt to be cheaper or more productive—or both—than workers in the United States. Around the globe, millions of potential workers are ready to underbid American labor.

- Some competitor nations—Japan, in particular—have created relationships among engineers, managers, production workers, and marketing and sales people that do away with the old distinction between entre- preneurs and drones. The dynamic result is yet another basis for chal- lenging American assumptions about what leads to competitive success.

Because of these global changes, the United States is now suscepti- ble to competitive challenge on two grounds. First, by borrowing the Big Ideas and process technology that come from the United States and providing the hardworking, low-paid workers, developing na- tions can achieve competitive advantage. Second, by embracing col- lective entrepreneurship, the Japanese especially have found a differ- ent way to achieve competitive advantage while maintaining high real wages.

Americans continue to lead the world in breakthroughs and cutting-edge scientific discoveries. But the Big Ideas that start in this country now quickly travel abroad, where they not only get produced at high speed, at low cost, and with great efficiency, but also undergo continuous development and improvement. And all too often, Ameri- can companies get bogged down somewhere between invention and production.

Several product histories make the point. Americans invented the solid-state transistor in 1947. Then in 1953, Western Electric licensed the technology to Sony for $25,000—and the rest is history. A few years later, RCA licensed several Japanese companies to make color televisions—and that was the beginning of the end of color-television production in the United States. Routine assembly of color televisions eventually shifted to Taiwan and Mexico. At the same time, Sony and other Japanese companies pushed the technology in new directions, continuously refining it into a stream of consumer products.

In 1968, Unimation licensed Kawasaki Heavy Industries to make in- dustrial robots. The Japanese took the initial technology and kept moving it forward. The pattern has been the same for one Big Idea af- ter another. Americans came up with the Big Ideas for videocassette recorders, basic oxygen furnaces, continuous casters for making steel, microwave ovens, automobile stamping machines, computerized ma- chine tools, integrated circuits. But these Big Ideas—and many, many others—quickly found their way into production in foreign countries: routine, standardized production in developing nations or continuous refinement and complex applications in Japan. Either way, the United States has lost ground.

Older industrial economies, like our own, have two options: they can try to match the low wages and discipline under which workers elsewhere in the world are willing to labor, or they can compete on the basis of how quickly and how well they transform ideas into incrementally better products. The second option is, in fact, the only one that offers the possibility of high real incomes in America. But here's the catch: a handful of lone entrepreneurs producing a few industry-making Big Ideas can't execute this second option. Innovation must become both continuous and collective. And that requires embracing a new ideal: collective entrepreneurship.

The New Economic Paradigm

If America is to win in the new global competition, we need to begin telling one another a new story in which companies compete by drawing on the talent and creativity of all their employees, not just a few maverick inventors and dynamic CEOs. Competitive advantage today comes from continuous, incremental innovation and refinement of a variety of ideas that spread throughout the organization. The entrepreneurial organization is both experience-based and decentralized, so that every advance builds on every previous advance, and everyone in the company has the opportunity and capacity to participate.

While this story represents a departure from tradition, it already exists, in fact, to a greater or lesser extent in every well-run American and Japanese corporation. The difference is that we don't recognize and celebrate this story—and the Japanese do.

Consider just a few of the evolutionary paths that collective entrepreneurship can take: vacuum-tube radios become transistorized radios, then stereo pocket radios audible through earphones, then compact discs and compact disc players, and then optical disc computer memories. Color televisions evolve into digital televisions capable of showing several pictures simultaneously; videocassette recorders into camcorders. A single strand of technological evolution connects electronic sewing machines, electronic typewriters, and flexible electronic workstations. Basic steel gives way to high-strength and corrosion-resistant steels, then to new materials composed of steel mixed with silicon and custom-made polymers. Basic chemicals evolve into high-performance ceramics, to single-crystal silicon and high-grade crystal glass. Copper wire gives way to copper cables, then to fiber-optic cables.

These patterns reveal no clear life cycles with beginnings, middles, and ends. Unlike Big Ideas that beget standardized commodities, these products undergo a continuous process of incremental change and adaptation. Workers at all levels add value not solely or even mostly by tending machines and carrying out routines, but by continuously discovering opportunities for improvement in product and process.

In this context, it makes no sense to speak of an "industry" like steel or automobiles or televisions or even banking. There are no clear borders around any of these clusters of goods or services. When products and processes are so protean, companies grow or decline not with the market for some specific good, but with the creative and adaptive capacity of their workers.

Workers in such organizations constantly reinvent the company; one idea leads to another. Producing the latest generation of automobiles involves making electronic circuits that govern fuel consumption and monitor engine performance; developments in these devices lead to improved sensing equipment and software for monitoring heartbeats and moisture in the air. Producing cars also involves making flexible robots for assembling parts and linking them by computer; steady improvements in these technologies, in turn, lead to expert production systems that can be applied anywhere. What is considered the "automobile industry" thus becomes a wide variety of technologies evolving toward all sorts of applications that flow from the same strand of technological development toward different markets.

In this paradigm, entrepreneurship isn't the sole province of the company's founder or its top managers. Rather, it is a capability and attitude that is diffused throughout the company. Experimentation and development go on all the time as the company searches for new ways to capture and build on the knowledge already accumulated by its workers.

Distinctions between innovation and production, between top managers and production workers blur. Because production is a continuous process of reinvention, entrepreneurial efforts are focused on many thousands of small ideas rather than on just a few big ones. And because valuable information and expertise are dispersed throughout the organization, top management does not solve problems; it creates an environment in which people can identify and solve problems themselves.

Most of the training for working in this fashion takes place on the job. Formal education may prepare people to absorb and integrate experience, but it does not supply the experience. No one can anticipate the precise skills that workers will need to succeed on the job when information processing, know-how, and creativity are the value added. Any job that could be fully prepared for in advance is, by definition, a job that could be exported to a low-wage country or programmed into robots and computers; a routine job is a job destined to disappear.

In collective entrepreneurship, individual skills are integrated into a group; this collective capacity to innovate becomes something greater than the sum of its parts. Over time, as group members work through various problems and approaches, they learn about each others' abilities. They learn how they can help one another perform better, what each can contribute to a particular project, how they can best take advantage of one another's experience. Each participant is constantly on the lookout for small adjustments that will speed and smooth the evolution of the whole. The net result of many such small-scale adaptations, effected throughout the organization, is to propel the enterprise forward.

Collective entrepreneurship thus entails close working relationships among people at all stages of the process. If customers' needs are to be recognized and met, designers and engineers must be familiar with sales and marketing. Salespeople must also have a complete understanding of the enterprise's capacity to design and deliver specialized products. The company's ability to adapt to new opportunities and capitalize on them depends on its capacity to share information and involve everyone in the organization in a systemwide search for ways to improve, adjust, adapt, and upgrade.

Collective entrepreneurship also entails a different organizational structure. Under the old paradigm, companies are organized into a series of hierarchical tiers so that supervisors at each level can make sure that subordinates act according to plan. It is a structure designed to control. But enterprises designed for continuous innovation and incremental improvement use a structure designed to spur innovation at all levels. Gaining insight into improvement of products and processes is more important than rigidly following rules. Coordination and communication replace command and control. Consequently, there are few middle-level managers and only modest differences in the status and income of senior managers and junior employees.

Simple accounting systems are no longer adequate or appropriate for monitoring and evaluating job performance: tasks are intertwined and interdependent, and the quality of work is often more important than the quantity of work. In a system where each worker depends on many others—and where the success of the company depends on all—the only appropriate measurement of accomplishment is a collective one. At the same time, the reward system reflects this new approach: profit sharing, gain sharing, and performance bonuses all demonstrate that the success of the company comes from the broadest contribution of all the company's employees, not just those at the top.

Finally, under collective entrepreneurship, workers do not fear technology and automation as a threat to their jobs. When workers add value through judgment and knowledge, computers become tools that expand their discretion. Computer-generated information can give workers rich feedback about their own efforts, how they affect others in the production process, and how the entire process can be improved. One of the key lessons to come out of the General Motors–Toyota joint venture in California is that the Japanese automaker does not rely on automation and technology to replace workers in the plant. In fact, human workers still occupy the most critical jobs—those where judgment and evaluation are essential. Instead, Toyota uses technology to allow workers to focus on those important tasks where choices have to be made. Under this approach, technology gives workers the chance to use their imagination and their insight on behalf of the company.

The Team as Hero

In 1986, one of America's largest and oldest enterprises announced that it was changing the way it assigned its personnel: the U.S. Army discarded a system that assigned soldiers to their units individually in favor of a system that keeps teams of soldiers together for their entire tours of duty. An Army spokesperson explained, "We discovered that individuals perform better when they are part of a stable group. They are more reliable. They also take responsibility for the success of the overall operation."

In one of its recent advertisements, BellSouth captures the new story. "BellSouth is not a bunch of individuals out for themselves," the ad proclaimed. "We're a team."

Collective entrepreneurship is already here. It shows up in the way our best-run companies now organize their work, regard their workers, design their enterprises. Yet the old myth of the entrepreneurial hero remains powerful. Many Americans would prefer to think that Lee Iacocca single-handedly saved Chrysler from bankruptcy than to accept the real story: a large team of people with diverse backgrounds and interests joined together to rescue the ailing company.

Bookstores bulge with new volumes paying homage to American CEOs. It is a familiar story; it is an engaging story. And no doubt, when seen through the eyes of the CEO, it accurately portrays how that individual experienced the company's success. But what gets left out time after time are the experiences of the rest of the team—the men and women at every level of the company whose contributions to the company created the success that the CEO so eagerly claims. Where are the books that celebrate their stories?

You can also find inspirational management texts designed to tell top executives how to be kinder to employees, treat them with respect, listen to them, and make them feel appreciated. By reading these books, executives can learn how to search for excellence, create excellence, achieve excellence, or become impassioned about excellence—preferably within one minute. Managers are supposed to walk around, touch employees, get directly involved, effervesce with praise and encouragement, stage celebrations, and indulge in hoopla.

Some of this is sound; some of it is hogwash. But most of it, even the best, is superficial. Lacking any real context, unattached to any larger understanding of why relationships between managers and workers matter, the prescriptions often remain shallow and are treated as such. The effervescent executive is likely to be gone in a few years, many of the employees will be gone, and the owners may be different as well. Too often the company is assumed to be a collection of assets, available to the highest bidder. When times require it, employees will be sacked. Everybody responds accordingly. Underneath the veneer of participatory management, it is business as usual—and business as usual represents a threat to America's long-term capacity to compete.

If the United States is to compete effectively in the world in a way designed to enhance the real incomes of Americans, we must bring collective entrepreneurship to the forefront of the economy. That will require us to change our attitudes, to downplay the myth of the entrepreneurial hero, and to celebrate our creative teams.

First, we will need to look for and promote new kinds of stories. In modern-day America, stories of collective entrepreneurship typically appear in the sports pages of the daily newspaper; time after time, in accounts of winning efforts we learn that the team with the best blend of talent won—the team that emphasized teamwork—not the team with the best individual athlete. The cultural challenge is to move these stories from the sports page to the business page. We need to shift the limelight from maverick founders and shake-'em-up CEOs to groups of engineers, production workers, and marketers who successfully innovate new products and services. We need to look for opportunities to tell stories about American business from the perspective of all the workers who make up the team, rather than solely from the perspective of top managers. The stories are there—we need only change our focus, alter our frame of reference, in order to find them.

Second, we will need to understand that the most powerful stories get told, not in books and newspapers, but in the everyday world of work. Whether managers know it or not, every decision they make suggests a story to the rest of the enterprise. Decisions to award generous executive bonuses or to provide plush executive dining rooms and executive parking places tell the old story of entrepreneurial heroism. A decision to lay off 10 percent of the work force tells the old story of the drone worker. Several years ago, when General Motors reached agreement on a contract with the United Auto Workers that called for a new relationship based on cooperation and shared sacrifice, and then, on the same day, announced a new formula for generous executive bonuses, long-time union members simply nodded to themselves. The actions told the whole story. It is not enough to acknowledge the importance of collective entrepreneurship; clear and consistent signals must reinforce the new story.

Collective entrepreneurship represents the path toward an economic future that is promising for both managers and workers. For managers, this path means continually retraining employees for more complex tasks; automating in ways that cut routine tasks and enhance worker flexibility and creativity; diffusing responsibility for innovation; taking seriously labor's concern for job security; and giving workers a stake in improved productivity through profit-linked bonuses and stock plans.

For workers, this path means accepting flexible job classifications and work rules; agreeing to wage rates linked to profits and productivity improvements; and generally taking greater responsibility for the soundness and efficiency of the enterprise. This path also involves a closer and more permanent relationship with other parties that have a stake in the company's performance—suppliers, dealers, creditors, even the towns and cities in which the company resides.

Under collective entrepreneurship, all those associated with the company become partners in its future. The distinction between entrepreneurs and drones breaks down. Each member of the enterprise participates in its evolution. All have a commitment to the company's continued success. It is the one approach that can maintain and improve America's competitive performance—and America's standard of living—over the long haul.

Notes

1. Andrew Carnegie, *The Empire of Business* (New York: Doubleday, Page, 1902), 192.
2. See Lee Iacocca and William Novak, *Iacocca: An Autobiography* (New York: Bantam Books, 1984).
3. George Gilder, *The Spirit of Enterprise* (New York: Simon and Schuster, 1984), 213.
4. Ibid., 147.

Executive Summaries

The Parable of the Sadhu

Bowen H. McCoy

When does a group have responsibility for the well-being of an individual? And what are the differences between the ethics of the individual and the ethics of the corporation? Those are the questions Bowen McCoy wanted readers to explore in this HBR Classic, first published in September–October 1983.

In 1982, McCoy spent several months hiking through Nepal. Midway through the difficult trek, as he and several others were preparing to attain the highest point of their climb, they encountered the body of an Indian holy man, or sadhu. Wearing little clothing and shivering in the bitter cold, he was barely alive.

McCoy and the other travelers—who included individuals from Japan, New Zealand, and Switzerland, as well as local Nepali guides and porters—immediately wrapped him in warm clothing and gave him food and drink. A few members of the group broke off to help move the sadhu down toward a village two days' journey away, but they soon left him in order to continue their way up the slope.

What happened to the sadhu? In his retrospective commentary, McCoy notes that he never learned the answer to that question. Instead, the sadhu's story only raises more questions. On the Himalayan slope, a collection of individuals was unprepared for a sudden dilemma. They all "did their bit," but the group was not organized enough to take ultimate responsibility for a life. How, asks McCoy in a broader context, do we prepare our organizations and institutions so they will respond appropriately to ethical crises?

The Team That Wasn't

Suzy Wetlaufer

"You have one responsibility as FireArt's director of strategy," the CEO had said to Eric on his first day. "That's to put together a team of our top people, one from each division, and have a comprehensive plan for our strategic realignment up, running, and winning within six months."

It seemed like an exciting, rewarding challenge. The team approach to problem solving was Eric's specialty; in his old job, he had managed three teams of manufacturing specialists. Clearly, this project would be difficult: FireArt was trying to combat an eighteen-month slump in sales and earnings. But Eric was sure that together, the glassmaker's top managers could find a way to reverse the trend.

Unfortunately, the team got off on the wrong foot from its first meeting. Randy Louderback, FireArt's charismatic and extremely talented director of sales and marketing, seemed intent on sabotaging the group's efforts. In fact, at the first three team meetings, Randy either dominated the discussion or withdrew entirely, tapping his pen on the table to indicate his boredom. Sometimes, he withheld information vital to the group's debate, or he denigrated people's comments.

Anxiously awaiting the start of the team's fourth meeting, Eric was determined to address Randy's behavior openly in the group. But before he could, Randy again provoked a confrontation, and the meeting ended abruptly.

What should Eric do now? Is Randy the team's only problem? Seven experts discuss the characters in this fictitious case study and examine what it takes to create a successful team.

The Discipline of Teams

Jon R. Katzenbach and Douglas K. Smith

Groups don't become teams because that is what someone calls them. Nor do teamwork values by themselves ensure team performance. So what is a team? How can managers know when the team option makes sense and what they can do to ensure team success? In this article, drawn from their recent book *The Wisdom of Teams*, McKinsey partners Jon Katzenbach and Douglas Smith answer these questions and outline the discipline that makes a real team.

The essence of a team is shared commitment. Without it, groups perform as individuals; with it, they become a powerful unit of collective performance. The best teams invest a tremendous amount of time shaping a purpose that they can own. The best teams also translate their purpose into specific performance goals. And members of successful teams pitch in and become accountable with and to their teammates.

The fundamental distinction between teams and other forms of working groups turns on performance. A working group relies on the individual contributions of its members for group performance. But a team strives for something greater than its members could achieve individually. In short, an effective team is always worth more than the sum of its parts.

Katzenbach and Smith identify three basic types of teams: teams that recommend things—task forces or project groups; teams that make or do things—manufacturing, operations, or marketing groups; and teams that run things—groups that oversee some significant functional activity. For managers, the key is knowing where in the organization real teams should be encouraged. Team potential exists anywhere hierarchy or organizational boundaries inhibit good performance. Considering the extra level that teams can achieve, the authors believe that teams will become the primary work unit in high-performance organizations.

How the Right Measures Help Teams Excel

Christopher Meyer

At many companies that have moved from control-oriented, functional hierarchies to faster and flatter multifunctional teams, traditional performance-measurement systems not only fail to support these teams but also undermine them, Christopher Meyer argues. Many managers fail to realize that traditional measures, which focus on results, may help them keep score on the performance of their businesses but do not help a multifunctional team monitor the activities or capabilities that enable it to perform a given process. Nor do such *results measures* tell team members what they must do to improve their performance.

How should performance-measurement systems be overhauled to maximize the effectiveness of teams? First, the overarching purpose of the system should be to help a team, rather than top managers, gauge its progress. Next, a truly empowered team must play the lead role in designing its own measurement system. And because a team is responsible for a value-delivery process that cuts across several functions, it must create new measures to track this process. Finally, a team should adopt only a handful of measures.

Senior managers play an important role in helping teams develop performance measures by dictating strategic goals, ensuring that each team understands how it fits into those goals, and training a team to devise its own measures. But managers must never make the mistake of thinking that they know what is best for the team. If they do, they will have returned to the command-and-control days of yore, and they will have rendered their empowered teams powerless.

How Management Teams Can Have a Good Fight

Kathleen M. Eisenhardt, Jean L. Kahwajy, and L. J. Bourgeois III

Top-level managers know that conflict over issues is natural and even necessary. Management teams that challenge one another's thinking develop a more complete understanding of their choices, create a richer range of options, and make better decisions.

But the challenge—familiar to anyone who has ever been part of a management team—is to keep constructive conflict over issues from degenerating into interpersonal conflict.

From their research on the interplay of conflict, politics, and speed in the decision-making process of management teams, the authors have distilled a set of six tactics characteristic of high-performing teams:

- They work with more, rather than less, information.
- They develop multiple alternatives to enrich debate.
- They establish common goals.
- They make an effort to inject humor into the workplace.
- They maintain a balanced corporate power structure.
- They resolve issues without forcing a consensus.

These tactics work because they keep conflict focused on issues; foster collaborative, rather than competitive, relations among team members; and create a sense of fairness in the decision-making process.

Without conflict, groups lose their effectiveness. Managers often become withdrawn and only superficially harmonious. The alternative to conflict is not usually agreement but rather apathy and disengagement, which open the doors to a primary cause of major corporate debacles: groupthink.

The Myth of the Top Management Team

Jon R. Katzenbach

Companies all across the economic spectrum are making use of teams. They go by a variety of names and can be found at all levels. In fact, you are likely to find the group at the very top of an organization professing to be a team. But even in the best of companies, a so-called top team seldom functions as a *real* team.

Real teams must follow a well-defined discipline to achieve their performance potential. And performance is the key issue—not the fostering of "team values" such as empowerment, sensitivity, or involvement. In recent years, the focus on performance was lost in many companies. Even today, CEOs and senior executives often see few gains in performance from their attempts to become more teamlike.

Nevertheless, a team effort at the top can be essential to capturing the highest performance results possible—when the conditions are right. Good leadership requires differentiating between team and nonteam opportunities, and then acting accordingly.

Three litmus tests must be passed for a team at the top to be effective. First, the team must shape *collective work-products*—these are tangible performance results that the group can achieve working together that surpass what the team members could have achieved working on their own. Second, the leadership role must shift, depending on the task at hand. And third, the team's members must be mutually accountable for the group's results. When these criteria can be met, senior executives should come together to achieve real team performance. When the criteria cannot be met, they should rely on the individual leadership skills that they have honed over the years.

Whatever Happened to the Take-charge Manager?

Nitin Nohria and James D. Berkley

In the 1980s, U.S. business experienced an explosion of new managerial concepts unparalleled in previous decades. Management schools, consultants, and gurus all offered their own special formulas for how to stay competitive in increasingly challenging marketplaces.

Many American managers felt that the emergence of new managerial ideas signaled a rejuvenation of U.S. business. By readily adopting innovations like total quality programs and self-managed teams, managers believed they were demonstrating the kind of decisive leadership that kept companies competitive. But their thinking doesn't jibe with the facts. American managers did not take charge in the 1980s. Instead, they abdicated their responsibility to a burgeoning industry of management professionals.

Furthermore, the management fads of the last fifteen years rarely produced their promised results. Between 1980 and 1990, market share in most key U.S. industries declined as much or more than it had in the 1970s.

If business leaders want to reverse this trend, they must reclaim managerial responsibility—and pragmatism is the place to start. Pragmatic managers are sensitive to their company's context and open to uncertainty. They focus on outcomes and are willing to make do. Pragmatic managers also avoid three common pitfalls, the "let's do it better this time" syndrome and the "flavor of the month" and "let's go for it all" approaches.

Information Technology and Tomorrow's Manager

Lynda M. Applegate, James I. Cash, Jr., and D. Quinn Mills

It came as no surprise to Harold Leavitt and Thomas Whisler when organizations started downsizing and flattening in recent years. Current trends are much like the predictions Leavitt and Whisler made in their 1958 *Harvard Business Review* article, "Management in the 1980s." Though their predictions have been harshly criticized, now, thirty years later, they seem quite correct. Where are we going from here?

As technology develops at a faster rate than ever before, it is creating wider options than ever before. In the twenty-first century, managers will be able to choose the kind of organization they want and eliminate some of the rigidities that keep them from being more responsive.

Information technology will allow cluster-type organizations to have the benefits of small scale and large scale simultaneously. Even large organizations will be able to adopt more flexible and dynamic structures. The distinctions between centralized and decentralized control will blur. And most work will be accomplished by teams formed to handle particular projects.

Sophisticated expert systems and knowledge bases will help capture decision-making processes, so decision making will be better understood. And the systems—not the people—will retain the corporate history, experience, and expertise.

Workers will be better trained, more autonomous, and more transient. The work environment will be exciting and engaging. Leadership will be shared and rotated among team members, narrow job descriptions will be obsolete, and the ability to track who does what will link individual contribution more directly to compensation.

Prepare Your Organization to Fight Fires

Karl Weick

Increasingly, work in today's corporations unfolds in small, temporary groups where the stakes are high, turnover is chronic, foul-ups can spread, and the unexpected is common. Karl Weick finds lessons for senior managers watching over such groups in an unusual source: Norman Maclean's 1992 book, *Young Men and Fire,* which reconstructs the circumstances of a deadly fire in Montana's Mann Gulch that claimed the lives of thirteen young men.

Weick recounts the basic details of the tragedy as they are provided by Maclean: On a hot August day in 1949, fifteen trained firefighters—smoke jumpers—parachuted into remote Mann Gulch to bring under control what they thought was a fairly routine blaze. They had help from one man already on the scene. However, within two hours of landing in the gulch, all but three of the men were dead—consumed by flames. The small fire had "blown up" and chased the men at terrifying speed up the steep slope, eventually catching most of them.

In the midst of the disaster, several things happened to the smoke jumpers' crew: Its structure broke down, confusion prevailed, and the men forgot their roles as firefighters. Weick believes that corporate leaders can learn from this example by developing groups capable of improvisation, wise behavior, respectful interaction, and communication. He explains how those things were missing that afternoon at Mann Gulch and why they are important to organizations today. When they are present, says Weick, small groups can function as resilient sources of what he calls collective *sense making.* In short, they can create a social context in which decisions evolve *before* a dangerous situation blows up.

Informal Networks: The Company Behind the Chart

David Krackhardt and Jeffrey R. Hanson

A glance at an organizational chart can show who's the boss and who reports to whom. But this formal chart won't reveal which people confer on technical matters or discuss office politics over lunch. Much of the real work in any company gets done through this informal organization with its complex networks of relationships that cross functions and divisions.

According to consultants David Krackhardt and Jeffrey Hanson, managers can harness the true power in their companies by diagramming three types of networks: the advice network, which reveals the people to whom others turn to get work done; the trust network, which uncovers who shares delicate information; and the communication network, which shows who talks about work-related matters.

Using employee questionnaires, managers can generate network maps that will get to the root of many organizational problems. When a task force in a computer company, for example, was not achieving its goals, the CEO turned to network maps to find out why. He discovered that the task force leader was central in the advice network but marginal in the trust network. Task force members did not believe he would look out for their interests, so the CEO used the trust map to find someone to share responsibility for the group. And when a bank manager saw in the network map that there was little communication between tellers and supervisors, he looked for ways to foster interaction among employees of all levels.

As companies continue to flatten and rely on teams, managers must rely less on their authority and more on understanding these informal networks. Managers who can use maps to identify, leverage, and revamp informal networks will have the key to success.

How to Integrate Work *and* Deepen Expertise

Dorothy Leonard-Barton, H. Kent Bowen, Kim B. Clark, Charles A. Holloway, and Steven C. Wheelwright

To be a leader in global manufacturing in the 1990s, a company must excel in two seemingly contradictory ways. First, it must constantly build and refresh its individual areas of expertise so that it has the critical capabilities needed to stay ahead. And second, it must get its ever-changing mix of disciplines to work together in the ever-changing ways needed to prevail in an ever-changing competitive environment.

Most manufacturers, especially those companies that have reorganized themselves by cross-functional processes, have already discovered how difficult it is to integrate various disciplines and still maintain functional excellence. But development projects offer a solution. Development projects are the critical juncture where functional groups meet and are therefore the true test of an organization's integrative abilities. More important, they can be used as a tool for strengthening the relationship among functions, while still giving those functions the room they need to advance their own expertise.

The Kodak FunSaver project illustrates how a company can encourage functions to work together effectively, enhance functional expertise, and create a winning product to boot. To design the camera as rapidly and efficiently as possible, the camera division's development team created a dedicated team of engineering, manufacturing, and marketing people. To help integrate the work of the team, the project leader championed a customized CAD/CAM system, which pushed team members to share information—and ultimately gave Kodak a new technical capability that it could apply in other projects.

Getting It Done: New Roles for Senior Executives

Thomas M. Hout and John C. Carter

A decade of process improvement has transformed the way most corporations operate and, at the same time, the job of the senior executive. Top-down autocrats are out and bottom-up teams are in. The message seems to be: Get the processes right, and the company will manage itself. But this message belies a simple truth: Managers, not processes, run companies. In fact, process-focused companies need *more* top-down management, not less. However, today's activist executives must operate very differently from executives of the past. Given the complexities of modern business competition, no single individual can do all that it takes to achieve success for a company. Success depends on the willingness and ability of the entire senior executive group to address not just their individual functional or divisional responsibilities but also their collective responsibility for the company as a whole. Only senior managers can rise above the details of the business, recognize emerging patterns, make un-expected connections, and identify the points of maximum leverage for action.

In fact, a study on innovation practices at some 550 American, Euro-pean, and Japanese companies across a wide variety of industries has shown that none of the best-known programs—total quality manage-ment, reengineering, the formation of self-managing teams, or the institu-tion of cross-functional processes—are enough to produce faster and more effective product development. What really separates the best per-formers from the rest is the role that senior executives play.

Real Work

Abraham Zaleznik

In this *HBR* Classic, originally published in January–February 1989, Abra-ham Zaleznik observes that many senior executives are substituting the rituals of "psychopolitics"—the balancing of social expectations in the workplace—for the real work of thinking about and acting on ideas relat-ing to products, markets, and customers.

That preoccupation with organizational issues can be traced back to the 1930s, when certain influential thinkers decided that maintaining workplace harmony was manager's most important task. The result was a new generation of managers who were more interested in cultivating the status quo than in changing their companies to thrive in a competitive world. Later studies showed that workers preferred managers who knew their own minds and understood the substance of their managerial work. Real proficiency in such work breeds self-confidence in managers, these studies showed, which in turn enhances workers' confidence and morale.

In his retrospective commentary, Zaleznik writes that senior executives seem to have established a healthier balance in the 1990s between their real work and psychopolitics. Executives are now leading their companies to deal with external, competitive conditions that require them to cut costs, create products, please customers, and develop markets. What worries Zaleznik today, however, is that under the guise of employee em-powerment, senior executives are beginning again to indulge in ritualized actions. For instance, they establish task forces to seek answers to ques-tions they themselves should be addressing. The real work of the execu-tive, says Zaleznik, should always include the thinking that informs and di-rects action.

Entrepreneurship Reconsidered: The Team as Hero

Robert B. Reich

Two stories illustrate the American way of thinking about entrepreneurship. The first is the story of the entrepreneurial hero—the plucky individual who uses energy, effort, daring, and good luck to rise in the world. This character, found in every story written by Horatio Alger, has been celebrated throughout American history and is still admired today. But the story has an unhappy ending. The second story holds more promise. It focuses not on the individual but on the team. One example is in Tracy Kidder's *The Soul of a New Machine,* a book that describes how a group of engineers pooled their talents to design a new computer.

The differences between these two versions of entrepreneurship are profound. The first celebrates the individual. The second celebrates the group—even the organization. In this approach, everyone in the organization makes an entrepreneurial contribution: invention and enterprise are continuous and take place at every level of the company. Products and processes constantly evolve and improve as workers share their ideas, pool their information, and engage in collaborative innovation. The company changes as well, finding new applications and new markets for the capabilities it commands.

In a world of global competition, only this second version of entrepreneurship offers real hope for the U.S. economy. Stories of individual heroism no longer embody the kinds of working relationships that yield competitive performance. We still need individual entrepreneurs. But for the United States to improve its competitiveness and enjoy a rising standard of living in the future, we will have to celebrate and honor collective entrepreneurship, just as we have always celebrated and honored the lone entrepreneurial hero.

About the Contributors

Lynda M. Applegate, a professor at Harvard Business School, teaches courses in general management, management information systems, and organization design. She is the author of two books and over twenty-five articles, as well as the senior editor for the *Management Information Systems Quarterly* and associate editor for the *Journal of Organizational Computing and Electronic Commerce.* Dr. Applegate serves on the board of directors of both MicroAge, Inc., and Extraprise, Inc., and on the strategic advisory boards for Mainspring Communications, Webline, and the Alliance Analyst. She is also a member of the Executive Council on Information Management and Telecommunications for the U.S. General Accounting Office and was a member of the roundtable of advisers to President Clinton's Commission on Critical Infrastructure Protection.

James D. Berkley is a Ph.D. student in comparative literature at the University of California, Los Angeles. Between 1990 and 1994, he worked as a research associate and case writer in organizational behavior at Harvard Business School, where he helped co-write *Beyond the Hype: Rediscovering the Essence of Management* (HBS Press, 1992) with Professors Nitin Nohria and Robert G. Eccles. His research focuses on the interrelations between science, literature, and society and the intellectual currents of the later nineteenth and twentieth centuries.

L. J. Bourgeois III is a professor of business administration at the Darden Graduate School of Business. He has consulted for a variety of North and Latin American, European, Asian, and Australian corporations on strategic management, corporate mission, and top management team building, and has designed and conducted various seminars in strategic thinking. He is the author of *Strategic Management: From Concept to Implementation,* as well as articles in various management journals.

H. Kent Bowen is the Bruce Rauner Professor in Business Administration at Harvard Business School. His research and teaching are in the field of operations and technology management. He was the Ford Professor of Engineering at MIT and a founder of Leaders for Manufacturing, a joint research and education program developed by MIT's School of Engineering and the Sloan School of Management. His research at MIT on advanced materials, materials processing, technology management, and manufacturing has led to over 190 published papers and a key textbook in the field, which he coauthored. He is a director of General Signal Corporation and Ceramics Process Systems and a senior adviser to Alcoa, Chrysler, Hewlett-Packard, and Pratt & Whitney.

John C. Carter is the founder and a principal of Boston-based Product Development Consulting, Inc. (PDC), a leading organization in advising *Fortune* 500 companies in the areas of research, development, and marketing. He has served as an adviser to the International Association of Product Development, the Gordon Institute, and the Management Roundtable. He has been a member of the core faculty at Case Western's Executive Program and is a cofounder of the Berkeley Software Forum (BSF). Before starting PDC, Mr. Carter was the chief engineer of Bose Corporation.

James I. Cash, Jr., is the James E. Robinson Professor of Business Administration at Harvard Business School. He has served as faculty chairman and/or instructor in several short executive education programs including managing business transformation, human resource management, achieving breakthrough service, and delivering information services. Among his publications are articles in accounting and computer journals, as well as a regular column in *Information Week.* Mr. Cash is also the author of several books, including *Building the Information-Age Organization: Structure, Control, and Information Technology.*

Kim B. Clark is the Harry E. Figgie, Jr., Professor of Business Administration and dean of the faculty at Harvard Business School. Currently, Dean Clark's research focuses on modularity in design and the integration of technology and competition in industry evolution, with a particular focus on the computer industry. He and Carliss Baldwin are coauthors of a forthcoming book on the topic entitled *Design Rules: The Power of Modularity.* Dean Clark serves on the boards of Fleet Financial Group, Guidant Corporation, and Tower Automotive.

Kathleen M. Eisenhardt is a professor of strategy and organization in the School of Engineering, Stanford University, and associate director of the Stanford Computer Industry Project. Her research and teaching focus on managing in high-velocity, intensely competitive markets. Her awards include the Pacific Telesis Foundation for her ideas on fast strategic decision making and the Whittemore Prize for her writing on organizing global firms in rapidly changing markets. She has written numerous articles and is the coauthor with Shona L. Brown of *Competing on the Edge: Strategy as Structured Chaos* (HBS Press, 1998).

Jeffrey R. Hanson is the director of Client Consulting Services and the chief operating officer of Milestone Capital Management, an investment advisory firm. Mr. Hanson specializes in consulting to financial and professional service firms on a full range of management, marketing, strategic, and organizational issues. His clients include banks and investment banks, investment managers, insurance companies, and other diversified service companies. Prior to establishing his consulting practice, Mr. Hanson worked for the investment banking firm of Goldman, Sachs & Co.

Charles A. Holloway is the holder of the Kleiner, Perkins, Caufield & Byers Professorship in Management at Stanford Business School. He is currently the codirector of the newly formed Stanford Center for Entrepreneurial Studies at the Graduate School of Business, which does curriculum development and research on smaller, rapidly growing companies. He is the author of *Decision-Making Under Uncertainty: Models and Choices* and the coeditor of *The Perpetual Enterprise Machine—Seven Keys to Corporate Renewal Through Successful Product and Process Development* and many articles in the field of management.

Thomas M. Hout was a partner of The Boston Consulting Group (BCG); during his twenty-seven year career with the firm he resided in Tokyo, London, Seoul, and Boston. He is the author of *Industrial Policy of Japan* and coauthor with George Stalk of the business best-seller *Competing Against Time.* Mr. Hout has contributed four articles to the *Harvard Business Review* and numerous op-ed pieces to the *New York Times, Wall Street Journal,* and *Boston Globe.* Currently he serves on the boards of an electric automobile company, a mutual fund, and a software producer, and as an adviser to BCG.

Jean L. Kahwajy coaches senior executives and teams, offering more effective approaches to meeting the challenges of change and negotiations. For nine years she has been a management consultant in strategy development and decision quality, and she regularly gives seminars worldwide on these topics. The author of several articles on organizational design, mitigating interpersonal conflict, and top management team decision making, Ms. Kahwajy is currently researching the social and psychological forces that influence decision makers—in particular, the powerful role of supporting others.

Jon R. Katzenbach is a director in the Dallas office of McKinsey & Company, Inc. During more than thirty-five years with McKinsey, his primary areas of focus have been strategy, organization, and leadership and change issues of large institutions. Mr. Katzenbach's experience and perspectives on teams, change, and the high-performance organization have been delivered to dozens of executive groups and management conferences around the world. His books include *The Wisdom of Teams: Creating the High Performance Organization* (HBS Press, 1993), *Real Change Leaders: How You Can Create Growth and High Performance at Your Company,* and *Teams at the Top: Unleashing the Potential of Both Teams and Individual Leaders* (HBS Press, 1998).

David Krackhardt is a professor of organizations and public policy at the Heinz School of Public Policy and Management, Carnegie Mellon University. He has held positions as a Marvin Bower Fellow at Harvard Business School and a visiting professor of organizations at the University of Chicago. Professor Krackhardt's primary contributions have been in the area of social network analysis and how these ideas can be applied to the management and change of organizations. He pioneered the concept of "cognitive social structures," showing the role that perceptions of networks play in power and politics in firms. He has developed measures of network structures that reveal the overall shapes and dimensions of the organization which in turn relate to profitability of the firm.

Dorothy Leonard-Barton is the William J. Abernathy Professor of Business Administration at the Harvard Business School, where she has taught in MBA and executive education programs since 1983. She researches and consults about new technology commercialization, new product development, and the transfer of knowledge across geographic, cultural, and cognitive boundaries. She has published more than two dozen articles based on field research in academic journals such as *Organization Science*. Her book *Wellsprings of Knowledge* (HBS Press, 1995) illustrates the managerial activities that sustain innovation and enhance strategic technological capabilities.

Bowen H. McCoy is a retired managing director of Morgan Stanley, a firm which he served for twenty-eight years. Recently he has been a business and real estate counselor. He is currently president of the Urban Land Foundation and a trustee of the Urban Land Institute. He has also served as president of the Real Estate Counselors, chairman of the Center for Economic Policy Research at Stanford University, and a member of the Executive Committee of the Hoover Institution. In addition to engaging in various philanthropic activities, he teaches ethics at several west coast graduate schools of business administration and Christian ethics in local churches.

Christopher Meyer, Ph.D., is Managing Principal of Integral, Inc., a management consulting firm specializing in strategy, technology, and innovation management. He is the author of *Fast Cycle Time and Relentless Growth*. He is an instructor at the California Institute of Technology, Industrial Relations Center and the former academic director of Stanford's Fast Cycle Strategy Program.

D. Quinn Mills teaches about leadership, strategy, organizations, and human resources at Harvard Business School as well as advising major corporations and consulting companies. He has written several books about organizations and business strategy.

Nitin Nohria is a professor of business administration at Harvard Business School. His research interests center on leadership and corporate renewal. His most recent of five books, *The Differentiated Network*, provides an innovative model for organizing multinational corporations. Professor Nohria is currently investigating the dynamics of organizational change through a series of projects that study the impact on *Fortune* 100 companies of corporate downsizing, the spread of strategic alliances, total quality management, and tighter corporate governance.

Robert B. Reich is the University Professor and Maurice B. Hexter Professor of Social Economic Policy at the Heller Graduate School, Brandeis University. From 1993 to 1997, he was the U.S. Secretary of Labor. Before heading the Labor Department, he was on the faculty of

Harvard University's John F. Kennedy School of Government. Mr. Reich served as an assistant to the Solicitor General in the Ford administration and headed the policy planning staff of the Federal Trade Commission in the Carter administration. He is the author of seven books and more than two hundred articles on the global economy, the changing nature of work, and the centrality of human capital. His most recent books are *The Work of Nations,* which has been translated into more than twenty languages, and *Locked in the Cabinet.*

Douglas K. Smith is a consultant and writer concerned with organization performance and change. He consults to leading organizations that span the spectrum from for-profits to nonprofits to governments. He is the cocreator of the "horizontal organization," and the coauthor of *The Wisdom of Teams* (HBS Press, 1993). He is the author of *Taking Charge of Change,* as well as *Managing Performance.*

Karl Weick is the Rensis Likert Collegiate Professor of Organizational Behavior and Psychology in the School of Business Administration at the University of Michigan. Dr. Weick is currently studying the leadership of wildland firefighting crews, the ways people make sense of adverse medical events, and the role of mindful action and improvisation in high-reliability systems. His most recent book is *Sensemaking in Organizations.* Dr. Weick's earlier writing about the social psychology of organizing provided significant background for the Peters and Waterman study, "In Search of Excellence."

Suzy Wetlaufer, formerly of the international management consulting firm Bain & Company, is a senior editor at the *Harvard Business Review,* specializing in the area of organization. In addition to "The Team That Wasn't," she is the author of several other *HBR* pieces, including "What's Killing the Creativity at Coolburst?" and, with Harvard Business School's David Thomas, "A Question of Color."

Steven C. Wheelwright is the Edsel Bryant Ford Professor of Business Administration at Harvard Business School, where he also serves as senior associate dean and MBA program chair. In his research, Dr. Wheelwright examines product and process development and their connection with competitive advantage and operations excellence. He has coauthored several works with Harvard Business School colleague Kim Clark, most recently *Leading Product Development: The Senior Manager's Guide to Creating and Shaping the Enterprise.* This and other related volumes present concepts and tools proven particularly effective in technology-intensive settings where rapid, efficient, on-target product and process development play a central role in competitive advantage. Dr. Wheelwright is also the author or coauthor of more than ten other books, as well as numerous articles.

Abraham Zaleznik is the Konosuke Matsushita Professor of Leadership, Emeritus, at the Harvard Business School. He is known internationally for his research and teaching in the field of social psychology in the business setting, and for his investigations into the distinguishing characteristics in leadership and the psychological aspects of executive behavior of managers and leaders. Professor Zaleznik has published fourteen books, most recently *Learning Leadership,* and has written numerous award winning articles. He is chairman of the board of King Ranch and a member of the board of Ogden Corporation, the Timberland Company, Freedom Communications, Inc., and Butchers, Inc. He is a consultant to both corporations and government.

Index